TO HELL AND BACK AGAIN

TO HELL AND BACK AGAIN

A True Account of Demonic Possession and Deliverance

JOSEPH WISDOM SESAY

WITH PAUL HARRINGTON

NEW HOLLAND

First published in 2021 by New Holland Publishers
Sydney • Auckland

Level 1, 178 Fox Valley Road, Wahroonga, NSW 2076, Australia
5/39 Woodside Ave, Northcote, Auckland 0627, New Zealand

newhollandpublishers.com

A record of this book is held at the National Library of Australia.

ISBN 9781760794309

Group Managing Director: Fiona Schultz
Project Editor: Xavier Waterkeyn
Cover Design: Corporality
Photo: Studio Reflections Photography
Designer: Andrew Davies
Production Director: Arlene Gippert
Printed in China

10 9 8 7 6 5 4 3 2 1

Keep up with New Holland Publishers:
NewHollandPublishers
@newhollandpublishers

CONTENTS

DEDICATION

I dedicate this book,
with all my life,
to The Holy Spirit –
the ultimate Source from which flows
Freedom, Restoration
and Transformation.

ACKNOWLEDGEMENTS

I would like to acknowledge the love and support of my family, in particular my wife, the ever-patient Fatmata, and my children, Mariama, Gabriel Wisdom and Esther Miracle, who not only inspire me, but who give up their time with Daddy so that he can continue his mission.

The team and congregation of Cross Purpose Church and the Divine Intercession Ministry have been invaluable in their contribution to making the world a better place.

And last, but not least, Paul Harrington and the other afflicted who cannot be named, for so generously sharing their stories and lives with me so that you, the reader, could have a better understanding of a hugely important part of life that so often remains hidden.

I hope that we can bring some light into the darkness through the Power of The Holy Spirit.

PRAYER FOR THE READER

May all who read this book be blessed by the divine providence of God and his son and savior Yeshua.

May you feel comforted and strengthened by this story.

May all who read it come to know themselves and their purpose in God's universe, regardless of religion, race or creed.

May the love and sunshine of The Holy Spirit protect you and all you love.

Amen.

TESTAMENT OF AN INTERCESSOR

17 January 2020 – Melbourne Australia

"The words of the Prophets are written on the subway walls."

God chooses from the unexpected, showing not only that God has a sense of humor, but also a sense of humility.

As an Intercessor, my role is to provide confidential support to the Deliverance Minister and to The afflicted One, through prayer, moved by direction from The Holy Spirit, providing perhaps another point of view, perhaps another layer of discernment – whatever the Deliverer or The Holy Spirit require of me in the moment. We leave little to chance. Nothing we do is unintentional.

There is nothing unintentional about Wisdom.

In him, God created an endless channel directly to his providence through the body of a gentle, small man. I suspect he was malnourished as a child. To me, he looks more Ethiopian than West African. His "third eye" is imprinted with a deeply clenched star of scar tissue, embedded into his forehead with a ferocity that makes me wonder where it came from.

A tribal marking?

An accident?

Or God?

From outside his room he radiates the calm that comes from one who has known great suffering but who remains elegantly defiant, with an internal strength that cuts its teeth on the devil itself.

It is an incredibly uninspiring room. Bare walls for the most part and meager furnishings, no sharp objects or weapons … apart from The Holy Spirit.

Paul Harrington could not be more physically distinct from Wisdom. His pastel white roundness is unmistakably different to Wisdom's dark angularity. They are an unlikely, odd couple, unlikely comrades in the battle for a soul. Outside this room, Paul emanates a frequency of agitated, suppressed energy, EVERYTHING about him gradually revealing few of the many tiers of his core.

Wisdom does not reveal himself at first either.

Paul does not relinquish control easily. He is like a man struggling to swim by grasping the water. For all his efforts all he manages is to hold himself just

above the waters of the abyss. By refusing to give up his pain and surrender it and himself to God and The Holy Spirit, Paul is lost in a constant battle of "keeping up appearances" at the cost of true healing, not dissimilar to the experiences of most of humanity.

Wisdom is familiar with this state.

Just as there are layers and tiers and stories attached to every human, there were layers attached to Wisdom. Until he learned to surrender.

"Pray for the baptism of The Holy Spirit," Wisdom says, speaking directly to God, "Father show us Your anointing …"

As Wisdom prays, Paul moans and groans and begins to writhe, reaching for an emotional and spiritual catharsis with a ferocity that is not of this world but well known to humankind nonetheless.

As Wisdom channels the power of The Holy Spirit he says, "Right now it's happening … the Power of God has been released."

The thing within Paul laughs quietly, "A-ha-ha-ha-ha … he-he-he-he-he-he-he-he-he …" and, then, another voice, perhaps The Holy Spirit itself speaks, "Eskara mo korlea popu du ara de keferdek …" There is a sigh and continues, "Ore kabu …ora kestelle a mutu al abutu alla kalicht … alla kamuste …" Then another voice makes a rolling, half-growl-half purr, "Ahhhhrrrrr …" an animal sound, but like no animal you've ever heard. Humans are so used to being under the illusion that they are the only beings capable of coherent thought that it is an alien thing to hear the sounds of another being that thinks. But this is not human and not animal either. It is nothing physical as we understand it. Its only physicality is in that Paul has allowed it, whatever it is, to use his body, through which it, whatever it is, is communicating, in its own fashion while the battle with The Holy Spirit continues for Paul's soul.

As Wisdom continues to speak in tongues the thing in Paul sighs and growls, sighs and growls.

Wisdom begins to speak in English again "Spirit of the Living God … Oh, You are pouring Your waters of life …"

"Paul" purrs, growls. He might be insane, but I don't think so. We know Paul from many encounters. He can be obsessive, compulsive – to the point of really getting on your nerves – but he's not mad. And he's not this good an actor either. In his normal state of consciousness he wouldn't be able to purr no matter how much he tried. This is something else.

A snatch of something from Wisdom, "… tu et laud," abruptly stops. Was that Latin? "You and [praise?]". Wisdom doesn't know Latin. Wisdom's Christianity is not a Catholic one. He continues, "Thank You Holy Spirit … thank You Holy Spirit … thank You Holy Spirit … thank You Holy Spirit … thank You Holy Spirit … thank You for releasing Your power … thank You for releasing Your presence … thank You for Your anointing … thank You for the breakthrough."

Are you in danger, reading this account, bearing witness to this, even as an observer?

But there is no danger here. Maybe whatever danger there is, you are being shielded from it.

"Thank You for the breakthrough … thank You for the empowerment … thank You for the baptism.

"Thank You for the baptism … thank You for the baptism … shi mama kaya kere keye narababa … Jesus! I speak to the salvation upon this man … protection of his spirit …"

All the while Paul just sighs.

And Wisdom drones on. It's almost hypnotic. "Thank You for the pouring of Your power … thank You for the pouring of Your anointing … thank You for the pouring of Your Grace … thank You for forgiveness … thank You for empowerment … thank You for filling this vessel … thank You for filling this vessel … thank You for filling this vessel, Lord … thank You for filling this vessel … thank You for filling this vessel … thank You for filling this vessel, God! … thank You for the filling of this vessel in the name of Jesus … shi kaba … mandelekeibusandarababa … i borukurabaya … shi kabayan delekerebus akala bayan daraba … makara yirebus se tarababa … dubarabayam derekerebus anda … mankayerebus setalabayandaraba … shibachayarebus senderbukum daraba … inlabrakuderebus setarabayan derekerebus sandaraba … mayarabus akereandaraba … Thank-You, Jesus … I give God the glory, and the honor, and the thanks and the adoration, for there is none like you, Jesus Christ."

People speak of the banality of evil.

There is nothing banal about evil.

Human evil might be banal – the faceless bureaucrat who rubber stamps sending people to the gulag or gas chamber, the man who looks like an office worker being tried for killing rabbits after he's raped them, or the ones that are even handsome, who kill women because it's easier to trust someone with a nice face – the ones of whom you say, "He didn't look like a murderer."

Human evil is often described as an absence – narcissistic negligence, an absence of a conscience, an absence of empathy.

Human evil is … superficial.

But this non-human evil is definitely a presence. It is palpable. It has purpose and intent. It doesn't harm just because it casually feels like it, it doesn't wound because it doesn't know any better and it doesn't rationalize by saying "I was only doing my job. I was only following orders."

Non-human evil – if you accept its existence – knows itself. It might lie to you, but it doesn't lie to itself, at least not about its work. It enjoys its job. It revels in destroying you. At least that's how it appears.

To the best of my knowledge this is the most focused and complete inquiry into an actual case study of the phenomenon commonly understood as Demonic Possession ever undertaken in Australia, and one of the most in-depth ever done in the world. But it is also an insight into the practice of Deliverance and Exorcism itself, direct from the experiences of both "the possessed" and the person charged with liberating that person from their possession.

What you do with this knowledge is up to you.

I was led by The Holy Spirit to record this observation of only a small part Paul's long struggle. His story is unique, but it is also the story of many.

It is certainly my hope that this account will dispel myths, shed light on a few things and provide clarity.

Above all, it is my wish that it might be of help to you and give you hope or give hope to someone you love.

PREFACE

You do not have to be a Christian to read this book. You do not have to be of any religious or cultural background. You can even be an atheist and find something of value here and you are free to interpret everything I tell you in terms that you are comfortable with.

However, please understand that I am an ordained Christian minister working within the framework of the Assemblies of God Church. My worldview is Christian. You no doubt recognize that the word "Christian" means different things to different people.

Speaking only for myself:

I believe that there is a Singular Being of Supreme Consciousness in the Universe, Creator of All Things.

I call this Being "God", and though this God is one, God manifests to humans in three persons – the Father, the Son and The Holy Spirit. I believe that God is all-knowing, all-present and all-powerful.

I believe that over two thousand years ago God manifested in human form in the person of Jesus Christ, and that Christ came to redeem us of our sins, our spiritual errors, and to lead us to a state of being in which we are one with God.

There are other spiritual beings in the universe. Some of them are kind, constructive and benevolent. They are the messengers of God and we call them "angels".

Others are destructive and malevolent – fallen angels – and we call them "demons". Chief among these destructive beings is an entity that goes by many names, but whom I call "Satan". Satan, together with his demonic minions, creates afflictions which have always plagued humanity, in turn, creating the afflicted. The afflicted are spiritually sick and broken and they require intervention and treatment to become healed and whole because becoming afflicted is just about the worst thing that can happen to you, because demons attack your connection with God.

There is much more to the Christian story, of course, and I will speak of some of that story here, but that is the gist of the worldview through which I operate.

My *particular* calling, guided by The Holy Spirit, is to deliver the afflicted from the influence of Satan and Satan's evil spirit minions. Demons torment us with scourges that go beyond the purely mental, emotional and physical, scourges that take us into the realm of the spiritual.

In that capacity I have performed Deliverance thousands of times on hundreds of people over the last twenty years. I can tell you one thing: Satan does not care if you are Christian, Muslim, Jewish, Hindu, Buddhist, Zoroastrian, Confucianist, Animist, Wiccan, New-Ager, or an adherent to any of ten thousand or more other beliefs or creeds. Satan does not care if you are Believer, Agnostic, Deist, Pantheist or an Atheist.

Satan is an equal-opportunity adversary, and if certain things happen and certain things are in place then Satan and the demons will take equal opportunity in tormenting you and making your life a literal hell on earth.

My hope is that whether you believe, as I do, that God and Satan are real, or whether you believe that they are figments of an over-active imagination, or products of a sick mind, or noises produced by faulty brain chemistry, that nevertheless, if you find that you or someone you care about is experiencing disturbances that might be resisting treatment through conventional means as currently understood by science and the scientific worldview, that you will *at least consider* that spiritual affliction is a possibility, and that there is a treatment and cure for it in the form of Deliverance and exorcism.

And most importantly, that there *is* somewhere that you can go to for help.

INTRODUCTION

It's hard to talk about this to a modern, educated, sophisticated audience steeped in the contemporary worldview of rationalism, science and materialism without sounding like a superstitious nutcase or a religious fanatic.

I'm neither superstitious or a fanatic and whether I'm a crazy and self-deluded person or not is for you to judge, but I recognize that parallel to our material world is a whole other realm of existence that affects us constantly and in profound ways, both good and bad.

The story of the human race is one of both success and failure, triumph and defeat, survival and extinction – health and affliction. And as long as humans have existed, they have been subjected to a group of afflictions that go beyond the mental, emotional and physical afflictions that are readily recognized in the modern world.

These afflictions, for want of a better term, are *spiritual* in nature and long before people even thought that there could be such a thing as a material basis for affliction they have understood that there was such things as profound disturbances that they recognized throughout history as *spiritual affliction*. It manifests in many ways, but no matter how it shows up, the manifestations are usually unpleasant and, as such, require a treatment and cure.

The processes for treating and curing spiritual affliction have also been recognized throughout the long story of humanity, and treatments often involve the recognition that there are *non-material consciousnesses* or *entities* involved, that are just as alive, active and potentially malevolent as any material being.

In Christianity, we call these malevolent beings "demons", and we recognize the need to get rid of them or expel them as part of the process of treating these spiritual afflictions, but the struggle against demons is far older than Christianity.

In tribal traditions, in shamanism, we think of this process as "the expulsion of evil spirits".

In the Roman Catholic and Orthodox Christian traditions this process is called "Exorcism".

In the Protestant Christian tradition, this process is called "Deliverance".

In other religious or spiritual traditions, it goes by other names, but they all mean roughly the same thing – the process of expunging demons.

This ability to expel demonic entities from the afflicted is a birthright of all of us.

The Bible explicitly states that Jesus gave to His apostles, "… to have the power to heal sickness and to cast out demons," – Matthew 3:15.

But while all of us are gifted with this ability, some of us are more gifted than others, even if that gift is thrust upon us.

DEMONS AND THE ORIGIN OF EVIL

Demons have always been with us. They are older than humanity itself.

In the Christian tradition, Lucifer was the most beautiful of the angels – second only to God. But somehow, Lucifer, the Carrier of Light – became full of pride, believing that "he" could do without God – a profound error, an insane idea if ever there was one. For this sin, this error, Lucifer was cast out of heaven, and because "he" was charismatic and convincing in "his" deception, "he" took one third of the angels with him. Thus, Lucifer became the Carrier of Dark Light, the light that shines on the recesses of the human soul, that illuminates what lurks in the shadows – became Satan, the adversary. The angels that followed him turned from being messengers of God, to demons.

This story is not *explicitly* in the Bible, as such. There are *hints*, but in fact there is, strictly speaking, no *overt or explicit Biblical telling* of many of the stories having to do with Satan and the demons. The story of Satan's fall has come down to us through traditions known as Exegesis, and in writings collectively known as The Apocrypha.

According to these traditions, the casting out of Satan from Heaven happened even before the creation of humans.

Once the human race was born, Satan took on the role adversary to the human race too, tempting humans into sin – by definition, away from God – and afflicting on them all manner of evil.

Many questions arise from this story.

Why did Lucifer become full of pride? What made "him" think that existence was even *possible* without God, much less than "he" could take God's place? Why would Satan take on the role first of God's adversary, and then later as the agent of evil for the human race? And, in a question that has dogged many for centuries, why would an all-powerful God allow such a situation to take place?

Many answers have been put forth to these questions. I can only offer some opinions and teachings here. I encourage you to seek your own answers if you do not find my explanations adequate.

This book is a combination of many stories. It is principally my story, the story of how a young man from Africa found God early in his life and how, through a series of extraordinary events, came to establish, in Australia, a Deliverance Ministry specifically devoted to helping the afflicted achieve liberation from evil, no matter who they are or where they come from, no matter their cultural or religious background.

But weaved within my story are also the stories of the afflicted themselves, principally of one man, Paul Harrington, who was a victim of the deepest and most persistent affliction that I have ever come across, and who tells this story in his own words in these pages.

But there are other stories here too, and each show a different aspect of the complex phenomenon that is Demonic Infestation and Spiritual Affliction.

The purpose of telling you these stories is to give you an understanding of Spiritual Affliction and its many forms, to describe the treatment for this affliction – commonly known as "Deliverance" or "Exorcism", and to give you insights as to what it is actually like to deal with this phenomenon both as an afflicted person, and from the point of view of the deliverer or exorcist.

My intention is to provide true and factual accounts, with some details changed only to protect the privacy of individuals who do not wish to be identified.

My ultimate aim is to educate, but also to let you know that if you find yourself in a situation of affliction, that there is something possible to do about it.

If you are suffering, you need not suffer alone, and there are people to whom you can come for answers and for support.

I hope to be comprehensive in my treatment of this subject, but I could not possibly be exhaustive. A truly exhaustive treatment of this subject would require many volumes.

Nonetheless, to my knowledge, until now no attempt has ever been made to bring the general public *both* sides of this story in one place – the story of both the afflicted and that of those whose calling is to bring them out of darkness.

I invite you now to take a journey down a rabbit hole into Hell … and back.

CHAPTER ONE

JOSEPH, A CHILD OF WAR

"I gave you this child. I will protect this child. He is a vessel for me. I am the Spirit of the Lord."

Joseph

My house had become a machine-gun nest.

It was the first night that the Liberian Civil War came to us.

My family had been delayed in getting out of the city of the town of Koindu, in Sierra Leone, near the border of both Liberia to the east, and Guinea, to the north. My mother's mother, my grandmother, was a woman of some standing in the community, practically a chief among the women in her own right. My grandfather, my mother's father, who was well connected, had been forewarned the day before of what was going to happen. Some soldiers from the government had come, "If you can leave, it is better for you to leave," they had said. "What is coming is something we will not be able to fight off for long."

My grandfather had wanted to get a bus to get us out, but there had been a delay, a mechanical problem. Surely, we could wait one more day?

But on that day, late in 1990, we had only been in bed a few hours, when we heard gun shot and we knew that the enemy, whoever they were, had come. They had set up a machine gun in front of our house. Our house was on top of a hill, with a clear view of the road that led to the center of town – a strategically advantageous place, a good place to kill people from.

There were other guns, elsewhere.

I don't know where they were. The sound of guns and explosions wracked the night. The fighters knew of my grandmother. They kept calling for her to come out, "We won't hurt you!" they said.

She didn't believe them.

My eight-year-old self, my grandparents, my mother, my stepfather, my elder brother, Moses, my two younger sisters – Mahawa and Mbalu – and an older, adopted sister, Meyatta, hid under our beds, praying that *they* wouldn't take us. Whoever *they* were did not come for us. They were otherwise occupied.

In the morning, after some hours of silence, my grandfather dared to look outside. The neighborhood was empty. The fighters had gone. In the eerie silence he made the decision to leave in that moment. We left the house, cautiously, not knowing if we would ever return.

We walked, avoiding the roads, through the jungle, stopping at villages that my grandparents had grown up in, through the border into Sierra Leone, in our pajamas. It took us four days of walking before we crossed the Moa river into Guinea and took refuge in the city of Nongoa.

We would be there for three years.

I was the only son my mother Mary and my father Attem had in common. My mother had my elder brother Moses as a result of a previous relationship.

My father, Attem, had come from a Muslim background but

was effectively using his religion as a cover. He was a man who was fascinated by the occult and was heavily involved in tribal sorcery. Sorcery in that part of Africa does not operate as an organized religion, so much as like a continual tournament between competing sorcerers and sorceresses and their apprentices. They have gatherings in which they perform rituals and enter trance states. They compete to attract spirits who will provide them with knowledge and power in exchange for sacrifices – animal sacrifices and sacrifices of other things of value. In these rituals there would be much invoking of spirits, rapturous dancing, drinking of strange brews and animal blood from creatures in their death throes. I never saw my father committing these acts myself, but they were common enough that anyone from that part of the world would not be unfamiliar with them as you would be, if you lived there for any amount of time.

I must remember when talking to a Western audience that not everything translates easily. It is probably best if you understand the sort of activities my father was involved with as being a cross between shamanic experiences and voodoo. He was actively involved in contacting non-physical entities from another plane or realm of reality in his search for influence and powers that were not available to those unable or unwilling to make such contacts and *contracts*. My personal belief was that he was actively inviting demonic possession, however else he might have framed it or spoken of it. People would come to these sorcerers or "witch doctors" for healing, or to curse. A sorcerer with talent, with a reputation for being affective, would see their reputation rise and with that, the opportunity to access knowledge of herbs, chants and other rituals of magic to invoke ever greater spirits and access ever more power.

What my father thought he was ultimately gaining; I was never clear about. What I was clear about was that his own journey into this aspect of spirituality resulted in him spending long periods of time away from his family and he did acquire a reputation for being a man of power, a man of some fame who was much in demand for his services, even by members of his political party.

Africa is a continent of blurred lines.

The line of language is blurred. My ethnic group and language is Kissi, but we mostly spoke Liberian English and Sierra Leone Kreyol at home – not so much languages as people in the West normally understand them but a spectrum of creole dialects – a jumble of words from many native languages built on a foundation of American English with pronunciation altered by the native languages around it, sometimes so altered and warped they becomes Liberian Kreyol and Sierra Leone Kreyol.

The line between biological children, stepchildren and adopted children is blurred. The line between family, friend and tribe is blurred. Family, friends and tribes are separated by lines between countries and borders created by colonialists who knew nothing and cared nothing for tribal lines, such as they were, or the lines that connect families and friends. Lines that have created wars.

The line between church and state is blurred. The line between the material and the spiritual is blurred. The line between formal religion, folk tradition and animism is blurred.

The line between The Holy Spirit and the Devil is blurred.

The line between life and death is *especially* blurred.

Sometime around the age of three, almost four, my mother came into my room to wake me up but couldn't.

I had stopped breathing.

I was pronounced dead.

But within a few minutes, in amongst the wailing and grief in the household, I simply came back to life again.

Tongues were already wagging about me. Now they were wagging more. In the community the story circulated that I was a cursed "spirit child", sent by evil spirits to ruin a family, and then, having completed my "mission", to die, leaving the family devastated, with nothing left. This is what many believe in Africa. I understand that this is strange to Westerners, but my "death" and how my family reacted to shows this blurring of the lines between the material and the spiritual.

Several weeks later, I died again and, in the same way, came back to life.

Tongues wagged even more.

Later, I experienced two occasions of sudden immobility. The spirits had not been able to kill me, but perhaps they could paralyze me. It is known / believed that sleep paralysis is common in cases of Demonic Affliction. Was this such a case? My mother didn't know what to do. She was exhausted and considered leaving me with her mother to raise. In church one day, she cried out to The Holy Spirit.

"God! What's going on? You made a promise. You told me that you would protect this child!" And she sensed a reassurance, that yes, I was protected.

I did not die again. I was not paralyzed again, but my connection to the spirit world remained unbroken.

Although I have no memory of most of these events, my mother says that as a child of about six I would suddenly say things that I couldn't possibly know, things about the future. I would even go so far as to bless my friends, acting in a way that "normal" children never do.

My father never married my mother and since Attem was never much around anyway, my mother was available to marry my stepfather,

Ibrahim, when I was six. Ibrahim was, is, a good man. He and my mother would go on to have three other children together, my two younger sisters, I have already mentioned, and at last, my younger brother, Mohammed. Such large, complicated families are not unusual where I come from. Because of blurred borders it is easy to have family and friends in three countries very close together – such is why we ended up in Guinea. In leaving in such a hurry, and because of the disruption of the war, we lost contact with Attem and I would not see my biological father again for many years.

A close friend of my grandmother, practically an aunty, took us in. It was March 1991. The UN had started building refugee camps for the thousands escaping across borders. We could have gone there, to one of the camps, but my great-aunty would have none of it, and insisted we stay with her. We had two rooms in her house. Later, more refugees came, and all nine of us moved into one, small room.

Somehow, we managed. But my parents decided after a few months that they would return to Sierra Leone, to Kono, where the war had not yet arrived, and they would take my brother and younger sisters with them, leaving my elder adopted sister Meyatta and I behind.

At about this time I began to experience prescient dreams.

Some of the dreams were ordinary. I dreamed that we were in the jungle collecting wood *in a very specific place*, and that a snake was chasing us. This later happened.

Another time I dreamt my brother and I fell into an open grave, where we found a skeleton. Three days after the dream, this happened.

Other dreams were worse.

There was a man living close by, another refugee. We had known him from back home. He had a tattoo near one shoulder.

In one very vivid dream, I saw this man. He was tied down.

Liquid fire dripped down onto one of his shoulders, onto his arm, onto his tattoo. He was screaming.

I woke up. I told my grandfather about the dream. At about midday that same day a van of Guinean military came to our neighborhood and abducted the man. They looked at his arm and interpreted the tattoo as a mark that he was a rebel terrorist. We could do nothing but stand by as they took him. We did not want to be accused of being associated with him. They tied him up. They poured burning plastic on him. They do this to lift off a rebel mark as proof of guilt. They took him into their van. We never saw him again.

We later learned that they took him to a prison where he died.

My childhood was over.

We did what we could to survive. For cxample, a friend of mine and I would go looking for firewood, that we would then bundle up with my grandfather to sell. We did the same with fish caught from the river. We would find people who had things to sell, then sell them at the markets, taking a cut of the proceeds. One of our projects involved picking coffee beans in plantations halfway between Nongoa and the next big town to the east, Gueckedou. For our trouble, the plantation owners would give us a few kilos of coffee that we would then sell in Gueckedou, where we would get the best price.

Income trickled in like raindrops in a bucket. I learned that you could do with very little, that the Lord would provide *just enough* to get by, but that the Lord also helps those who help themselves, especially if you learn basic economics. You learn, for example, that the closer you get to a big town, the better the price you'll get for what you're selling.

The UN had started up schools in the refugee centers, so we worked in the morning and went to school in the afternoon, between one o'clock and four thirty, after which we would buy some things in the market that my grandmother could cook for dinner.

As hard as it was for my adopted elder sister and I, who had been left behind in Guinea, it must have been harder for my grandparents. They were used to having money, to being people of means, power and influence. My grandparents had a lot of property in Sierra Leone – farmland that grew rice, plantains and bananas and they had considerable influence there. Such are the advantages of being descendants of chiefs. Unfortunately, given the current political instability, it was impossible to access these resources. They had come down in the world. They were now relatively poor, without means and powerless. But in Africa you make money by hustling and hustling is a set of skills – like riding a bike – you never forget.

And, as I was to learn much later, having hustling skills, what in The West is called, "the art of negotiation" is particularly useful when you are creating a Deliverance ministry.

My spiritual experiences continued. People were getting sick all the time. I would "feel" a voice saying to me, *"Go and pray for them."* I would do that and tell these sick people I was praying for them. Some instinct, perhaps some imitation of what I might have seen others do from time to time, told me to lay hands on them as I prayed. And they got better.

There was a young man with a bloated belly. The "voice" in my head said, *"Pray for him."* I went to the room where he was lying in pain.

"I want to pray for you," my nine-year-old self said.

"OK," said the young man.

I laid my hands on him. Prayed. A week later, he was much better. I had only prayed for him once, because I hadn't received any "instruction" from "on high" to do it more than once.

When I prayed for people, they got better. Consistently.

Tongues wagged again.

It didn't stop at healing people.

My grandmother got it into her head to start selling beans and bread. She came to me.

"I know that you have a gift," she said. "I want you to bless my beans. I want you to bless the business."

So, I did. I stood in front of some bags of beans and bread and said, "I bless this business of my grandmother's." The business became successful. It fed the whole family, all four of us, from that moment on.

Tongues wagged again. I became in demand.

"Joseph, I have a business. Could you bless it?"

"Joseph, my daughter is sick. Could you bless her?"

"Joseph, I've just opened a restaurant. Here's some money. Could you be my first customer and buy a meal from me and bless the restaurant?"

I didn't really know what I was doing. Remember, I'm just a nine-year-old boy, but I was happy to oblige. This was *normal* for me.

In gratitude, people would give me money or food. Without realizing it, I was paying my way as a "channel of spirituality". It wasn't much, but it didn't have to be. I was grateful enough that The Holy Spirit was keeping body and soul together.

In a sense, these were the early days of a spiritual apprenticeship.

I should point out that even though I was *sincerely* doing what I could to help people, without any expectation of reward, and people were simply expressing their gratitude, there are such things as other "spiritual hustlers" who pretend to offer "spiritual services" in exchange for money. You have these sorts of charlatans in the West too.

My grandparents had chosen to stay in Guinea because that's

where they felt safest. I stayed with them because my grandmother was very attached to me and didn't want to let me go. School was an interrupted thing. The UN was renting spaces from the Guinean government that often had to be used for Guineans, at short notice, so school might be called off for a week at a time. The Liberian Civil War showed no signs of abating, and was, in fact, getting worse. Nongoa continued to fill with refugees from Liberia and Sierra Leone now. After a couple of years of this the situation was becoming so unstable that my grandparents and I feared for our livelihoods and for my education.

It is now 1993, so at the age of eleven, I decide to take matters into my own hands.

One day I go to Gueckedou with some friends to sell five kilos of coffee.

I do not plan to come back.

Meanwhile, on the other side of the world, in a place and in a life that I could not even imagine at the time, a slightly older boy who I would not yet meet for many, many years, had been undergoing his own spiritual "apprenticeship".

CHAPTER TWO

A CHILD OF THE SUBURBS

"I can call on Mary, and I will weep.
And when I pray to Mary, they will be tears of joy."

Paul

Nothing about this whole infestation, oppression, obsession and possession thing is *easy*.

When I think about all the weirdness that happened to me over a period of many years, there's a part of me that thinks, "This wasn't me. This wasn't my life. This was *somebody else*. This happened to *somebody else*."

What I'm about to tell you is so unbelievable that I won't blame you if you think that I'm making it all up, or if you think that I was, and still am, some insane drug-addict.

And what I want you to know is that when it comes to "matters of the spirit" it's nothing like the way that movies, TV shows and books like to portray them. The real-life story isn't, say, "neat". It doesn't fit into tidy boxes or within sharply defined borders. Things don't always have a clear beginning … or ending.

The real-life story is a matter of a series of events that aren't always even seen as being connected, at least not at the time. And often, when extraordinary things happen, things that fall outside of what you're used to, to what's ordinary, it's easier to disregard them, to "conveniently" forget them, to not look at them *too* closely rather than reflect on them, especially when you're young, and scared. When you're living through events that are truly horrifying, you're not thinking, "Gee, I'd better remember this clearly, because some day this is going to make a great book," you're just trying to get through it, you're trying to *survive*. And often, when the weird invades your life, you're in an altered state of consciousness, you're not even *you*, you really are someone, or something ... else.

So, you end up making a justification, some "reasonable" explanation, at that time, as to what happened. Just so that you can get on with your life.

I'll share with you what I can, on the understanding that my memories are incomplete, and on the understanding that when I've had to rely on the memory of witnesses that their memories are incomplete too and that they were scared and just trying to get through "it", whatever "it" was, too and that they too, at the time, would also create their own "reasonable" narratives and explanations as to what was going on. But to this day, I still struggle with everything that happened.

And it's only recently that I've become spiritually mature enough to make some sense of this, and to tell you what I went through, without feeling covered in fear, without feeling emotionally overwhelmed, without this ever-present sense of ... *dread*.

And even though, at the time, I thought I was the only one in the world going through this. I know now that there are thousands, probably millions of people who have had experiences similar to mine, and I want you to know that if anything I went through speaks to you, then all I can tell you is that you are not alone.

If you, or somebody that you care about is going through something like what I'm going to be describing, *please, know that you are not alone.*

Nobody should have to go through this alone.

Everything that I am about to tell you and will continue to tell you is true. For what it is worth to you I swear on the Holy Bible that these events happened as I described them. At the time, they happened irregularly and over a long period of time. Often, so much time passed between events it was easy for me to rationalize them or write them off, but over the years so many things happened, so many things that compelled me with their reality, that in the end I couldn't ignore them.

Eventually, I could not deny that something of a profoundly evil spiritual nature was deeply embedded in my life.

I was brought up a Catholic and educated within the Catholic system. As far back as I can remember I've had a strong connection with the Virgin Mary and God. I was also relatively sensitive to the spiritual and the paranormal. When I was a child, stories of ghosts and witches and things that go "bump in the night" terrified me, *but also fascinated me.*

But it wasn't until I was about fourteen, that I had what you could say was my first paranormal experience.

Full disclosure first.

I'm asthmatic and at the time I was overdosing myself on asthma medication. Ventolin opens up the passages that allow air into your lungs. You over-breathe and get high. I'm pretty sure I was not the only teenage asthmatic who ever abused their medication, but I've never heard of anyone doing that who experienced or who reported anything like what happened to me.

I was lying on the couch in the upstairs lounge room of our house, when suddenly I found myself outside of my body, looking at myself. In this other, non-physical body I found myself in, I turned and ran and then I flew out the window, and I felt as if I was going through something to … somewhere … and I found myself in Heaven, or at least something that I interpreted as Heaven.

I found myself in a place where there was white light coming from above, a river embankment, and a tree.

I still felt as if I was in a body, complete and whole like a normal person, but at the same time still felt that *I was a spirit.*

I found myself in front of the Virgin Mary. She was in her robe and looked just like she usually looked as she was depicted in Catholic imagery.

In this vision, I also saw my grandfather. By this time he had been dead for six years. He was sitting down, in a garden, by a riverbank, with his arms outstretched, forward, hands resting on his knees. He was looking up at me. He appeared just as he had been when I had last seen him.

Standing there, in front of Mary, I had the most amazing feeling of peace and joy at a level that was beyond anything in ordinary experience. It was as if every cell in my body was bathed in pure love. And there was an unbelievable amount of something that I can only describe as *trust.*

Some people take drugs, like ecstasy, and they feel this overwhelming sense of happiness. If you've ever had that sort of experience, it was like that, only the feeling was of love, and multiplied a thousand-fold, a million-fold. This was a level of love that was almost unbearable, that would, afterwards, make me question how much love a mortal human could stand.

And in the face of this almost unbearable love, I never wanted to leave that presence. There was nothing on earth that could compare, or that *could* ever compare to what I was experiencing. Wherever I was, I did not want to return. It would be even more accurate to say that it didn't even occur to me that I would want to go back.

And I felt this need to go to my grandfather and be with him, but before I could even take a step Mary intervened and she said to me, "It's not your time. Go home."

I found myself back the lounge room, running and jumping back into my body.

I "woke up" and that feeling of overwhelming love and trust had gone and in its place was *pure terror*. I was confused and utterly and completely petrified with fear.

I had recognized that in that moment just passed, that I had nearly died, that I had nearly caused my own death, and that I felt guilty about that. The heavenly bliss had gone, and I was back in my mortality.

I went downstairs to where my parents were. Now, I didn't want to tell them that I was abusing my medication, overdosing on Ventolin to the point where I was high on, of all things, oxygen. But even so, I couldn't explain to them that I had just had an out of body experience, because I was in shock, but I tried anyway. So, I told my father, "I think I've just left my body," and he just laughed.

But I also knew that they could see the hint of terror as it dawned on them that whatever had happened to me had left me in a mess.

So, at the time, they did what they could to comfort me, without their really getting a clear explanation as to why I was feeling the way that I was feeling.

Having given so little to my parents, there was nothing much that they could do for me.

To be clear, the experience that I had wasn't part of some deliberate new-agey practice. I wasn't *setting out* to leave my body, so I had no preparation and it wasn't in any way controlled. It just spontaneously happened. It wasn't until a long time after that I heard that when people are blind-sided into an out-of-body experience that whatever comes to help them through it shows up as somebody that they trust. And, because at that age I had a strong connection to the Virgin Mary, it would be natural to assume that she would appear to me. In similar circumstances other people might see Jesus Christ, or Buddha, or a saint, or a wise imam, or a deceased loved one, or even a spirit animal.

So, I did what I could, which was to deny what had happened. I couldn't fathom that what I had experienced was even possible. So, I rationalized it, and put it down to some very vivid dream. What had happened couldn't have really happened, so it didn't, and in a matter of a few weeks I had swept it under the carpet, as I would later sweep so much else under so many other "carpets".

Years later, I've come to learn that there is such a thing as spiritual maturity – a capacity to know and feel comfortable in the realm of the non-physical, in the things that are not material, or easily measurable, or easily explainable.

I can call on Mary, and I will weep. And when I pray to Mary, they will be tears of joy.

But that's *now.*

Back then, when I was fourteen years old I was a long, long way from being spiritually mature. So, I did what so many other people would have done in the face of the "impossible" – I dealt with it either by pretending it was not real, or by not being dealing with it at all. If this were a movie script, this is the point where the hero is utterly changed by their experience, and, transformed and begins a greater journey. But real life isn't like that and it wasn't like that for me. I didn't become a bigger and better version of myself for having had a profound spiritual experience.

But it did, for a while, deeply strengthen my faith. I had had a deep confirmation of my faith, but it was a *private* thing. I didn't suddenly become all evangelical. In fact until now, here in this "confession", maybe only four other people have ever known what happened to me.

Then, shortly after, within a few months, something did change.

I began to pick up on what I could best describe as "negative energy".

Weird things started happening to me.

Weird things started happening within the house.

The first time I experienced some weirdness was in my bedroom. It would have been around 1:00am. I had just woken up and the right-hand door of wardrobe, that had been securely shut, swung slowly open, far enough to reveal the mirror on the door's inner surface. The left-hand door remained closed. Through research and accounts of people who had experienced similar phenomena I later learned that "spirits" can "come through" mirrors but long before learning that I intuited that this was what was going on. Up until the age of thirty-eight I covered mirrors with a cloth and hung a cross or a rosary over the cloth, to stop "them" coming through.

In that moment, I felt and intuited a *presence.*

And, at least at first, I felt that it was a harmless, playful spirit.

So, I challenged it. I said, "I'll pray to Mary and she'll get rid of you." And I rolled over and went back to sleep.

A few nights later the same thing happened again and again I challenged it, "I will pray to Jesus, and you will have to go."

And then again, a few nights after that it happened again. Sensing that things were escalating slightly I was beginning to get annoyed.

"I'm not afraid of you. Fuck off!"

But it, whatever "it" was, kept coming back. About once every few weeks or so.

About the fifth time it happened the bedroom door started opening, *and closing*, of its own accord too.

"If you don't go, I will pray to Jesus and I will tell on you!"

These encounters went for about six months, and about eight or nine times.

At about the sixth encounter, there was a change in the feeling. The door games continued. That hadn't changed, but I started feeling *threatened*.

About the sixth time the bedroom door opened and closed. Fed up, I got up and tried to leave my bedroom, but the door wouldn't open.

Now I was angry.

"If you don't go away, I'll tell Jesus what you're doing, and you'll be in a lot of trouble." Only after I'd said that was I able to open the door.

Then about the eighth or ninth time, things escalated further, dramatically.

I had been asleep for hours, and then I woke up, and my eyes were open, and I could move my eyeballs, but I couldn't move any other muscle in my body. I couldn't move or even twitch. I had no control over anything other than my eyes which could at least move my limited gaze around my darkened bedroom.

Others finding themselves in this situation might have thoughts going through their heads like, "Have I finally done something to myself that I can't undo? Is this a stroke, or worse? Is this permanent?"

But no such thoughts occurred to me in that moment.

Instead …

Fear covered me, like a thick blanket.

I was completely certain that *I was in danger*.

Sheer panic and terror.

This started happening, on average, once a week, or once a fortnight.

On another night I was paralyzed again, and I thought, "If the door locks again, I can at least escape through the window," but as I had that thought, I could see the window slam down shut, and lock, by itself.

Suddenly, I could move again.

I got up. I immediately tried to unlock the window, but it wouldn't unlock. It would not budge.

I went to the door. I tried to open it but couldn't open it.

I knew that "It" wanted me to know that it was in control, that it was in charge.

I went back to my bed, and with more bravado than confidence, I said, "I don't care about you. Just go away."

I was very concerned, because my escape route had been cut off. But I didn't show it. And within a few minutes I felt that the presence was gone. It's energy just, *dissipated*.

I had an overwhelming sense that "it" lived in the wardrobe, "behind" or "in" the mirror or that in some way the mirror was a door to wherever it did live. I don't know if it went back into the wardrobe, or somewhere else.

I immediately went to my parent's room.

"There's something in my room. I don't want to sleep in there. I'm terrified."

But they just brushed me off, probably thinking that I was just having a bad dream.

"Go back to your room."

They didn't want to hear about it.

But, not wanting to waste time arguing with their crazy teenage son, they let me take a mattress into their room, and I slept at the foot of their bed. But my father was a no-nonsense type of man and wasn't going to put up with this sort of crap. So, when his patience ran out, I took to sleeping on a mattress in the hall outside of my room, or in the upstairs lounge room, next to my bedroom. It was better than being trapped *in there*.

One night, my nanna, my mother's mother, stayed over, and she stayed in my room. I was told to sleep on the couch in the lounge room. In the morning, I heard my grandmother and mother talking in my room and I heard my nanna distinctly say, "The wardrobe door opened in the middle of the night."

My mother, in turn, whispered back something I couldn't hear. My mother wasn't a believer in anything that was going on, aside from the fact that maybe her younger son was having a troubled adolescence, and I got the impression that her reply to my nanna was just a "So, what?". As dismissive a "So, what?" as any that she'd ever given to me, but I got the distinct impression that my grandmother had picked up on something too.

I felt at the time that now, *finally*, there was some confirmation from someone else that it wasn't all "in my mind" or whatever, that at least now my mother would start to believe me. I felt validated. But this didn't magically start up any dialog or any open discussion. I kept waiting for my parents to make a first move on the situation, but it never came. In hindsight maybe they didn't want to acknowledge anything and risk, I don't know, "feeding" the situation or exacerbating it.

So, I was on my own.

It got to the point that every few weeks when I'd sense "it", I'd just leave my room before it got aggressive and I'd sleep on the couch in the upstairs lounge room.

Some nights, when I felt it was safe to stay in my room, I'd keep the bedroom door open with a doorstop.

The doorstop was a glazed, grey, ceramic gargoyle with beady little red eyes. Perhaps not such a best choice for a doorstop, given the circumstances. I'd think to myself, "Well, that's pretty scary. I wouldn't want to look at that!" And I figured "it" wouldn't want to look at that either. It's the same sort of logic that medieval designers of cathedrals had when they used gargoyles to frighten off demons.

The first time I tried it, it didn't work.

I woke up in the morning, the door was shut, and the doorstop gargoyle was strategically placed in the center of the room so that it was staring right at me with its red, beady, glass eyes.

No one, no human anyway, had moved it.

I tried the same strategy on other nights and the same thing happened over and over. I'd find the gargoyle at different places on the floor, staring at me, with those red eyes.

I was never awake when the gargoyle moved.

In my usual way of trying to find some "rational" explanation the story I told myself was that I had been sleepwalking in the night and moved the gargoyle myself, in the same way that I tried to rationalize the overwhelming fear I'd feel on some nights as some sort of night terror that I still hadn't grown out of. But I never came up with a definitive test as to whether it was me doing all this, or whether it was something else. Unfortunately, the technology didn't exist at the time to have a camera in the room recording this at night to see what was really going on so that option didn't even occur to me.

To be honest, I don't know what I or anyone else would have done if we had ended up with video footage of a wardrobe and bedroom door opening and shutting, or of a gargoyle doorstop mysteriously moving by themselves.

And maybe I could convince myself that maybe, just maybe, all this was down to some unusually active sleepwalking.

But then there were things that happened when I was wide awake, and nowhere near my bedroom.

My parents worked hard and long hours, and my brother and sister were a lot older than me and had their own, independent lives. I'd be home about four o'clock in the afternoon, and my mother and father wouldn't be home until around six o'clock, or later, if they had to go out for some reason. So, I had quite a bit of time on my own and this had been the situation since I was about eight.

In the interests of even more full disclosure, but at the risk of leaving even more room to discredit myself, I have to admit that at the time that I was fourteen to fifteen I was a cannabis smoker as well, regularly, but only on weekends, as a recreational thing. I can only say that the weirdness kept happening to me even when I wasn't using cannabis. Later consultation with mental health professionals would confirm that nothing I experienced could reasonably be put down to "drug psychosis" or psychotic illness. Later events also unfolded that were witnessed and corroborated by third parties. I swear on my grandparents' graves that the cannabis had nothing to do with what was going on with me, again as many things happened in the middle of the week when I was not using cannabis and could not have possibly been under its influence.

So, there was no one around when, all of a sudden one day the TV started turning itself off.

Then turning itself back on.

Then turning itself back off.

Then turning itself back on again.

At this point I didn't have the sense of danger that I would later have.

I thought, "This thing is playing with me." So, I decided to play back.

When the TV turned itself off, I said, out loud, "Turn yourself back on", and, within a second or two, it did.

I said, "Turn yourself off", and, again, it did.

I got the feeling that "it" liked to play these games, particularly when I was ignoring it, in order to get my attention.

Other things would happen, like some standard, staple scene from a cheesy horror movie.

The family dog was an outdoor dog. My father wouldn't let him in the house. But the dog would bark and growl through the back door in the direction of some space in the middle of an otherwise empty hall room, at something, that, as far as I can tell, wasn't there.

Sometimes the dog would growl at me. Viciously. It wasn't until I said, "Cobber, it's me", that Cobber would stop. It was like he wasn't seeing or sensing me, and he was in some sort of, I don't know, dog trance that he'd only snap out of when he heard my voice.

My parents later told me that at other times Cobber would growl at this invisible thing even when I wasn't there.

Another time, at about 6:00pm I was sitting with my father in the downstairs lounge. We thought that my mother hadn't come home yet, but then we heard her voice shouting out for me from upstairs.

This wasn't unusual. My mother would often come home late, and get dressed upstairs before calling down for something, usually to nag me into cleaning my room, or something.

"Paaaaauuuuuul", my mother called out.

"Your mother wants you", my father said, unnecessarily.

So, I got up and walked to the stairs to stare up at the banister, expecting to see my mother.

But she wasn't there.

And in that instant the light from the headlights of my mother's car, driving into the driveway, shone through the front windows. She wasn't home. She wasn't even in the house.

As far as my father was concerned, since my mother showed up within a minute of this incident occurring, he must have assumed that she had been in the house all the time.

He didn't know any better.

But *I* did.

Another night I was home alone, again.

It was about 7:00 pm when I heard my mother scream over the stair banister again.

But this time I ignored "it". I didn't want to give it any attention.

And then because I ignored it …

Suddenly, I heard this great, crashing sound and a shaking of the whole house.

I was terrified, but even in my terror, I wasn't going to go upstairs to see what had happened. I didn't want to give "it" any more attention, give it the satisfaction of knowing that it had rattled me. I also had no idea what it was going to do to me when I got up there.

By the time my mother got home at around 9:00 pm I *still* hadn't gone upstairs. When my mother did, I heard her scream "Paaaaauuuuuul!!! Come here now!!!!!"

I went upstairs and in the TV lounge the entire TV cabinet, including the TV and all the books on the shelves had come down.

"Why did you do this?!!!" my mother screamed at me.

"I didn't do this! I've got to tell you what happened. Something yelled my name out and then this thing came crashing down."

"You're lying to me! You're lying to me! This could NOT have happened. Nothing but a human being could have done this. This cabinet could NOT have come crashing down on its own!!!"

I couldn't have lied and said that I was somewhere else, because my mother would have wanted to know where I was and would have wanted to corroborate my story. But telling the truth wasn't getting me anywhere either. And the truth was unbelievable.

When I saw it, *I* couldn't believe it! What *force*, could have brought down a wooden wall unit that was at least six-foot-high by eight wide, with all thc stuff on the shelves? Something with *power* and *strength* had done this.

If "it" could do *this*, what *else* could it do?

I don't even know how my mother could think that I would have done this, given that I grew up in a "spare the rod, spoil the child" household and I was well aware of what would happen to me if I stepped out of line. But it was easier to believe that I had done this than what had actually happened.

I was still terrified and in shock, but my mother wasn't having any of it and made me put the whole unit back up and tidy everything up too and to do it before my father came home and decided that I needed to be taught a further lesson involving his hand and my bottom.

And after I had put the shelf back in its place and fixed everything, I continued to play the denial card and put it out of my mind.

CHAPTER THREE

DOWN BUT NOT OUT IN GUECKEDOU AND CONAKRY

"Let the Church be your mother."

Joseph

After selling my coffee in the market at Gueckedou I left my friends. I had some money from the sale.

That night I slept on a table in the now empty marketplace. I told myself that I would give it a week. If somehow some help didn't come to me so that I could continue my education, I would return to Nongoa and to my grandma.

In the morning, I saw a lady called Fatmata, but we had always called her Aunty "F.A.". She was one of the many people that my grandma's friend had, over time, taken into the same house where we had been staying.

"What are you doing here, Joseph?" Aunty F.A. asked.

"Oh, I was just hanging around," I said. "It got late, I didn't have a place to sleep, so I slept here."

"Does your grandmother know you're here?"

"Um, ah, nooo …"

"Joseph! What are you thinking? She must be beside herself with worry about you! Are you crazy, boy?"

"Yes, I suppose so."

Aunty F.A. took me in. She got a message to my grandparents that I was OK, and that she was trying to get me into school.

Aunty F.A. was a prostitute, something I didn't realize until I had been living with her for a week. Many nights she would not be home. Sometimes she would bring men home and I would make a discrete exit for a while. My grandmother would not have approved.

But Aunty F.A. was, at heart, a good woman. She was doing what so many women have done so often. She did what she could to survive and taking me in was her way of paying back the kindness and support that she had received when she had needed it.

That is how it is where I come from. People help each other if they can. We "pay forward" if we can.

We do not expect to be "paid back" by the same people we help. We trust that there will be somebody who will help us when and if we ever need help. I guess we believe that the Lord brings the helpers and those in need of help together at the right time. With Aunty F.A.'s help I was able to go to a school that wasn't getting closed down every five minutes. I was with her a year.

Among the refugees returning to Guinea were my parents and sisters who had had to flee Liberia all over again.

The moment my mother caught up with her mother she asked, "Where is my son? Did you sell my son?" When my grandmother told them the "details" of Aunty F.A.'s life they both decided that they had to come and get me *straight away*.

Reunited, my family decided that since I was already going to school in Gueckedou, that they would move to Gueckedou too, where my stepfather had a house owned by his extended family.

At this point religion became a problem.

My stepfather's family where devout Muslims. They didn't mind that my mother was a Christian, but they couldn't tolerate the idea that my stepfather's children would not be brought up Muslim, and I was counted among his children, obviously, since my stepfather had been more a father to me than my biological father had ever been.

My mother, while always respectful of my stepfather's wishes, didn't feel it was his family's right to dictate how her child would worship, so the whole family moved out. Ironically, I started going to Mosque with my stepfather anyway. And so, we had some stability for a while.

Then, when I was fourteen, I had a vision. A sort of "waking dream" that came upon me suddenly when I was just sitting down and taking a moment of repose.

I was sitting on a log of wood outside the house. I was half-asleep, half-awake. In this vision, I was running. People were chasing me. I felt that their intention was to kill me. I found myself in an open space, flying. I flew for a while and then I descended. I looked back to see if the people were still chasing me. Instead, I saw a huge throne. I turned fully around. What I saw had my full attention. No one was sitting in the throne, but there was *the presence of a vast light in a human form.* I glanced back. A large crowd of people were there now behind me.

Thousands.

Uncountable.

I turned around again. A huge book came out of nowhere, between me and the throne. There came a voice that sounded as if thunder could speak, or as if roaring, rolling river rapids could make words. The voice called out names. As the roaring, rolling thunder voice called out names, pages in the book turned.

I was terrified.

I heard my name called. I did not answer, so scared I was. I looked back again, into the crowd. I had an impulse to bring people from the crowd forward, so that they could hear this voice for themselves, because somehow, I felt that they could not hear the roaring, rolling thunder-that-spoke.

In that moment that voice spoke to me from the throne.

"I AM GOING TO USE YOU TO BRING FREEDOM TO MANY. YOU ARE MY VESSEL."

This is Jesus talking to me!

It is difficult for me, even now, to describe this. I can tell you the events of this trance / vision / sending / visitation – whatever you want to call it – but the events that happened in this vision do not adequately convey the *feeling*.

Imagine that you are very thirsty. Imagine that you have been exhausted with heat and thirsty for so long that you aren't even aware of how thirsty you are. Imagine that suddenly, you are washed over with cool, sweet water and you surrender to this flow and you feel this incredible relief as you drink in the water while also being surprised at how thirsty you must have been all this time without ever knowing that you thirsted in the first place.

That is what it felt like.

I felt refreshed, restored and very … pure.

Clean.

Revived.

And a fear that I had had for so long, a fear I had not even realized I had … had gone away.

It was at about this time that my grandfather was dying. Because the adults in the house were busy making ends meet, and the other children were too young, I ended up spending the most time with him. One day he called me to him and said, "Joseph, the time has come to give you a name."

It is the custom in some parts of Africa for an elder to bestow a name upon a child if an elder is moved to do so.

"But I have a name, Grandfather," I said.

"This is a new name. This is the name that you will carry with you. This is the name that represents who you are."

"And what is that, Grandfather?" I asked.

"You are 'Wisdom', because I see that in you."

And that is how I became "Wisdom". I know it sounds strange to the Western ear, but that is yet another example of how we do things differently in Africa. This is why I am "Wisdom". Hardly anyone calls me Joseph.

Shortly after, my grandfather died, but not before he had given this name, this final gift, to me.

I had never had any attraction to or feeling for Islam. I do not want you to think that I have no respect for Muslims or for Islam as a religion. God speaks to us in many ways. But for me, personally, Islam had always been something *imposed* on me. It did not speak to my heart and much less so after my experience before the Throne.

I went to my dad, my stepfather and said, "I don't want to go to the mosque anymore. I want to be a Christian."

"Well," my dad said, with the sort of cold fury a parent has when they think that their child is in the process of doing something particularly stupid, "you can be a Christian if you like but, if you want to still live under the same roof as this family you will go to the mosque. You keep going to mosque or you can get out."

I knew that he didn't understand the depth of my conviction. He probably thought I was just being a rebellious teenager. People who haven't experienced it don't understand how a profound spiritual experience can change you forever *if you let it*. My Dad also failed to realize that I was still the same person who had decided to leave home *at the age of eleven* to get an education. My Dad really didn't know what I was capable of, once I got it into my head to do something.

"With all due respect then, OK," I said, "I'm leaving."

I was fully confident that The Holy Spirit would look after me. Of that, I had no doubt.

My mother, bound as she was by our culture to "obey" her husband, didn't have much to say in the matter. But she didn't mind that much. She too had her connection to The Holy Spirit, who had kept the promise to protect her child, and whom she *knew* would always keep that promise. So, she *knew* that I was making the right choice. She *knew* it wasn't going to be easy, but she still *knew* in that way of *knowing*, with complete certitude, that people of deep faith have.

And I *knew*, with absolute certainty, that I was doing the right thing too.

So I left for the Guinean capital, Conakry, some 400 kilometers, some 250 miles to the north-east, by the shortest route through Sierra Leone. By bad roads entirely within Guinea, the trip would have been more like 550 kilometers, some 350 miles.

As I said goodbye to my mother at the bus station, she said, "This is not going to be easy."

"I know."

"I'm going to be praying for you."

"I know."

"Remember the reason that you're making this decision is because you have encountered the Lord."

"Yes."

"Always seek him, Joseph. Seek the Lord in everything you do."

"I will."

"Treat the Church the way you treat me," she said. "Let the Church be your mother."

Under the radar, my mother had arranged for me to stay initially at my dad's nephew's – my step-cousin's – house in Conakry. I began to go to the local Assemblies of God Church to get a feeling for what my next step might be.

I was there at my cousin's place for a couple of weeks before my dad found out and instructed my cousin to kick me out because I had been "disobedient". My cousin was in no position to defy his uncle, so I had to go. Fortunately, in the way that things happen in that part of the world, I reconnected with an acquaintance, a man called Fodah. I told him my story and even though he and his wife Agnes were already hosting three other boys, they welcomed me into their home so I slept on a bench at their place – for the next three years.

I'll admit that in spite of my faith in what The Holy Spirit was leading me to do I did feel wounded and a little bitter about a lot of things – my dad's hardline attitude, the way my biological father had effectively abandoned me to chase his dreams of power through sorcery, the war that had disrupted my family, the poverty we had so often experienced in spite of our wealth, how everything was *just so hard all the time*.

And yet, even in the worst of times, I would feel the presence of The Holy Spirit and with that have a deep sense of encouragement. Sometimes it was more than that. I would be gently seized by visions of being in front of thousands of people talking to them or praying for others in more intimate settings – moments or flashes of my future life that would come to me in trance-like states or in vivid, intense dreams. A couple of times, I'd ask for clarity and I would see a vision in front of me as clear as if it were on a large television screen in front of my open eyes. These visions would last maybe two or three minutes at a time. After them I would feel edified, but that feeling would fade and I would fall back into moods of not feeling so great.

Freshly kicked out of my cousin's house, I went to the Assemblies of God Church. There I approached Pastor Apie, a French-speaking Togolese who headed up the Deliverance ministry there. I told him my story. Pastor Apie, being a man of discernment, knew that I had a *calling*.

"You have a gift for Deliverance," he said. "You have a calling upon your life for a Deliverance Ministry." I knew only at the time that Deliverance was the process of "casting out demons". I was both a little shocked that he had discerned this in me, but some part of me knew this was true too. I had had my doubts about who I was, and who I might become, but Pastor Apie had confirmed what some part of me had known all along.

"You also need some inner healing," he declared.

As I said, he was a man of discernment, that talent, capacity or skill to be able to look beyond the surface of things and intuit a truth often through a connection to The Holy Spirit.

In that first meeting he put me on a three-day prayer program that involved fasting from midnight to 6:00 pm.

"We need to put you in to a state where you can receive the light of The Holy Spirit," he said.

Prayer is a powerful tool for strengthening the conscious spiritual connection to the healing power of The Holy Spirit – at least it is for me. It is also a powerful tool for psychological healing. To be its most effective, really, to be effective at all, the Inner Healing Prayer Work must be conducted in a spirit of *ruthless* honesty.

In Christianity, we relate to God in three principle ways, "God the Father", "God the Son" and "God The Holy Spirit". Without going down a theological rabbit-hole, one way of understanding the difference between these three aspects is that "God the Father" is God in the role of creator. "God the Son" is the "human face" of God. "God The Holy Spirit" is God as a transformative power through which we undergo transformation. It is through relating to God as God The Holy Spirit that we ask for Divine Intercession – the active participation of God in our lives – through which we call upon God for the expulsion of conscious evil, in the form of demons, and through which we draw upon God for healing the damage that demons have caused. Even in the face of this definition, I tend to use the term "The Holy Spirit" to refer to God, because the term "God" is so loaded and I don't want theological quibbles to get in the way of appreciating the experience of the Spiritually afflicted and those who treat these afflictions.

There is an old movie called *The Nun's Story*. In it, a postulant nun is being told by her Mother Superior that only she herself can ultimately determine if she can commit herself to a life dedicated to God. Only she herself can ultimately determine if she is willing to become a pure instrument for The Holy Spirit. To make this determination, she must be *ruthlessly* honest with herself. As her Mother Superior says, "You might be able to fool us. You might even fool yourself. But you cannot fool God."

After my first three days of prayer, Pastor Apie put me on a further four-day prayer program and prescribed deep self-examination.

And so, in that spirit of *ruthless honesty*, over those four days I looked into my heart and soul. I did not realize until I really looked how much resentment, anger and bitterness truly I had in me. I had not been aware of the extent of my feelings towards my fathers, my mother and so many of the people in my life and the things that had happened to me. I will explain the absolute necessity of forgiveness later, but for now let me just say that a first, vital step in becoming strong enough to perform my spiritual tasks is to work on myself first. I work to uncover things within myself that I might have long-repressed or denied – things that could be denied no longer. It is far better to do this work first, before Demonic forces find a way of exploiting your shadows and find a way of turning them against you.

And then I had to share these things, again, with ruthless honesty, with Pastor Apie. Every night for those four days, for a couple of hours, he and I would sit while I opened up to him.

There is something profound in this sharing. There is something powerful in having someone listen to you without judgment, while you truly express your inner world, even if, *especially if*, you do not like what you see. There is undeniable value, I think, in saying these things *out loud and publicly to another person*, to hear yourself speaking what, until then, has only been said by your own voice in the privacy of your own mind. The Catholics are right when they say that confession is good for the soul, but it must be a confession that comes from a place of deep sincerity.

"I will give you some prayers, specific to your situation," Pastor Apie said. "Say these prayers in the middle of the night, just before you go to bed."

These prayers emphasized forgiveness. And if the purely practical psychological aspects of forgiveness weren't enough, from a purely practical *spiritual* point of view, unforgiveness is a very low spiritual state and it leaves the door open to Spiritual Affliction.

Having a door negligently open to Satan was a luxury that

someone like me, with a nascent calling for Deliverance, *could not afford to have*.

That is what Pastor Apie saw in me. That is what first had to be dealt with, what I first had to deal with.

Forgiveness was the first step in cutting any ties I might have to negativity, to evil, to spiritual chaos.

And there were other ties too.

I never really knew what happened to me when I was very young and Attem would take me away. I might have spent time with witchdoctors and sorcerers, contaminated by whatever entities they were dealing with. There might have been ties there, there might have been contracts entered into and curses and spells cast and however young I was, however unwittingly, I had provided an entry to these forces. Now I had to declare that those ties were cut, those connections now broken. Naturally, I had to forgive my father for anything that he did, and anything he *might* have done.

Again I emphasize that in Africa, and in most of the world for that matter, the existence of demons and the reality of witchcraft and the power of witches, witchdoctors and sorcerers is a given, it is part of our construct of reality. Only in the Western hyper-scientific and hyper-rational worldview are these realities at best questioned, and at worst scorned as superstition. Where I come from, the world of spirits is *normal*. For us to say that we "believe" in spirits is as nonsensical as saying that we "believe" in gravity. For us, faith is not a matter of "believing" in the existence of God, in spirits and the dimensions in which God and the spirits reside. For us our crises of faith is not that we might falter in our faith in the *existence* of God and the spirits. When we falter, is in which *power* we trust the most. Do we trust in the power of the spirits, or do we trust in The Holy Spirit?

And there were times when my mother too, might have despaired, might have faltered in her faith, in her trust in The Holy Spirit. There might have been times that my mother, however innocently, however ignorantly, however subconsciously, might have made a pact with a demon or entity, if only to save her sickly young son from dying. This was a very real possibility because when, as a child, I experience extended paralysis my mother sent me to live with my grandmother for a couple of months and during this time The Holy Spirit visited my mother through the medium of powerful vision, a waking dream, and said, *"YOU HAVE FORSAKEN YOUR RESPONSIBILITIES TO THIS CHILD."*

The Holy Spirit is not one to pull punches. My mother came back to her mother, and in taking me back said to her, "I have a responsibility to this child. If he's going to die, let it be on my watch."

The possibility, however slight, that my mother had compromised us spiritually in some way also needed to be broken too, and any connection to demonic entities had to be cut.

This whole process of soul searching and finding forgiveness did not happen all at once or in one sitting.

"Spirit of the Living God, shine your light upon this child," Pastor Apie would say. "Shine your light in every part of this child. Let the light be known and let the truth be known so that this soul can be healed."

Prayer and the Word of God lightened my heart and with each lightening more "stuff" would come up. Over several sessions with Pastor Apie we rooted out the weeds from my inner garden.

It was not always easy, but in the end, I felt so much better for it.

"In one sense," Pastor Apie said, "This will never be over. God will continue to challenge you. But anytime you find yourself needing it, go through this process and use this same method."

And I always have.

Above all else and all other preparations though it is the process of forgiveness that I prescribe to all who come seeking liberation from their afflictions.

Carrying unforgiveness is like weighing yourself down with chains, like driving with the parking brake on, with the steering lock on or sailing with the anchor down. Carrying unforgiveness is effectively handicapping yourself, and really, I had enough challenges without making my life more complicated or burdened than it already was. Forgiveness therefore had to be an essential part of my initiation into the work I would be doing.

Beyond my spiritual health, my priority, as always, was to secure my education. As soon as I was able to I enrolled in school. I was able to attend classes between about 1:00 pm and 6:00 pm. Fodah, the man who had taken me in, and his wife, Agnes, were generous and kind people. They never asked for money from me for my board, but I felt that I had to contribute to my upkeep, and I had school fees, school expenses and bus fares, so I had to work. School fees were very cheap, maybe $50 for a three-month semester, but wages were also ridiculously low. This is why when you donate to an African charity a little can go a very long way.

I started working in a plastics factory from midnight to about 8:00 am, earning about $25 per month. I'd go home, have a nap, and then get myself ready for school. After school I'd go home, get something to eat. Have another nap and then go off to work. Because there was so little money, on most days I would walk to school. It was about an hour's walk each way.

I lived like this for about two years. Then one day the chief engineer of the factory where I worked, a Pakistani man by the name of Sede, approached me.

"Would you like to be a caretaker in my home?" he asked. "I need a cleaner. A cook too."

NECESSARY PREPARATION

It is said, quite rightly, that "Fools rush in where angels fear to tread."

I have, in one way or another, been battling with demons for my entire life.

Any time I am faced with a case of an afflicted person I feel humble but also know within me that this is what I am here to do. Even when I am involved with a very serious spiritual battle I become filled with a capacity, a power, to stand between these destructive and malevolent spirits and the soul of a human being. To be able to channel that power must be a calling, and yet I must stay humble within my true relationship with The Holy Spirit.

My priority, first and foremost and always, is to maintain my relationship with The Holy Spirit.

I do this by being in a constant fellowship with The Holy Spirit, in constant conversation with that which bears witness with my soul. I that I do, all that I accomplish comes from The Holy Spirit and this relationship is what strengthens *my* connection, *my* spirit.

I know the Divine Voice in my heart. I know Divine Instruction in my heart. I know Divine guidance in my heart because my relationship is a relationship of the heart.
I know when He instructs me from my heart.

I see The Holy Spirit in my Heart's Eye. It is a sense that calls strongly even in the midst of chaos.

This was not a sense that I fully developed overnight. This takes practice. It requires me to practice getting out of the way and allowing The Holy Spirit to work through me.

And I am not alone. Intercessors who work behind the scenes play their part through prayer to create a cohort of power. I would not tread did I not have these angels behind me.

But these general preparations are just the beginning.

Before every individual procedure I dedicate a certain amount of time so that I might be open to where The Holy Spirit leads before I engage.

Before every deliverance session I seek the approval and assurance of The Holy Spirit.

I say my protective prayer for both myself and the afflicted.

I get the participant to repeat certain prayers to keep them protected and assured.

I know that we are all protected if The Holy Spirit gives me the green light. This green light is an undeniable sense that it is appropriate to proceed.

During the session, The Holy Spirit is in control of what happens so we are all safe. I always ask that manifestations be reduced to a minimum. Too many theatrics, I think, indicate a lack of preparation, like a patient who wakes up on the operating table because the anesthesia has been improperly administered.

What do I do after a session? It depends on how the sessions went. I do different things. Again, The Holy Spirit prompts me on what to do immediately after a session.

What is it that the holy spirit asks of a Minister of Deliverance? The Holy Spirit requires that I rely on the Wisdom of The Holy Spirit as a gift. The Wisdom of The Holy Spirit is the perfection of my faith. As a Minister of the Spirit, I am required to position myself to understand the works of God and to move beyond human faith in myself toward a faith in the Divine Process.

It is vital for me to depend on the counsel of The Holy Spirit by which I am able to judge how best to act. I submit to Spiritual Intuition, and thus, I can perfect my Spiritual Prudence. I have to be courageous to face Satan in the name of the Lord through the power of The Holy Spirit. I am called to rely on the knowledge of The Holy Spirit.

If I have done my groundwork correctly I can perceive the afflicted as God sees them.

I do all this with humility and respect, and through this I am free to take on the Spiritual Authority to create a positive intervention for the afflicted and to aid in their liberation.

I share this with you because I want you to use your own prudent judgment. Unless you are in an emergency situation and you do not have access to a suitably experienced Minister of Deliverance any untimely or unprepared intervention on your part is likely to do more harm than good.

Do not try this at home.

"You do?"

"I'll pay you double what you're getting here. You work too hard and you need to go to school."

"I'll need to talk to the boss," I said, mentioning the owner of the factory.

"Don't worry about that," he said. "If you want the job, I'll take care of it."

So I started working for Sede. From 7:00 am to about 11:00 I'd clean his house. I'd cook something. Then I'd go to school, finally able to afford the bus. I'd come back, do my second shift at Sede's house and then go home.

Sede was a kind man.

"Listen," he said. "If it gets too late for you to go home, I have a spare room. You can sleep there."

People don't always have much. They want to help, but there isn't always much to go around. But I've found that by and large, when people have the means to help, they do.

All my life I have found that when I need it the most, some angel in human form comes to help me for the next step of my mission.

It was now 1997, I was fifteen, but because of all the delays and interruptions in my education, I was only in Year 7 – the first year of high school. Nevertheless, I was doing well in school, always in the top five, and I was school captain. If I had been growing up in the West, I would have been the goody-two-shoes, bookworm nerd that's the butt of so many jokes on TV and in the movies. In Guinea, I was just one of thousands and thousands of kids who had been displaced and disrupted by circumstances not of our own making. Not all of them had had a Fodah, or an Agnes, or a Sede to help them on their way. For all that I had been through so far, it was nothing compared to what some other kids had been through, as I was later to learn.

I spent the next eighteen months working and studying. Doing what I could to catch up on my education. Classes were conducted in English, but because the rest of my life was spoken in Kryol, I was not yet inhabiting the English language. That had to change.

During this time of work and study my real life was at the church and so I settled into a new routine for this next two-year period of my life.

I was seventeen before I saw Attem, my biological father, again. It had been almost ten years.

The Civil War had stopped in August of 1997, when I was almost sixteen, but peace is a fragile thing in Africa, and hostilities had started again in April of 1999 and, as such the earlier war became known as The First Liberian Civil War and part two would be known as the Second Liberian Civil War.

Somehow, friends of my father had found me and contacted me to tell me that my father had been shot by rebel forces. He had escaped into Guinea, and bribed his way in, to convalesce. They told me that I had to see him. I agreed.

We met in Guinea, in Gueckedou.

It had been ten days since my father had been shot on his right side, upper chest, close to his right arm. I could smell the wound. It had become septic. I knew my father was on the run, which is why he hadn't been able to go to the hospital. I knew he would die if he didn't get medical attention soon.

"I'll talk to Mother," I said. "I'll get you a doctor."

"Thank-you," he said. "I'm in living in regret, Joseph," he said to me. "I've had a selfish life. It's been all about me and what I wanted, and I allowed myself to be open to … how do I put this? Negative spiritual influences …"

"To demons", I said, calling a spade a spade.

"To demons," he said.

My father had aged a lot. Since we look rather alike, I saw in him a vision of what I might become one day, if I were to make the same decisions that he had. I determined in that moment, that I was not my father, and that I would continue to follow my own path. My father had had a good education, but he had not made good use of his education. I was determined that I would make good use of mine.

"I'm sorry I abandoned you," he said. "I'm sorry that I wasn't a father to you. I hope that you can find a place in your heart to forgive me.

"I forgive you," I said, and I meant it. But at the time, in spite of all the work that I had done with Father Apie, I still did not truly realize what forgiveness was.

Now that I understand it a little better, I can perhaps better explain it.

People often misunderstand forgiveness. They think that forgiveness is a process whereby you are saying to the one that you need to forgive that it's "OK", that what they did was "acceptable" and that "it doesn't matter." This is what we are so often told.

But forgiveness isn't about being "OK" with something. If you have been the victim of, or on the receiving end of, mental, emotional, physical or spiritual negligence, injury, violence or abuse then *that is not "OK"*.

It is not "OK", it is never "OK" for the perpetrator to have done what they did. Abuse, in all its forms, is not "nothing". It is never "nothing".

So, forgiveness is not about dismissing what a perpetrator has done to you. Forgiveness is also not about rationalizing abuse or injury and saying, "they didn't mean it", because sometimes people are malicious, sometimes they are cruel and sometimes they *do* mean it. Forgiveness is also not about denial, that something that did happen, never happened. Forgiveness is not about "OK-ness" or "making it better" or "making the best of things" as it is usually understood.

Forgiveness is first and foremost a decision to undergo a *process*.

Forgiveness begins by honest acknowledgment of what happened to you.

Forgiveness continues with honest acknowledgment about what *you feel* about what happened to you.

Forgiveness continues with the brutal realization that what happened in the past *actually happened*, and that there is nothing you can do to "unmake" that past. That past will always exist.

Forgiveness continues with the brutal realization that whether the perpetrator acted out of clumsiness or ignorance at best, or nasty, cruel petty maliciousness *and the intention to do harm* at worst, that *the motives of the perpetrator are irrelevant.*

Forgiveness continues with the acknowledgment that what happened to you was and *cannot be dismissed or made acceptable.*

Instead, having gone through all these steps, forgiveness is the act of cutting your mental, emotional, physical and spiritual ties to your injury.

It is about releasing yourself from bondage.

This is the most important part of forgiveness.

Unforgiveness leaves you in bondage. Forgiveness releases you from that bondage.

If forgiveness is about one important thing it is about saying, "Enough is enough."

It is about saying, "It's time to move on."

On the other side of forgiveness, we should be able to say:

"Yes, that was terrible. Yes, I was hurt. But now I have to stop endlessly

picking at the scab and further injuring and scarring myself. I must now release the past and no longer keep dragging the pain and suffering and further injury into the present, contaminating the present and compromising my conscious spiritual connection and my ability to love. I now just have to heal and get on with it."

This does not mean the perpetrator "gets away with it". It does not mean, especially in extreme cases, that something should not be done about the harm that the perpetrator – who is often ignorant or sick – is doing or could continue to do unless stopped, somehow.

This does not mean you automatically "forget", because the perpetrator might still be in a position to continue to harm and *that has to be dealt with too.*

*But it does mean that you can move on from being a victim, because as long as there is resentment or unforgiveness in your heart, the perpetrator keeps winning, and it is **that** which cannot be allowed to continue.*

This does not mean that all feelings of victimhood are justified either. Sometimes you can play the victim and victimize yourself over imagined abuses, offenses and injuries that exist only in your own mind. False victimhood might give you some sense of power, at least for a little while, but it is a pathetic sort of power, because in playing the false victim you might become the abuser. This too must be examined with ruthless honesty. You must also look to the times when you were the genuine abuser too and you too created injury out of ignorance at best or malicious intent at worst. This too must be healed. We call self-forgiveness "repentance".

On the other side of self-forgiveness, we should be able to say:

"Yes, that was terrible. Yes, I hurt someone. But now I have to stop endlessly picking at the scab and further injuring and scarring myself and them. I must seek forgiveness, even on the understanding that I might not get it because I cannot control the decisions of another. In either case,

I must now release the past and no longer keep dragging the pain and suffering and further injury into the present, contaminating the present and compromising my conscious spiritual connection and my ability to love. I now just have to heal, ***make whatever amends I can****, and then get on with it."*

This "making amends" part is crucial. If it is within your capacity to make amends, but don't, then your "self-forgiveness" an empty gesture, and there is no healing in this, and there is no release, at least not for those of us who shirk our true responsibilities – our "ability" to "respond".

Forgiveness is about our responsibility to our own liberation.

My mother was able to arrange for a private doctor to extract the two bullets that were still inside my father. I saw him several times again over the next few months while he healed. Then he decided to go to Freetown, the capital of Sierra Leone.

I did not see him again for several years, until after the war.

I was later to learn that psychic wounds and mental trauma are a primary entry point for demonic entities. Unforgiveness is a gaping, unhealed psychic wound that is like a huge pile of manure to Satan, to *The Lord of the Flies*. The issues surrounding forgiveness are therefore crucial to understanding the phenomenon of Spiritual Affliction and confronting unforgiveness is crucial to the treatment and healing of Spiritual Affliction.

Whatever happens, healing requires confrontation, often many confrontations.

If there is to be healing, these confrontations cannot be denied.

CHAPTER FOUR

DOWN AND OUT OF IT IN ELWOOD AND ST KILDA

"If you kill her now, I will do a year in hell."

Paul

Denial works wonders, which I guess is why it's such a popular way of dealing with the undealable.

But it comes at a cost.

Over time, I became less and less religious. I was slowly, but surely, disconnecting from and losing my faith. These experiences with the paranormal were eroding my faith.

Where was God?

Where was the Virgin Mary?

Why weren't they protecting me from "it"?

Maybe none of them, God, Mary, Jesus, were real.

But whatever this "thing" was, it *was* real.

I started to receive psychic intuitions – messages and warnings –

more often than not as I was waking up and still in that half-asleep, half-awake state that psychologists call "hypnagogic".

One such message warned me not to walk down an alleyway near my house.

But did I listen to this warning?

No, because a message like that was just another of example of something that I could deny.

So, I found myself walking down this alleyway when a neighbor jumped a fence and started to attack me. I later learned that he attacked me because I looked like someone who had burgled him. I managed to run away but it wasn't long before, driving around in his car, he found me waiting at a bus stop. He threatened to beat me up and put me in the trunk of his car. He didn't do that, but he took away my concession card ID, with a threat that he'd come for me later. I went to school terrified but somehow managed enough courage to get a group of school friends with me, go to his house and to confront him, "You've got the wrong guy," I said. He was screaming in my face, looming over me, but somehow, because I'd come to confront him, he thought that was "honorable" in some way so he changed his mind about coming around to my house and "fucking me over". So, I dodged that bullet, sort of. But none of this would have happened if I'd listened to the "message" not to walk down that alley in the first place.

I started seeing "things".

My aunt and cousin were regular visitors and my cousin would often stay overnight and sleep in my room on a trundle bed.

On one occasion, my aunt, cousin, mother and I were in the downstairs living room. I saw a shadowy adult female form, holding the hand of a shadowy child, run from the laundry, across the hallway and into the cupboard underneath the stairwell.

"Did you see that?!"

"Shut up, Paul," my mother said. "You didn't see anything."

But it turned out that it wasn't *just* me.

One night my cousin was staying over. I woke up in the middle of the night and was bolt upright, staring at the ceiling. Something must have woken my cousin up as well, because she saw me just staring while I said, "What do you want?" It wasn't just her cousin's weird behavior that caught her attention because she too felt a presence that spooked her so much that she went into my parents' room, saying, "There's no *way* I'm staying in that room." That night, she slept at the foot of my parents' bed. I had no recollection of this myself and only found later out after my cousin told me.

Some of the manifestations of this rot that had started to creep into my life were of an entirely different level of power.

One night I woke up and I was levitating off the bed. Very high. About two meters (six feet).

Again, I was terrified, but whatever had me then let go, and I came crashing back onto the bed.

I know what you're thinking, but these things weren't dreams. I k*now* what dreaming feels like.

But I also know that demons distort the perception of reality, so that even Exorcists and Ministers of Deliverance can perceive levitations while under their zone of influence. Whether the laws of physics as we understand them are truly being violated or whether it's just our distorted perceptions, who can say?

These things happening to me were nothing like a dream. But dreams would come, and one night when I was about seventeen, I did dream that some entity was entering me through my mouth – some black, substance, like a thick mist.

By this stage, the paranormal stuff had been continuing for about three years, from the time I was 14½ to about the time I was 17½. These abnormalities became the "new normal" – a "stage" that, my family assumed, I would eventually grow out of.

My faith got so broken that I completely and utterly turned away from God.

But the subject of the Devil was on my mind in the form of persistent, obsessive thoughts.

Many of them.

And I did not know at the time that these thoughts were not entirely my own.

I'm not sure now, but I think at one point I prayed to the Devil and asked him for a girlfriend.

And not long after I met a girl.

A coincidence? Maybe. Maybe not.

I quickly became besotted with her. In my mind she walked in the clouds among the angels. She was all and everything to me. I worshiped the air she breathed and the ground she walked on.

I gave up smoking weed, because I'd found a new drug, *her*.

She became my salvation.

And because I lost myself to her, the relationship was totally unhealthy and became a total disaster.

I wanted to "do the deed". Very much. But we couldn't make that work. Every time we tried, it would hurt her, and she'd make me stop.

But in every other aspect of the relationship I put her on an impossible pedestal and smothered her.

This went on for about ten months. With the wisdom of hindsight this smother love killed our relationship. Neither of us knew what we were doing – on a number of different levels.

And then some other man entered the picture and she ended up sleeping with him, which left me feeling totally inadequate.

We broke up, in the way that people do when they don't know what they're doing, and the breakup wasn't clean. We were still communicating, in fits and starts.

The paranormal stuff had stopped, having been replaced by other ways that the thing, whatever it was, had devised to screw my life up.

While all the stuff with my girlfriend was happening, I became convinced, I truly felt, that somebody in my family was going to die – either my brother or my father. There was no question in my mind and heart that this was going to happen. This … what do I call it? … *profound intuition* … was very clear to me, and I started grieving and crying.

And then we found out that my father was diagnosed with terminal heart disease.

I had become so pathetic that I tried using my father's death as a way of getting back with my girlfriend, playing the victim card, in the hopes that somehow, she'd take enough pity on me to give me one more chance.

"Things are really bad. My father's business is failing …"

Of course, my father's business was failing, he was dying.

And of course, that didn't bring her back.

Confronted by my father's illness and everything that was going on with their problem-ridden youngest son, my parents decided that there was something SERIOUSLY wrong with the house we were living in.

Although they had never given me even the slightest acknowledgment that what I was telling them about what I can describe as my "haunting" was true or real, they were still Catholic.

They were still "believers". They still believed that God and Satan were realities, while, perhaps, also believing that incursions by the Devil were things that happened "to other people", in the same way, I guess, that no one denies the existence of car accidents, but they always happen "to other people" – until they happen to you. But things had gotten to the point that whatever denial my parents were in just wasn't working any more, and somehow, they had come to the conclusion that the house we were living in in Elwood was, in some way, *cursed.*

So, they called a priest in to help.

Looking back at it now, I think that it's profound, that they were willing to take that step.

The priest did a blessing. He walked around the house with a candle. Said prayers, especially in the doorways. Sprayed Holy Water around. Did some more praying and basically said, "OK. Well, you're done!"

And it did absolutely fuck all.

Six months then passed since my parents had tried to "cure" the house with a priest's blessing.

My life continued to get worse.

Things had finally ended with my girlfriend.

After my making yet another pathetic attempt to get back with her, she very publicly humiliated me and totally rejected me in front of my friends. She made things abundantly clear, "Go away! Get out of my life! I never want to talk to you or hear from you again! Paul, I didn't want to do this or tell you like this but *fuck off!!!*"

The rejection had been so absolute, the humiliation so deep, that I became suicidal.

Since *she* wasn't my drug anymore, I started smoking marijuana again, and I was also abusing alcohol, drinking every day.

Even the dog died.

Since the blessings of Mother Church had failed, my parents then decided that the most prudent course of action was to sell the house and to get the whole family out of there.

Fortunately, since my father owned more than one property, he had decided to keep one of his investment flats, and, since my sister and brother had already moved out, we were able to get out of the house relatively quickly and put it on the market, while, at the same time, starting construction on another house. We didn't know how long my father had, but at least, in the time he had left, he could build the house that he'd always wanted to live in.

My parents had gone back to denial mode and dumped the "cursed" theory. To this day, if you ask my mother why we ended up moving she'll say to you that the real reason we moved was because we needed to fund the new house and we needed the cash.

In the face of all these things that were tearing my world up, I was so filled with rage and grief that I found myself praying to the Devil.

Without realizing it, I had stumbled upon a classic occult practice. It's one thing for demons to "infect" you because trauma leaves a gaping psychic would that they can take advantage of. It's another thing altogether to *invite them in*.

You pray to the Devil the same way that you pray to God. But they're not the same prayers, obviously.

I wanted revenge on my former girlfriend.

I prayed to the Devil for her early death – "If you kill her now, I will do a year in hell."

I became obsessed with the idea that I had to have sex *in order to become a man*. I didn't even know what being a man meant. Maybe it was about being powerful and in control when I was feeling increasingly powerless and out of control. Maybe it was about being worthy and accepted, when I was feeling increasingly worthless and rejected.

And because I had never had sex with her, or anyone else for that matter, a few months later I also prayed to the Devil for sex, because, by now, after all, what was I doing as a virgin? Because, by now, my opportunity was gone and now *I would never get sex – ever.*

And if I never had sex, I would never *become a man.*

So, while my father was dying, I wanted *her* to die and I wanted *sex* – in order *to become a man.*

Even in the face of my father's death, somehow, and I don't even know how it happened, I had sunk to the point where my priorities were revenge and sex – in order *to become a man.*

I didn't know it at the time, but through these prayers I entered into a process of making some sort of pact, some sort of contract, some sort of *deal*, with the Devil.

And even though I can't confirm it now, because I don't have any conscious recollection of it, there exists the possibility that sometime around this period of my life, I also made a deal for money. And I say "there exists the possibility" because, now, years later as I'm telling you all this, I get spiritual intuitions, messages from "good spirits", that inform me of what was going on for me during a time when I was, in all probability, in an altered state of consciousness. To the best of my knowledge I said the deal for money as a joke, something along the lines of, "I'll spend another year in hell, in exchange for my getting a lot of money."

When we finally moved into the new flat in the suburb of Saint Kilda the paranormal stuff had stopped altogether, except that now and then the TV would switch itself on and off for no reason, and never at my command. Since we were no longer anywhere near the old house, I felt relatively safe.

But I had sunk into a deep, deep depression.

I was in the pits and nothing was working.

For example, I was almost cripplingly lonely. Now, I don't want to give the impression that I was a *complete* loser when it came to women, because later I did get the occasional fun here and there, but they were drug-fueled encounters, and I don't know how I would have fared if both parties had been sober at the time.

I'd approach women and usually get nothing but rejection. They could *smell* the inadequacy and would tell me in no uncertain terms to fuck off. I was oozing rejection and failure. And again, at the time I did not know that this too was a sign of Spiritual Affliction. The Spirit of Rejection is real.

They could smell the fear, and just like when a dog smells fear they become aggressive the women would in their turn smell the fear and they would become aggressive and be complete bitches to me. They would exert their dominance over me. I just didn't have the confidence *to be a man* at that point. I was being tested and failing *all the time.*

So, no matter how much I wanted to move on from the disaster of my first relationship and from everything else, I couldn't. I was using marijuana again, heavily. Drinking every day, heavily. I had left school and was working in a shitty dead-end job as a carpenter's assistant where the owner was constantly "encouraging" me to get a proper carpentry apprenticeship but somehow never *quite* managing to allow me enough time off to actually attend classes. I was working ninety-hour weeks for $6 per *hour*, taxed.

My mother even caught me on the phone to the suicide hotline one night – hardly surprising, under the circumstances.

In the morning my mother said, "I'm really worried about you. We need to do something."

"I know." But we took it no further at the time because the need to kill myself went away, at least for a time.

I had started using ecstasy, in a fruitless effort to get more relief.

The one thing that ecstasy did for me was give me confidence, a sort of pill-popped Dutch courage.

After eighteen months we finally moved into the new house. The TV maybe did its off/on trick once or twice but then we got rid of it, got a new one, and it never happened again.

But one night I was asleep and woken up by the bed's violent shaking. I ran into my parents' bedroom, terrified, again, and told them what had happened. "I am NOT going back to my room!"

My father just laughed at me, "You were just dreaming.".

"I wasn't dreaming! That fucking bed was shaking."

I got my mattress and put it at the foot of my parent's bed and slept there – twenty years old, as if I were still fourteen.

My mother had worked in the health industry for twenty years. In early 2001 my father was extremely sick. He was in unbearable pain. When one day it got too much and my mother called for an ambulance, she knew that this was the beginning of the end. She knew that he was not coming back.

And yet, even though my father was in a hospice, through his contacts, he managed to get me a job as a in a legal firm. My father told me I had a gift for negotiation. But he told me that my whole life I had an inborn skill at being able to argue my way to what I wanted – particularly with my own parents – that I would argue my position, incredibly well, and never, ever take "no" for an answer.

I thought he was just being nice.

What did I have to lose, in leaving the carpentry slave-job, other than cutting myself and getting splinters repeatedly because I was constantly exhausted? At least I wouldn't be covered in sawdust all the time.

My father died in August, a few weeks before my twenty-second birthday.

The night he died, I prayed to God. I asked God for some assurance that my father was is a better place.

Somehow, I got it into my head that I could make a deal that I could trade another year in hell in exchange for my father getting into heaven. I don't know where this idea came from. Perhaps it was an idea planted in my head by demonic influences that there was the possibility that my father had gone to hell.

That's where I left it.

And not long after my father died, and before I started my new job. I needed to get away for a while. I went on a camping trip around Australia with a friend of mine. At some point during that trip I prayed for sex again. I was so totally clueless about women that I had no faith in myself to even recognize a proposition when it was being made to me. So, I remember saying to the Devil, as part of the deal, "When you do send a woman to me, I want you to make it *abundantly* clear to me who the woman is whom you have sent." Within a few days I was drinking at a bar when a woman dressed in black gothic garb tried to pick me up and take me home with her. I knew it was the "her" I'd prayed for, *but I didn't go through with it.* I ended up rejecting her.

Coincidence?

Or not?

In either case my strategy was to put her off by telling her I was a virgin. She instantly rolled her eyes and I knew that she wanted nothing to do with me. I made sure to deliberately ruin the situation for myself, and that worked! I had consciously chosen not to go through with the contract. At least some part of me was still salvageable, or so I thought at the time.

Having lost my girlfriend and my father within a relatively short period of time and having already contemplated suicide many, many times. I entered a part of my life where even though I was bluffing my way through my new job as a paralegal, through which I would eventually be able, by some miracle, to gain admission into a law course, in other ways I was still spiraling out of control in a constant, unrelieved state of despair and grief.

A couple of years after my father died a colleague had lost a friend and that had left him grief stricken. He had heard of this medium and visited her, and had been very impressed, and, knowing a little of my history, he recommended that I see her myself. She was so in-demand that I had to wait six months for my appointment.

I had never visited a medium before and had only the vaguest idea of what they were and what they did, but I was open-minded. My mother warned me beforehand, "Don't give her any information. Don't give her any space to ask leading questions. And observe her. Don't give her either a positive or negative response to what she says. Just observe her."

I need not have been concerned.

"I know how you got here today," she said, "because I can see the truck that cut you off at the intersection."

I was impressed.

"I have no reason to lie to you. There's nothing in it for me if I did. There is an afterlife. I lost my own son to heroin addiction. He died a few years ago on Christmas Day. The police called me because the heater in his flat had been left on and the neighbors knew that something was wrong because of the smell coming from his apartment."

And, possibly because I felt such a connection to my own grief, I could feel hers.

"And, in the midst of my pain, I felt my son communicate with me, and tell me that he was OK. The trauma of my son's death opened up the channel for me. I get intuitions, hunches and then I interpret the messages that are behind those intuitions and hunches. I'm not a predictive psychic. I'm not here to forecast your future. I'm only here to tell you about the past, and where your loved one is. I'm just here to pass on the message to let you know that your father is in a better place and that he's all right. So that you can move on.

"I know that you're in finance," she continued. "Your sister's about to get married. Your father died of heart disease. I know you had a girlfriend, and the breakup was ugly. But she wasn't just your girlfriend, she was your soul mate. You lost her and then you lost your father."

And even though I was surviving in my numbness, she saw the pain that I was in, and that I had gone through, and she was crying uncontrollably. "And you've been rejected by women, over and over again, because of the pain of that relationship, when all you wanted was just a partner. And now you're struggling to find one."

Things were starting to make sense. In my mind at the time I had already had the best possible girl that I could ever have had. As disastrous as the relationship had been, in the back of my mind there was always the chance that *if only* we'd been a little more mature, *if only* we'd understood ourselves and each other more, *if only* we'd known what we were doing, we could have been the love of each other's lives. I had lost my soulmate, and no amount cheap, one-night stands propped up by ecstasy and alcohol was going to replace that. In my mind, I had to go further than where I had gone, or I'd be a failure, and I couldn't go further because the love I had … had died.

It was, well and truly over.

She continued. "You were besotted with her. You were under a spell, and the love turned into obsession, and it was that obsession that turned her away."

That was true. I had over-worshiped her. I had suffocated her emotionally to the point where she couldn't breathe.

She continued, "I know you won't believe this, but you're strongly spiritual, and this is why I can read you so well. And I know you pick up on things, through thought, and I want you to just acknowledge that, that sometimes you have thoughts, and I know you think they're your thoughts, but they're not. Have some recognition of that. I want you to acknowledge that even though you're smart, and you can give yourself credit for having your own thoughts, you also get the thoughts of others and those are the thoughts of the spirits who are helping you. They are guiding you. Clairvoyance happens when people "see" things. But there's also clairaudience. That's when people "hear" things. But you have clairsentience. Like me, you pick up on things through thought, through just *knowing* things.

I believed her because I had already had a significant experience like this. A year earlier when I was about twenty-two, I was about to go a boating trip when I had a dream that the boat would capsize. But in the dream my father appeared and told me to take his inflatable navy-issued life jacket. Sure enough, the boat did capsize, and I used the life jacket.

So, I asked, "How do you know all this? How is this possible?"

"There's another life. There's another level of life through which we can know these things."

"OK," I said. "I'm open to that. I'll stay open to the idea that I'm being guided."

I left the reading feeling much better about everything, particularly my father.

I threw myself into my work.

The psychic reading had helped. It hadn't been a miraculous cure-all for everything, but at least I had a focus. And even though in every other aspect of my life I was still comfortably numb, I took on a crazy, crazy work ethic and a drive to make something of my life and to correct the wrong. So, I did anything and everything to learn how to broker mortgages. I was so driven that I impressed a mentor enough to take me under his wing and help me bring out my potential. I read every possible book on selling and psychology I could get my hands on. I attended seminars. I took every opportunity to get ahead in my job.

Work during the week and alcohol on the weekend had now become my life.

There was now Jekyll and Hyde Paul – the dedicated professional and the dedicated binge drinker. I was becoming, simultaneously, a genius solicitor and a dysfunctional drunk.

But in spite of the effort that I was putting into my job, my employer at the time didn't have enough real work for me, so after two years I left and joined up with my brother and mother who were working in our legal firm. After I'd worked with my family, very successfully, for about six months, word got around that I was very good at what I did and I started to create my own business. At least, *professionally*, I was empowered.

I met a woman. And during the two years we were together nothing paranormal happened. Except that my partner revealed that sometimes, in the middle of the night, I would seem to wake up, startled, and then go back to sleep. I was completely unaware of this. There's not much further to say about these two years, and although we were content for a time, the relationship for me was a rebound from my first love, even though so many years had passed. The relationship helped me heal a little, if not enough. I couldn't really develop feelings for this woman beyond a certain point, because I was still emotionally numb. I wanted to fall in love again, but I couldn't.

The walls around me were still strong, protecting me because I knew I couldn't have survived another traumatic breakup.

By now I had turned twenty-six. The relationship was over. The breakup this time was amicable and not traumatic in the slightest.

But I still needed something to fill the void.

So, I started using cocaine.

For a long time, nothing particularly "paranormal" happened except on one occasion, around this time, I was in the bathroom one morning in my boxer shorts, when my mother noticed that my back was covered in claw marks, as if some three-clawed animal had scratched me. I hadn't noticed because I hadn't felt anything. There hadn't been any sign of this the day before. It had to have happened overnight, but I hadn't been with anyone – at least not with anyone human.

But then something happened that was to haunt me for years to come.

One weekend afternoon I was sitting on my couch, in my usual binge drunk stupor, and I was once again in that, half-awake, half-asleep hypnagogic state. I entered into a trance-like vision.

In that vision, I was shown that in my childhood I had undergone some abuse.

I don't want to go into the details. I'm sure you can imagine a scenario for yourself that makes the point that I felt traumatized as a result of that hypnagogic vision.

This vision had come out of nowhere. Prior to that moment I had never had even the slightest recollection that this abuse had happened, and I couldn't tell if the experience had been real or not. Immediately after the vision ended I didn't know if it had been a real memory that I had suppressed for years, that was finally coming to the surface again, or if, somehow, I had fucked myself over so much with alcohol and other drugs that my mind how now found a new way to torture me.

The experience of having that vision so traumatized me that the only way I could calm myself down was to take a few valium and beers. I was still living with my mother, and I tried to talk to her about it. She did what she could in the moment. She did what I imagine any loving mother would do in such a situation, but she was as much at a loss on how to handle this as I was. It was too big a problem for either of us.

I sought help immediately. I started seeing counselors.

The first counselor I saw said, "I don't know what really happened, but this thing that you're describing didn't happen to you. You need to accept that."

I wish I could tell you more, about these early counseling sessions, but I think I was still in such a state of shock that nothing much that anyone was saying was sticking. Natural questions at this point would have been, "What made the counselor think that this hadn't happened to you? What criteria of reality testing did they use?"

I can only say that if the counselor, and all the later counselors I saw did explain to me *why* they thought that the experience wasn't real, they didn't do a very good job of it. Without exception, the counselors determined that the vision that I had received was of an experience that had *never actually happened*. It wasn't real. And yet, over time, partly I think because the counselors never adequately answered the question as to why they thought this experience wasn't real, I acquired the persistent, niggling feeling that it *was*. I didn't believe in their professional diagnoses and I couldn't shake the ever-growing conviction that this had really happened to me. It didn't matter how many times they tried to tell me otherwise, it was feeling more real all the time.

Then for some reason, gradually, my cocaine usage dropped.

But I became paranoid. In my paranoia I convinced myself that the counselors were lying to me in order to protect me from a truth that was too difficult for me to deal with. I started grieving and I was in a constant state of fear. I had all the signs of a trauma victim and I started to develop the see-saw symptoms of Post-Traumatic Stress Disorder – obsessively playing over the event in my head and reliving the feelings while at other times, obsessively avoiding reminders of the event. I was on continual high alert, all wound up, easily startled and then I'd flip back into emotional numbness. I'd blame myself and tell myself I was worthless, then feel this rage against the perpetrator and I'd have to deal with a trigger temper and stop myself from exploding at any innocent person who just happened to cross my path at the wrong place and at the wrong time. This only exacerbated my self-destructiveness, and the alcoholism got worse. I didn't know that I was suffering from PTSD at this point, but then again, as so often happens, when you're in trauma, you don't always know what's going on with you and you're not thinking clearly enough to make an accurate assessment of what you're experiencing.

The counselors that I would later see would always say the same thing in various different ways in order to get through to me. "Stop obsessing over this event. It's unhealthy. Let it go."

But I couldn't.

I saw a psychiatrist. In her professional opinion I had created the vision to victimize myself. She thought that the vision was a representation to myself of the worst thing that could happen to me and that, in some screwy way, I had created it to punish myself out of self-loathing. She too told me to "Let it go."

But I couldn't.

Between the ages of twenty-six and thirty-two and over so many sessions I lost count of; I saw four mental health professionals and they all said the same thing.

Hundreds of thousands of dollars in counseling, but this thing would just not fucking go away.

In order to make some sense of this I started to read accounts of victims of trauma and abuse. The more I read their stories, the more I could relate to them, all the while feeling intermittently suicidal.

Again.

I had not planned to still be living with my mother until the age of thirty-two, but the flat that I'd bought at the age of twenty-nine took three years to build. By the time the flat was finished I was more than happy to move into my own place. The intensity of the abuse thing would come and go, but I felt I was at least a little on top of it and I was looking forward to independence.

And then the paranormal shit came back.

With a vengeance.

CHAPTER FIVE

FIRST STEPS AS AN EXORCIST

"Before the Throne of God demons are compelled to tell the truth."

Joseph

Father Apie was more comfortable in French than in English. By now, in the year 2000, I had spent the majority my life in Guinea, and I had picked up French in the same way that meat picks up a marinade. I could not speak it at all well, but I could understand it well enough to understand Pastor's sermons, so I began my church career interpreting the services from French to English. It is said that one of the most common fears is speaking before an audience, but that was never a problem for me. I was doing God's work. That was all that mattered to me and through my work as an interpreter my French and English improved and I absorbed theology at the same time.

Pastor began taking me along as his personal assistant / apprentice on his pastoral work, interpreting for him while he explained the process of Deliverance to those who needed it. Unlike many, who conduct Deliverance processes "in public before a live audience" Pastor preferred to conduct most Deliverance in private. Now because I was too busy at school or at work, somehow, in spite of having worked with Pastor for a number of years, I had never gotten around to attending an actual Deliverance service, but I had explained it to so many people for so long that although I had never seen a Deliverance myself, I was theoretically very familiar with the process.

One day, Pastor surprised me. "I want you to come to the next Deliverance I do. I think it's time you saw this for yourself. I think that you're ready for it."

It was on a Friday evening that I came.

For those unfamiliar with the process of Deliverance, I should begin by telling you that every Deliverance is different.

I use the term "Spiritual Affliction" because not every case we deal with is technically a "possession". In fact, "perfect possession" itself is relatively rare, though not as rare as you might think. Still, it is more accurate to talk of Spiritual Affliction as an overarching blanket term to describe a number of related phenomena, all of which have in common the incursion into the material world of spiritual energies or entities that can create varying degrees of havoc. These related phenomena include forms of "partial" possession – oppression and obsession and others – none of which are anywhere as rare as you might think they are or would like them to be.

Spiritual affliction is a highly individual experience. It is as if demonic forces use their intelligence to tailor-make an affliction, preying upon and exploiting idiosyncratic weaknesses of the victim, with the goal of inflicting as much damage as possible to a particular person.

Imagine something looking into your soul and finding what you most fear, what makes you feel the most vulnerable, most worthless.

What is your personal hell? Imagine something entering you, occupying you, possessing you. Something that preys on all your insecurities, your guilt, your *shame* – everything that most disgusts you about yourself, all the things you never look at because they're just too painful. Something that hates you and will do anything to destroy you. Something that patiently but obsessively eats away at you. Something that will destroy your relationships, your life, *you*, mockingly, gleefully.

And yet, in spite of the tailor-made hells which the demons would put you through, there is a generalized pattern to the process of identifying and removing inhabiting or attached entities in a situation of Spiritual Affliction.

Preliminary and Initial Manifestations

The Christian-based "possession industry", such as it is, historically recognizes four or six types or "degrees" of Spiritual Affliction, depending on whom you talk to. I have my own views, based on my own experience, which I describe below.

Listed in the degree of incursion, escalation and seriousness:

Infestation occurs when entities inhabit or attach themselves to a **physical object**. This object can be as small as a piece of jewelry or a talisman, a statue, painting or other a piece of art or a piece of furniture. The object can also be a house, an apartment or an entire building. It can also be a part of nature, like a brook or a river. Some consider an attachment to a tree or to an animal to be infestation, but because trees and animals are living beings, I do not share this opinion. For me, infestation is about habitation. Because spirits and demons are non-material, and their "home turf" is a dimension of existence beyond the material, there is no reason why their incursions into the material world need be limited in any way.

The spirit is simply "inhabiting" or, more accurately, I think, "attached" to a physical object, using that object as an "anchor" into our physical realm.

When a living being is involved, it makes more sense to me to consider this type of demonic affliction to be a case of *oppression*, which I describe below.

Because there are limits to what an entity or demon can do with what is usually an "inanimate" object, the manifestations of infestation are usually creepy, but mostly innocuous – apparitions, the sound of footsteps or voices, odors that come from nowhere, objects that move without human agency. Classic "hauntings", while often interpreted as the activities of "restless spirits of the dead", might well be the doings of spiritual beings with the simple intent of amusing themselves at the expense of humans.

Have you ever experienced a sense of unease when walking into room, or a sense of wrongness in a thing?

Have you ever felt that there was something wrong about that piece of art, or statue, or decoration?

Have you ever had something that seemed to bring you bad luck?

Then perhaps you have felt the first stirrings of evil – Entities of Infestation have a childlike nastiness that isn't quite bad enough to cause serious damage, but just enough to disrupt your peace of mind, or your life.

Or, if the entities are more malicious, or perhaps more experienced in the material realm, the Infestation can escalate to Oppression.

Oppression ups the ante of infestation and is **the first level of inhabitation or attachment to a human being.** Although the classical interpretation of oppression is to human beings only, I see oppression more as occurring with *any* living being. Oppression implies the first level of affliction or violation of the personal boundary of the mind or body of a living being. It might well be that demons too have their "apprenticeships" and that once they pass the "class" in infestation, they can move on to oppression. Perhaps they start with animals first, before moving on to human beings, but this is speculation on my part.

Oppression is the area of operation in which "psychic attacks" happen.

With manifestations at a personal level, the afflicted experiences feelings of unease that can escalate to anxiety, or a weight on the soul that can escalate to depression. Sleep disturbances are common and can escalate to recurring, persistent, increasingly disrupting nightmares and night terrors. Health problems can occur and can become frequent, severe or even life-threatening illnesses – mental, emotional, physical – either originating in, or exacerbated by, spiritual illness. I would also argue that many substance abuse and addictions have their origin in some form of demonic oppression.

At an interpersonal level, relationships can experience disturbances and, in the more serious cases, recurring patterns of dysfunction, abuse, exploitation and failure.

Inexplicable problems with employment or financial difficulties are also common although, sometimes, paradoxically, the afflicted might be doing very well at a material level, if only so that the afflicted has sufficient material means to continue to be demonically exploited at other levels.

After all, if you eventually want someone to fall far and hard, it's a good strategy to ensure that they rise far and hard too. You need to get behind someone before you stab them in the back.

The important thing to note about oppression, is that since

there are no demonically related thoughts or feelings at this stage, it's very easy to simply shrug the signs and symptoms of oppression as manifestations of "conventional", low-level, mental or emotional illness, or even just the failures of a "weak" personality.

The Catholic Church recognizes another stage – **physical pain**. This is perhaps more a symptom rather that a stage of incursion, since to produce pain some level of oppression must have already occurred and is manifesting as a physical sensation rather than just a collection of negative thoughts and feelings.

The Spirits of Oppression have no respect for the boundaries of your body. Their goal is to violate you. I would not be exaggerating to call Oppression a form of Spiritual Molestation, or in more severe cases, Spiritual Rape. The Spirits of Oppression delight in making you feel soiled and dirty. Oppression works in the realm of *feelings*. Feelings of wrongness, attacks on your sense of reality can escalate from a state of almost zombie-like detachment to profound depression and nihilism. And in Oppression your thoughts are hijacked to give you a story, a running commentary, on why you feel the way you do.

It's important to recognize here that Oppression can be all-too-easily dismissed as a material or psychological affliction because it isn't "paranormal" in the way that we usually imagine it. That's what makes it so insidious. You think that a bit of talk therapy or some pill will fix you up. It's only when you've tried the talk and the pills and there's still no improvement that you have to consider that there might be something altogether different going on – something that can't be fixed with conversation or chemistry.

Obsession occurs when the thoughts and feelings of the afflicted become **a preoccupation with demonic activity**. While even severe manifestations of Oppression are often dismissed as simply "bad luck", "poor decision making" or "mental illness" or "emotional illness" (all of which might be true), it is at the point of obsession that the afflicted first begin to suspect that there is something more going on than just a "conventional" or "material" problem. This feeling, however, can vacillate because, especially in the West, there is little cultural support for the idea of Demonic Affliction.

In a state of Obsession, the afflicted endlessly ruminates on thoughts related to The Devil or demons. The afflicted also obsesses with existential feelings of dread. If their worldview allows it, *there is a persistent feeling in the afflicted that it is not just one's sanity at risk, but one's very soul.* Thoughts of death and suicide predominate, accompanied by the fear that if one actually goes through with self-murder, that an eternity in hell awaits. The feeling of fear and terror is almost constant.

In more extreme cases, the afflicted is tormented with impulses, fantasies or outright visions of injuring, abusing and killing or of being injured, abused or killed in every way imaginable. In this sense, the obsession with particular thoughts and feelings evolves into **Compulsion** to act on those feelings.

If substance abuse has not already occurred, then by this stage it will begin as the afflicted desperately attempts self-medication. Sleep is virtually impossible, as the afflicted is constantly worn down by an exhausting, inner struggle. In the more extreme cases the afflicted becomes so dysfunctional that they require hospitalization. In the most tragic cases they commit suicide.

I would argue that ***Compulsion*** is a degree of demonic possession that should have more recognition, because obsession focuses on thoughts (mental phenomena) and feelings (emotional phenomena) while compulsion takes a step further into acts (physical phenomena) – acts which can lead to horrific consequences.

I should note that since Spiritual Affliction is a deeply personal, even tailor-made experience, the afflicted will tend to interpret their obsessive thoughts and feelings through their own socio-cultural and religious filters. One man or woman's demon or vision of Hell might be startlingly different depending on where in the world they come from. The Devil certainly shows up in very different ways in The West as opposed to everywhere else – a point I shall frequently return to. It is for reasons of cultural relativism and accuracy that I also tend to prefer the term "The Afflicted" rather than a term that you might often hear, "demoniac" – one who is possessed by a demon.

In a spiritually healthy person there is either a conscious or subconscious sense of spiritual security. There is a sense that you are a child of God, unconditionally beloved, absolutely inviolate, eternally safe.

The goals of the Demons of Obsession are to take you as far away as possible from that feeling of security of being loved. The Demons of Obsession will use every trick in their very thick book of tricks to make you feel that it is not only your physical life on the line, but your *immortal soul itself*. Obsession is the place where the peace and love of God are replaced with a constant war of fear and hate. Obsession is not only a vision of Hell; it is the experience of being *in Hell*. Obsession is where you are confronted by visions and feelings of your annihilation and the destruction of everything you cherish, or of an eternity of abandonment and perpetual condemnation. Obsession is where you will feel what it is to be forsaken by God and from any possibility of redemption. And Demonic Obsession is where your every thought and feeling will fill you with an all-encompassing guilt, that you have brought this entirely upon yourself, through your own weakness and worthlessness.

And again, because Obsession is very much a personalized Hell, there is no immediate reason to believe that this hell is anything other than a culture-bound mental or emotional illness. Especially in the West, if you tell people that you're being persecuted by demons, you run the risk of simply not being believed and your cries for help go unheeded while they put a straitjacket on you and pump you full of drugs, thus adding the hell of isolation to the hells that you are already experiencing.

In truth not all forms of possession are "bad". A medium who is deep channeling spirits of light is experiencing possession. Even an Exorcist or Deliverer is possessed of The Holy Spirit and there are many accounts of mystics and saints giving themselves over entirely to The Holy Spirit. But even though the process is essentially the same, the quality and nature of Angelic or Divine Possession is entirely different from the quality and nature of Demonic or Satanic Possession. There's a world of difference between drinking a glass of water and drinking a glass of hydrochloric acid.

Possession can be **voluntary** or **involuntary** too. And there's a world of difference between being subjected to an involuntary act of Grace and an involuntary act of Demonic Possession.

Perfect Possession is the most extreme form of spiritual affliction. Although in truth the afflicted never totally lose their agency or free will, in the case of Perfect Possession **the autonomy of the afflicted is so compromised that they give control over to the entity or entities inhabiting them**. In such cases, for all practical intents and purposes, the afflicted at this point *has no effective free will at all*, the consciousness of the afflicted is completely subjugated. If the entity chooses to release them then the afflicted frequently has little or no memory of anything that happened while the entity used them as a meat puppet because, to all intents and purposes, the human consciousness *simply wasn't there*.

Partial Possession occurs when the possessed still maintains some "control" over the situation and the possessed is aware of what's going on and can take control again whenever they want to.

As I've already explained, if you've left an unhealed psychic wound open you leave yourself open to Affliction, but **Subjection** occurs when the afflicted makes, for whatever reason (and there are many) a conscious invitation to submit to Satan or to demons.

It's more likely to occur in cases of Subjection because of the "consensual" aspect of Subjection. The important point here is that we are talking about two different things – voluntary vs involuntary and perfect (or complete) possession and partial possession.

I suspect that my biological father indulged in both Perfect and Partial Subjection in his desire for power. This is the sort of activity that is often portrayed as trance mediumship or voodoo rituals when things go horribly wrong.

But it is the more "involuntary" or "unconscious" type of **Perfect Possession** which is the form of Spiritual Affliction most commonly portrayed when we speak of "possession" in popular culture.

Perfect Involuntary Possession has a compelling, intriguing and, one could add, fascinating dramatic quality.

In Perfect Involuntary Possession the afflicted loses consciousness or enters a state of consciousness where the demons take over and the afflicted can do nothing about it – at least nothing on their own.

The body of the afflicted becomes essentially a puppet to be used by the demonic entity for its own purposes.

The fortress has been breached and even though, theoretically, the afflicted never *really* loses agency, and could theoretically regain control at any time, by this stage they are so worn down by the cumulative effects of infestation, oppression, obsession and compulsion, that they seem to have no "fight" left in them. I must make an important point here.

Think of your soul as drawing its very existence, its very source of life, from the Source of The Holy Spirit in the same way that a tree draws its nourishment from its roots, or the way that a lamp draws the power for its light from a cord.

This spiritual cord, your spirit, is unbreakable. No force in any universe can sunder it.

Your connection to The Holy Spirit is eternal and unbreachable, whether you are consciously aware of this or not.

This is important to remember because **your *conscious* spiritual connection is the Source of your Spiritual Authority.**

However, you are also endowed with free will. As such, in your free will, you can enter a state where you *believe* that the cord has been cut, where you *believe* that The Holy Spirit has abandoned you.

You can enter a state where you are no longer consciously aware of your inviolable connection to the Source. This is the ultimate point of Obsession.

It is your potential to deny your connection to the Source that is The Holy Spirit that demonic entities can exploit. This feeling that The Holy Spirit has abandoned you is, by far, the worst experience a human being, or *any* being can have. Some perceive Hell as a place, a region on another plane of reality where souls are in eternal torment. But for the purposes of this discussion it is useful to see **Hell as an *illusion* of the absence of God because the true absence of an omnipresent God is an impossibility.**

It is often said that Satan's greatest trick is to convince you that the Devil does not exist. But the Devil has an even greater trick – the ability to deceive you into believing that God can be absent, that God can forsake you. This *illusion* of the absence of God is Satan's greatest lie of all. In fact, I could argue that for all the many tricks in the demonic book of tricks that Satan is in fact a one-trick pony.

But this trick is, *literally*, a hell of a trick. Everything that demonic entities do to the afflicted is in service to the endgame of leading you to believe that you are eternally cut off from Source.

Demonic possession is the ultimate gesture of defeat, the conscious surrendering of your spiritual authority through an act of misplaced free will. It is, in effect, the ultimate spiritual error, and therefore the ultimate sin.

But how do we know that the horrors that the afflicted experience are the work of evil spirits, entities, demons or whatever else you want to call them?

One tool is **discernment**. Discernment is a spiritual detector of both truth and falsity that The Holy Spirit grants us to intuit the presence of demons. And it's more than that. Discernment is an ability granted to those who are aware of a connection to a higher consciousness, from which we can connect to knowledge that we otherwise would not have access to. We all have the potential for discernment, but for the most part it is undeveloped. However, if you are called upon by The Holy Spirit to do this work, The Holy Spirit bestows on you a developed sense of discernment, whether you want it or not. The Holy Spirit does this when, usually with your consent, the blockages to that divine connection are removed. In truth, we could live with a high level of discernment all the time, if we would only use our free will to submit to the gift of higher consciousness that The Holy Spirit is always offering us. That of course, is something I could write a whole other book about.

Another thing we look for is **signs and manifestation** that defy the conventional.

The manifestations of possession include, but are not limited to, the classic symptom of an aversion to sacred or holy objects. There can also be radical changes in appearance and behavior with the afflicted possessing abilities beyond what is considered "normal":

- Speaking fluently in languages that the afflicted have no knowledge of
- Having intimate knowledge of things that they could not know through conventional means
- Having super-human strength, having psychic or paranormal powers, or even, deceptively, the power to heal, but most often to harm.

These powers belong to demonic entities acting through the afflicted. The powers might also be "granted" to the afflicted. It is precisely the opportunity to access these powers that makes people pursue Subjection, or *voluntary* demonic possession, as, again, I believe was the case with my father, Attem.

And while it is potentially within all of us cast out demons and to spiritually heal, some of us are better at it than others. Just as it is within all of us to administer first aid, this does not mean that all of us can perform open-heart surgery. While in extreme cases *some* intervention might be better than nothing, in most cases you need help from someone experienced in these matters, someone who knows what they are doing.

It is because infestation, oppression, obsession, compulsion and especially possession create such disturbances, disruptions and chaos that those who suspect that they might be afflicted, or those who have a loved one whom they suspect is afflicted, seek out the help of a Deliverance ministry in one form or other.

The Treatment

As I began to attend Deliverance sessions with Pastor Apie, I learned the process of diagnosis and treatment. This treatment for the problem of Spiritual Affliction has been discerned, elaborated and refined over thousands of years and varies considerably according to tradition and locality. Think of this as a long tradition of apprenticeship where exorcists have accumulated knowledge about demons and how do deal with them. Naturally, over the course of millennia, there have arisen many points of view about theory, diagnosis and treatment of these "spiritual illnesses" just as there have been many different traditions of medicine – with equally varied results and rates of success.

And yet, for all the variations, just as the manifestations of spiritual affliction follow a classic "textbook" pattern, the treatment and ultimate cure of spiritual affliction also follow a general, classic, textbook pattern.

Step One – Discernment

As I've already described, some individuals, through a developed sensitivity, have the ability to detect the presence of entities. This ability is one aspect of the skill of *discernment*, as I have already described above.

Note that not all discerners are deliverers or exorcists and not all exorcists are necessarily very good at discernment. Nor are we, no matter how experienced we might be, infallible. We all have our strengths and weakness and it is our responsibility to recognize them. Often, a wise and cautious Deliverer will rely on helpers who have shown a talent or predilection for discernment, if only for a second opinion.

Of course, in the spirit of due diligence, one should take steps to rule out "conventional" explanations for events, circumstances and behaviors. Often the "patient" needs a medical doctor or a psychologist more than a deliverer. Nevertheless, sometimes if it walks like a demonic duck and quacks like a demonic duck, it's probably a demonic duck and demonic ducks should not be ruled out of hand just because you do not believe in demonic ducks. There are more things in heaven and earth …

Discernment is a major spiritual diagnostic tool. Like any diagnosis, it might not reveal everything there is to be revealed at once. the afflicted present themselves to the Discerner. The Discerner, guided by intuition mediated by The Holy Spirit, then senses the presence of demonic entities. Each case is different. Sometimes there is an ugly energy "in the air", sometimes the signs are more overt – a dead stare in the eyes. Sometimes there is a feeling of revulsion.

And sometimes you just *know*.

Step Two – Prayer

Having established the presence or influence of demonic entities, the participants, who comprise the Deliverer, the Discerners, the afflicted and any witnesses or supporters, then begin a process of prayer. They might follow a script, or the words will arise from inspiration.

In this initial stage the prayers involve a request to seek help and guidance and a willingness to be a vessel through which The Holy Spirit can work. One should also invoke protection to shield oneself from the energies that one might encounter.

Ironically, the treatment for demonic possession is based on allowing oneself, in turn to be subjugated by, to be possessed by, The Holy Spirit.

So the treatment for demonic possession is, effectively, *divine* possession.

It is important to recognize that *Deliverance requires the exercise of spiritual authority* – a recognition of the strong connection of the participants to The Holy Spirit, a recognition that it is also that *the power to expel demons is not a human power*, but that *humans are the instruments through which the power of The Holy Spirit acts.*

Neither I, nor any genuine Deliverer, makes *any* claim to power for ourselves.

The power always comes from The Holy Spirit.

Always, always, always.

I CANNOT stress this enough.

To claim this power of healing as originating in the human self would be as ridiculous as a light bulb claiming that it generates its own electricity.

Nevertheless, if the deliverer claims their spiritual authority, they have the license and guidance of The Holy Spirit to discern, root out the truth and later to expel.

Step Three – Compulsion and Inquiry

Demons have an agenda and will almost never voluntarily give up information truthfully, so they must be *compelled* to tell the truth. This involves the Exorcist giving orders, "in the Name of Jesus" or "By the Power of The Holy Spirit". Since demons are notoriously proud, stubborn liars, they will not usually submit to interrogation or expulsion without a fight.

So the Exorcist or Deliverer must use their spiritual authority to compel the demons to testify before The Holy Spirit. One way this can be done is to ask God to point the "Finger of Truth" and to "Shine the light of truth, to come before the "Throne of God" with an invocation "in the name of Jesus" where the demons are compelled to speak the truth.

Only after the demons are placed in a position where they have to speak and speak the truth at that, can the Deliverer start asking for, and later demanding, answers to questions.

It's vitally important to realize that as an Exorcist your capacity to deal with demonic forces depends on your Spiritual Authority, so when you're compelling demons to tell you the truth you need to use whatever terms, words or phrases would be meaningful to you in terms of *your* tradition and that helps you draw upon *your* own Spiritual Authority.

The words are less important than the Authority you use to deliver the words. Words or gestures without Spiritual Authority are basically worthless.

My knowledge about Judaic or Muslim or Hindu or Buddhist processes of Exorcism or that of any other cultural or religious tradition is virtually non-existent, but since I draw *my* Spiritual Authority from the Christian Ecumenical Protestant tradition of Deliverance and my own personal relationship with The Holy Spirit, it is the imagery and language of that tradition that I use.

So, I ask that whatever demons are present be placed before the Throne of God. I believe it was the Throne of God that I saw in the vision in which I first truly felt my calling.

Before the Throne of God demons are compelled to tell the truth. Once they are there, common questions and demands include:

"Spirit, reveal yourself!"

"What is your name?"

"Have you harmed this person's mind? Their heart? Their body? Their spirit? Have you harmed their soul? Have you harmed their relationships?"

This is where things generally become interesting to film and documentary makers. It is at this moment when demons – disturbed as they have been through *the Exorcist's assertion of Spiritual Authority* through prayer and invocation – begin to speak through the afflicted. At this point the afflicted often experience disturbances ranging from as subtle as grimacing and chuckling to as violent as writhing around on the floor, growling, screaming and cursing.

From out of the mouths of the afflicted we hear all sorts of horrible things in what we call the "demonic voice" – a sort of guttural voice that sounds as if a wild, predatory animal has found the power of human speech.

Through this all, the process of inquiry continues. Guided by The Holy Spirit the deliverer might even begin praying "in tongues", making sounds that sound like words and sentences in a foreign language.

Speaking in Tongues is usually interpreted and experienced as some sort of holy rapture in which the deliverer is entering into a closer union with The Holy Spirit and is attempting to articulate a reality for which there are no words in the language the deliverer normally uses. Speaking in Tongues can also be a prayer, or communication, from the depths of your Spirit directly to God that is conducted in a language that neither Devil nor Demon can understand – a means to bypass their intelligence so that they cannot counteract or interfere with the prayer. Think of this as a very secure form of "encryption".

The Deliverer, at this point of the proceedings, might have begun a process of fluctuation between a normal state of consciousness and the higher state of consciousness necessary to do the work. This Holy Rapture is something that I often experience and it is always a profound experience. All the consciousnesses involved can Speak or Pray in Tongues – the afflicted, demons, the Devil, and sometimes even The Holy Spirit.

In some cases the words in the "languages" spoken actually are from a real, historic language either living or extinct. The fact that these utterance often come from the mouths of people with no prior knowledge of the languages is something not easily explained through conventional explanations of where knowledge comes from. Spiritual entities have had a long time to acquire many languages.

Other questions you might ask of the demon(s) are of a more technical nature.

If the afflicted has entered into a contract with the entity – either consciously or unconsciously – then the entity has established a "legal right".

"How do you come to be here? Do you do this harm because of legal right?"

If they did, you must inquire as to the nature of the agreement and what was agreed to and whether or not in fulfillment of that contract a curse was placed. You must then, again and always, draw on words, symbols, imagery, or acts that reinforce your Spiritual Authority. So for me I demand that "in the Name of Jesus" or "by the Power of The Holy Spirit" that the contract be broken. If they have a "legal right" then "legal right" effectively means that you, of your own free will, *asked* them to be there. An intact contract implies *consent* and allows them ongoing free access.

So binding are these contracts that it is impossible to cast the demons out *until the contract has been broken!*

This is a trap that many inexperienced Exorcists fall into. They will "cast out" the demons and the demons will pretend to be cast out but in fact they are still there. The naive Exorcists will think they've don't their job, but as the contract hasn't been broken the demons retain their legal right. No effective "treatment" has occurred, much less a "cure" and the afflicted remains afflicted, allowing the demons free reign to continue their process of damage and destruction.

The contract can be broken, but only through the intercession of a higher power, and the Exorcists better know what they are doing or they do more harm than good.

If there was never any legal right in the first place then there is nothing to be broken and one can proceed to other inquiries that are even more involved and would be too detailed to outline here. For now, I can only give you a broad idea of Spiritual Affliction and Deliverance, rather than a "Manual for Exorcism".

One must then ask if there are any other demons associated or connected to the demon whom you are now addressing and how many of them there are.

Demons often work in "packs". There is often a "strongman" demon who is operating like a "captain" at the top of a chain or cohort of demons. It is important to identify the cohort by asking the strongman demons how many other demons are operating with or beneath the strongman. You then need to join them together as a group. This is called "binding". When demons are bound to each other the victim becomes "loosed" of the demons. Once bound to each other, the cohort can be expelled as a group. This expulsion is also called "casting out". It is not unusual for cohorts comprising twenty or more demons to be exorcised or "cast out" at once. Depending on how many "strongman" demons there are this process might have to be repeated and the program of binding, loosing and expulsion could go on for a number of weeks. The limiting factor is the energy available to the Exorcist and the afflicted as Deliverance and Exorcism are equivalent to spiritual surgery and can be incredibly taxing on the mortals involved in the process. The ongoing "bindings", "loosings", "expulsions" and "castings out" can take weeks or even years depending on the severity of the case.

As Paul's story progresses, I'll provide examples of how binding, loosing and casting out occurs.

Step Four – Expulsion

With the preliminary information out of the way, having established what we are fighting and why, the next step is to order the loosing and expulsion of the demons. As usual, this is not straightforward. Only very smart or very weak demons leave when you ask them to. Most of the time they stubbornly resist and they need to be compelled. In my tradition, compulsion often requires that you place them in the Fire of The Holy Spirit. My understanding of the Fire of The Holy Spirit is that it is like an energy so pure, so Holy, that it is totally incompatible with the evil energies of the demons. The result is that in the Fire of The Holy Spirit the demon experiences a torment similar to what I would imagine we would feel if we were being burned alive. Perhaps the strongest demons can tolerate it for a little while, but in the end, they *all* succumb.

The Fire of The Holy Spirit is not a fact that is well known, even in many Exorcist traditions. It is simply invoked by saying "I call upon the Fire of The Holy Spirit" or "Demon/Devil I set you on fire with the Fire of The Holy Spirit". You continue to do this until they are expelled. It's important not to give up because even with this effective invocation it sometimes takes some time before a breakthrough becomes apparent.

There are many things that the Devil does not want us to know. Among them:

- The effectiveness of the Fire of The Holy Spirit.
- The truth of the omnipotence of God.
- That we have Authority over the Devil through God.
- That Jesus took away any Authority that the Devil had when he died on the cross.
- That each time a demon is expelled your spirit gets stronger, you

get closer to God and you become more resistant to their attacks.

Since all demons are familiar with the Fire of The Holy Spirit, and its *power*, one wonders why they bother resisting. But if there is one weakness that demons have it is the weakness of *pride*. "Pride" has different meanings depending on context. We are not talking here about the pride you feel in a job well done, of a genuine positive creative accomplishment, or the pride you might feel for a child or a friend who has achieved something extraordinary through an act of courage or discipline. No, here we are talking about "pride" in a context where the meaning is closer to "arrogance" – a mistaken overestimation of your power. Then again demons are so proud of their work that they can't resist telling us of all the damage that they've done – and that is ultimately their undoing.

Satan "fell" because "He" felt that "He" could outdo God, even surpass God. This is insane, and one wonders about God allowing an angel to fall into insanity, but this is the story we are told.

The fallen angels "He" took down with "Him" shared the mistaken belief that a life without God was not only possible, but better. This demonic pride contaminates everything they do. They believe that they can stand anything we throw at them. On the face of it, this is true. Demons are more ancient, cleverer and much more experienced than human beings. We are nothing to them, except perhaps, playthings, or possibly food. But when we invoke the Power of The Holy Spirit, or otherwise invoke and access our Spiritual Authority, then we acknowledge the Power of The Holy Spirit to work through us. And when we have established Spiritual Authority The Holy Spirit and the Deliverer can work together.

It is then that we are the majority power.

And at this point, if it hasn't already happened, the afflicted might sway a little, or collapse on the floor, or, in more extreme cases writhe and thrash about, dry retch and vomit. I have never *personally* known of the afflicted to either harm themselves physically or anyone else through this process, but that is because I was taught the necessary precautions. Others do not take the necessary precautions, and there have been tragic results because of this.

When The Holy Spirit manifests and exposes the demons, I have known afflicted men to speak with the voices of women, women to speak in the voices of men and adults to speak in the voices of children, but not children as you've ever heard them.

But whatever the voice, the demons are always so full of *egotistic, arrogant pride*.

They'll say things like:

"I have destroyed him."

"I have taken love from him."

"I caused him to hate."

"I torment him."

"I caused him to lose his mental balance."

And this is always said with a tone of such assurance, such confidence that you might find yourself doubting if the afflicted can ever get out of their hole.

And this is always said with a tone of such pleasure, such *relish*. They really *enjoy* their work.

And sometimes there is also the smell – *the odor of evil*. It can be like rotting fish, or fermenting feces.

One thing I can say though: the afflicted in my charge have never reported *physical* pain, but by their actions and the moaning and the yelling and the screaming coming out of their mouths the demons in the Fire of The Holy Spirit seem to be in agony. I don't think they're faking it. They are still before the Throne of God and compelled to “tell the truth”, and that involves demonstrating the truth of their experience. If they are suffering, they have no one to blame but themselves. We did, after all, give them an opportunity to leave without all the hoo-ha. We did, after all, give them a “no penalty, way out.” They just didn’t take it. They hardly ever do.

Demonic stubbornness can reach ridiculous extremes. Even under the torture of the Fire of The Holy Spirit I will ask for permission that God issue one or two judgments on the demons so they can’t ever come back. The first might be that they get thrown into the Pit of Hell for eternity, where they no longer have access to the earth, and the second might be that they are set on fire with the Fire of The Holy Spirit for eternity. They hate this! They are terrified of this! They always scream and curse at this point and yet even in the fact of the compelling tool of judgment some will still resist. However, more often than not the threat of eternal judgment is enough for them to leave right there and then rather than waiting for the judgment to be passed.

Step Five – Healing and Closing Up

It is usually obvious when the demons in questions have left. Usually there is a noticeable expulsion of energy! The afflicted begins to act “normally”. The theatrics are over with. The semblance of sanity has returned. Of course, it is not always that simple. There might be other entities still lurking within who have, for the moment, escaped the Deliverer’s attention. But demons are prideful and can’t *wait* to tell you they are still there. Unfortunately this means starting the same process all over again. The Holy Spirit usually deals with the most wicked demons first or the most important issue first or deals with what the afflicted and the Exorcist can handle energetically first and moves down the line accordingly. In these cases, I presume that The Holy Spirit has done everything necessary for the moment depending on what the deliverer and the afflicted is able to stand or tolerate. There have been notable cases of Deliverance that have been a little too enthusiastic, resulting in very unfavorable outcomes. These cases are occasionally reported in the mainstream press. I suggest you google "exorcisms gone wrong."

Besides preserving the safety of all involved, The Holy Spirit might also have other reasons why not everything has been dealt with at once. If so, the Exorcist or Deliverer is not always privy to everything going on in the Mind of God. But, at least for the moment, it is done.

And sometimes, the afflicted, now liberated, begins to speak in tongues, or even sing in tongues, in a language known only to God. This is the Baptism of The Holy Spirit and it is a good sign Deliverance has been completed up to that particular point. However, a trap for the inexperienced or ignorant is that we must be sure it's not the Devil speaking in tongues through the mouth of the afflicted!

The Devil and the demonic minions have no qualms about masquerading as Angels of the Light to fool the naive into believing the Deliverance was successful. This is yet another reason that Deliverance and Exorcism should not be conducted by people who don't know what they are doing.

It is a fact that during Deliverance the afflicted are also sensitive to information from the Spiritual Realms. They hear thoughts of both good and evil and they often relay these thoughts back to the deliverer. At first they might hear thoughts such as "You will never be set free!", "We are too powerful!" or "God has forsaken you!" Demons will persist as long as they believe they have some chance of winning. But as the process continues the voices of demons are replaced with the voices of angels, and ultimately, The Holy Spirit.

But the process isn't perfect because the afflicted generally lack reliable discernment on their own state of being. So experienced Deliverance Ministers *always* seek confirmation through their own Discernment and Mediumship directly from The Holy Spirit. They can never rely *solely* on what the afflicted might be telling them.

There remain only three things to do right now.

First you identify what wounds the demons have caused the afflicted. How and when and where the wounds were created and how they affected the afflicted. The demons are compelled to provide that information.

Secondly, the Exorcist then assumes the role of Healer and invokes the Power of The Holy Spirit to repair the damage.

"Oh, Holy Spirit, heal the wounds that Your Servant has suffered. Heal them of their injuries. Heal them of the violations against them."

And after invocations of healing, the third and last thing to do is to "close the afflicted up".

"Please, Oh Holy Spirit, fill Your servant with your illuminating and healing light. Close the wounds that have been opened because of this affliction. Heal the wounds that have not yet healed. Restore the integrity of Your servant and may they continue to be safe in your protection. May they go now in peace Amen."

… or words to that effect. The Deliverer has, after all, performed the spiritual equivalent of major surgery, and one should not leave any "holes" through which entities might reenter and reinfect. Surgery is trauma, albeit trauma for a good cause, and the Deliverer has a duty of care to dress the wounds so that the healing can continue.

It might take more than one operation and in exceptional cases, many, many more before all the rats have been expelled from the building. Unfortunately, in extreme cases, this can take years.

And, if the afflicted is in the hands of a practitioner who does not know what they are doing, or who has taken on more than they can handle, then the results are terrible and might leave the afflicted worse off than before, especially if the rats have been invading for years, even decades.

CHAPTER SIX

FURTHER STEPS INTO DARKNESS

"… – underneath, something was laughing. Laughing through me. Laughing at the prayers. Just laughing and laughing."

Paul

I must have had some inkling, some intuition, that *something* was going to happen. Even though nothing paranormal had happened for years, at least to my knowledge and awareness at the time. But there was always, in the back of my mind, the lingering possibility that something could start up again. There had always been, in the back of my mind, some sense that some "thing" was following me, waiting for me, biding its time.

So, the first thing I did, when I moved into my apartment, was to say:

"OK. If there are any bad spirits here, you do NOT have permission to stay. Please leave!"

Nothing immediately happened.

Shortly after I had moved into my flat, my cousin's husband, Peter, suggested that he, a friend of his called Simon, and another cousin of mine, Ed, go on a camping trip to a log cabin that Simon owned.

We were there, in the woods. I was sitting on a log. I had had a couple of beers and – and this is the best way that I can describe it – I sensed an *entity*, an entity in the woods.

Don't ask me why I said the next thing I said, but for some impulsive, prankish reason I said to this entity, "You can take over my body. Take over my body and scare them."

I don't remember the next four hours.

What I'm telling you next I only know because of what Peter and Ed told me afterwards.

I started telling Simon things about his mother that I could not possibly have known. Deeply personal stuff. This was completely out of character for me, but apparently "I" was unrelenting, to a point where this man wanted to punch the living daylights out of me. Simon had a gun with him. At one point he was so enraged by what I was saying that he said, "If he doesn't fucking stop, I'm going to shoot him."

To make things worse, I was growling.

Frothing at the mouth.

Pacing back and forth like a zombie.

Peter convinced Simon to go. Peter, who is a religious man, was terrified as to what was going on and left too. My cousin, Ed, who was only twenty-two at the time, was also terrified, but stayed with me because he was concerned that if he left me alone I would walk off into the woods and never be seen again.

I was sitting on the log again, when I snapped out of the state I had been in. I said, "He knows he's too strong for us."

"Who?" Ed said.

"The Devil," I replied.

"Riiiiiiiggghhht …"

And then I looked around and asked, "Where's Peter?"

"What do you mean, Paul?"

"Where'd Peter go?"

"Don't you know what just happened? You've been in like this crazy state for the past four hours. We couldn't talk to you. We couldn't communicate with you. You were talking about Simon's mother – something you shouldn't have known. You have been, absolutely, completely … *gone*."

"Really?"

"Yeah, Paul. And both of them went home, shit scared."

"Oh … OK … well , that's … um … really bad."

And I just didn't think anything of it. I just left it there.

By that time it was too late to go back, so Ed just suggested we go into the cabin and sleep it off.

A couple of weeks later I was attending a family gathering. Peter had invited Simon. I approached him and said, "Hey, Bud. I don't know what happened or what I was saying to you, but I just wanted you to know that I have no recollection of what went on. I'm really, really sorry."

"I've actually had visions of getting into my car, finding you and shooting you," he said more in fear than in anger. He was still terrified of me. He didn't want to talk to me. He didn't want to come anywhere near me.

"Well … um … OK," was all I could think of saying.

We parted awkwardly. He spent the rest of the evening avoiding me.

I never spoke to him again.

With time we've left this whole incident behind, but not completely. Peter and Ed almost treat it as a joke, but I've said to them, "Look. I know that this is funny to you, but I was possessed."

"We know. But let's not talk about it."

They still don't want to look at it, at me, in the eye.

So though this turned out to be an isolated event I have to admit that *I asked for it.* For whatever reason I did ask this entity to take over me and I got what I wanted. Didn't I?

But I never did *that* again.

Back in my flat, the cocaine fairy was regularly pulling on my strings and saying, "It's time for a hit," so I'd be getting $2000, quarter-ounce bags at time.

On weekends I was getting drunk and going to poker machines at two in the morning, high as a kite.

I remember one weeknight I went to the drug dealer's house and I bought a bag that the bastard had adulterated with something like, I don't know, washing powder. I didn't know this, obviously. "I'll just do a gram," I told myself. I did, but something wasn't quite right. I was getting a little high, but I was sweating profusely, and my heart rate was going through the roof. I decided to lie down, but something in me kept saying, through thought in my mind, "Have another line!"

So, I did.

But then, something in me that was more powerful than that first voice or impulse said, "Stop! Stop now! Stop doing this! Stop right now!" And while I was sweating like crazy and my heart was just thumping, thumping, thumping, thumping I felt as if I was in the middle of a tug-of-war between something that was telling me to "Do some more!" while another thing was telling me to "Stop!" Both were independent voices, in my mind, clear as day.

I focused on the voice that said, "Stop!" and then it said, "Go to the bathroom and tip it down the sink."

I did.

And the voice said, "You're going to be all right now." Then I crashed on the bed and slept.

Later, I came to understand that if I had continued, I probably would've overdosed. I confronted the dealer over what had happened. He denied everything – of course.

Ironically, it was this incident that made me stop using cocaine. It wasn't because I made some heroic moral stance. I stopped because I couldn't trust these seedy, greedy cheats to give me what I was paying for. So it was a blessing. I guess.

But even though I'd given up on the cocaine, I was in a lot of trouble still, and really starting to recognize it. I was reaching the point when things were getting so bad that even I, with my well-practiced capacity for denial, couldn't ignore those problems anymore.

One night I was in the apartment, just lying in bed, when I got this overwhelming feeling that there was someone standing at the foot of the bed. I couldn't see it, but I could sense it and again it was speaking in my mind.

"Kill yourself. Kill yourself," it kept saying. "Kill yourself. Kill yourself."

By about the thirtieth repetition of "Kill yourself." I was certain that this wasn't me telling me to kill myself, but something else.

I retaliated.

"Fuck off! I'm not going to kill myself. Shut the fuck up and go away."

It stopped. And it was gone.

In the following weeks I was visited by another voice telling me to, "Repent! Repent! Repent!"

In one drunken haze I texted a fellow cocaine buddy, saying, "Repent!"

"Fuck off!" he texted back.

So, the message was intermittently coming through to me to, "Repent! Repent! Repent!".

Also, intermittently, the vision of abuse would haunt me and taunt me, playing over and over and over again, filling me with these almost overwhelming feelings of *shame* that, in their own way were goading me to kill myself.

"You're not a man! You're nothing! You're disgusting."

I felt at this stage, in spite of the "Repent! Repent! Repent!" I had only spent a few weeks living on my own and dealing with all this shit on my own and I felt that I was completely cut off from God. Jesus had never lived. God was just a fiction. The Bible was just a pack of lies. There was just, maybe this tiny little flicker of hope that God, maybe did exist.

I did what I hadn't done in years.

I prayed to God.

"God, I'm in trouble. Help. If I don't get help, I'm going to die. Would you please bring a woman into my life quickly or I'm going to die. I don't have any choice here."

I asked for this because I *knew* that a woman would give me some foundation to heal. A good strong woman with a good strong personality would not let me do cocaine again, not let me drink and then I could sober up and get my shit together.

I was praying for this at a time when I was in total despair. I don't value myself. I had lost touch with my more positive qualities and didn't hold much hope that someone else would see those qualities either. My self-worth was gone. I was in the pits.

And within weeks, and I don't know if this was God's doing, Kristy came along.

And she was exactly what I prayed for.

Coincidence?

But I have no idea how *any* woman would have stuck with me during what was about to happen.

It took the sort of woman who sees a wounded animal on the street and either takes it to the vet or takes it home and nurses it back to health. I was a major wounded animal project for Kristy.

Even after our first date I had her phone number, and in a drunken stupor called her and told her I was in real trouble. She rushed over to my flat and was banging on the door but by that time I was in an alcohol coma. When I woke up the next day, I saw that there were all these messages from her, "I hope you're all right." I don't know how at that point she wouldn't have just concluded, "OK. This guy's a total loser. I'm outta here!" But she stuck around.

Why?

Later she told me.

"I saw your potential, not your failing."

And somehow, this sick, wounded animal managed to convince this woman to move in with me within thirty days of our first date.

And whatever was haunting me didn't like it. It did not like it at all and did it's best to destroy that relationship. I think it knew that Kristy would give me the opportunity and the foundation to get better.

One night, we were in bed, asleep, and Kristy woke to find me in the middle of a deep, dark, and I can only say, demonic, growl. I slept through it this time. In the morning, she told me about it, and with smooth understatement she said, "Um, it didn't sound very good."

And on one occasion I did wake up and found myself doing it. I had no control over it. "It" was growling through me. It took over. It took *authority*. "It" was comfortable. "It" felt natural. And it stopped after a minute or so.

Kristy slept through that one, but in the morning, I told her what had happened. She admitted that the growling had occurred for several nights over the course of weeks, always between around midnight and three a.m.

Strangely, I wasn't particularly scared.

Yet.

Even under the best of circumstances, even in relationships that aren't contaminated by paranormal weirdness, there are going to be disagreements and arguments. Kristy and I were no exception and we did get into some fights early on – nothing relationship breaking, but we did get pretty close to the edge a few times. It would be accurate to say that we were testing our relationship.

But we were also *being* tested.

On one occasion one of our fights had gotten so bad that Kristy completely lost it and tried to choke me.

Several nights later I was lying in bed after one of our more animated arguments and out of the blue Kristy came into the bedroom and started to strangle me. I held her back. Kristy had a look on her face that was half shocked and half surprise.

"Why are you grabbing me?" she asked.

"Because you just tried to strangle me!"

"No, I didn't! I haven't even touched you! Let go!"

"But you tried to strangle me!"

Shaking me off she said, "No, I didn't! That didn't happen. Paul, you're acting like someone possessed."

I disengaged and let it go.

On reflection something was trying to drive a wedge between us and to destroy the relationship. On that night, it came close to succeeding. I'm still not sure that I was imagining the strangling although Kristy denies that she even laid a finger on me. Maybe *she* was the one who'd been possessed in that moment. I don't know.

After that the relationship nearly did fall apart. Kristy moved back into her parents' house for about a month. I moved out of the apartment and went to live with my mother again for a month because I was terrified. But something in Kristy told her to come back and do her damnedest to make things work, so we agreed to kiss and make up and only then did we both move back into the apartment, together.

But pretty soon after we moved back, she started telling me, "I don't like this place. There's something in this apartment. I hate it here."

So here we are. The apartment spooks Kristy for no obvious reason in and of itself.

But I was growling in the night. We were fighting and squabbling all the time. Violence had broken out in the relationship either physically or energetically and I was either actually being strangled, or imagining that I was being strangled, or wanting to strangle someone else.

I was lying in bed one night, rolling over, half-asleep, half-awake and the thought of the Devil came into my mind. But also in my mind came the thought: "Fuck the Devil".

No sooner than I'd thought of those words, something took over my power of speech. I felt it in my vocal cords. Beyond any power to control what was going on in my body, I said, out loud, in a deep, primal, guttural, animal voice: "You will be sorry you said that."

Startled awake I rolled over again. I woke up my partner and said, "Kristy! Kristy! Did you hear that!"

"Oh, shut up, Paul," she mumbled. "Nothing happened. Just go back to sleep."

"But, Kris …"

In that moment, I felt suddenly isolated. Up until that time Kristy had been my support, she knew that there was something wrong with the apartment, she was on my side. But now, in that moment, just after something had taken over my body and *I was aware of what had happened*, all the old feelings of being discounted and brushed aside and knowing that I was all on my own with this came back. I felt that she didn't believe me and I was terrified, again.

I was just lying there, not knowing what to do and feeling totally alone, again.

Not long after that Kristy and I realized that we were sharing dreams. I'd start telling her my dream, and she'd tell me, word for word, what I'd dreamed, because she had dreamt it too.

And the bedroom would all of a sudden be filled with the most awful smell. Kristy would accuse me of the obvious cause. "It wasn't me," I said.

"Yes, it was! You're an animal! Stop it!"

She wasn't convinced, but I knew I hadn't done anything, so I was scared. If "it" was doing this now, was it building up to something worse later?

Some subconscious thing, in the back of my mind, *finally* clicked.

The long-dormant Catholic in me kicked in. I knew that demonic possession was at least a possibility. It was part of the Catholic way of looking at the world. I know that Catholics did this sort of stuff and that exorcism was a "thing".

I got it into my head that I had to see an exorcist.

I didn't know where else to take that thought. It was 2011, the internet was there, but resources to help the possessed weren't as available then as it is now. In any case people like me still hadn't started the automatic habit of looking online for answers before doing anything else.

So, I started praying to God.

I don't know where these thoughts came from, but I said: "Please, God. Grant me the authority to exorcise myself."

So, I attempted a do-it-yourself-make-it-up-as-you-go-along exorcism.

"God gives me the power to exorcise myself." I'd say that over and over again.

This eerie feeling came over me – a tingling that started in the crown of my head and rushed through my body until it reached my feet. I knew that my prayer had been answered to some extent, but nothing much else would happen.

Since that hadn't really worked, I did go online and googled "exorcist". It took a while to find someone. Even now, in an era when you can find practically anything after a reasonably short search, you're hard pressed to find an exorcist at the touch of a button. It's not like there's a directory or anything. Back then, I was practically wasting my time.

I didn't necessarily believe that Kristy would believe me or support me in this. But there were signs that she was at least open to some sort of intervention. She had, in the past, bought some sage for ritual purification through smudging. She was a Catholic herself and I'd find her sometimes saying "Hail Mary"s and "Our Father"s. She had done something, but I wasn't sure if she was going to be willing to really own the situation, bring out the bigger guns and take it to the next level.

Eventually, I found an exorcist in Perth. His name was Father Barry May and he'd featured in a number of media stories. I didn't know anything else about him besides that.

So, I made an appointment to travel across a continent, alone, to work with the only guy I could find to fix me, or "it", or whatever it was.

I quickly realized that going alone was probably a very bad idea. I didn't really know who this "Father Barry May" was. I didn't know *at all.* I had no idea if he would actually be able to help me, or what would happen. There was some risk involved here.

My original plan was simply to tell Kristy that I was going to Western Australia "for a business meeting."

But then I decided to tell her the truth, because, say, what if these people were a bunch of lunatics? I wasn't going to let someone strap me to a chair, when I was in some sort of "state", on my own. Who knew what they would do to me?

"Look, Kris. Something's wrong. You know it. I know it. I'm going to Perth to see this exorcist. I wasn't going to tell you, but I'd really like you to come with me."

"Yes. I agree. I'll come too."

During the phone conversation at the time that I made my appointment to see him, Father May made it quite clear what the deal was. It would be a two-day process. On the first day there would be an interview with one of his "discerners" to see if I qualified. I'd never heard the term "discerner" before, but it meant someone who had a gift, or training, or both, to be able to tell if we were confronting a legitimate case of demonic activity. He naturally wanted to determine if I was mentally sound, and he wanted to hear my story, because people don't get an exorcism just because they ask for it. I left that phone conversation feeling that, at the very least, this guy was legit.

We met him the very same day of our arrival. We were in his home. I don't know what I was expecting but his home was nothing out of the ordinary. Father Barry May looked like a grandfather you'd go fishing with. Kristy and I were also introduced to his discerner, Anne, who also totally ordinary-looking – a woman whom I guessed was in her late thirties, early forties.

Father Barry asked me many questions, most of which I've forgotten.

"Did anything strange happen to you while traveling on your way here?"

"We lost our luggage temporarily," I said. "It was on its way to Bangkok, but we got it in time."

"People often find that strange things happen on their way to see me," he said.

One question stood out more than the others, so I remember it clearly years later.

"Have you ever received a hunch or intuition that someone in your family was going to die?"

"Yes. My father. And then he did die."

Over the course of an hour or so he teased out most of the story I've already told you. He then turned to Anne and asked, "What do you sense? What do you think is going on?"

"Yes," she said. "This is real. This is a real case. I sense something inside him. In his eyes."

Then Anne talked to me. At least, she talked *at* me. Her words were directed at me, but as if I wasn't there.

"I know you're in there, you wicked beast!"

Is this chick on something? Are you for real, lady? What the hell is going on?

Things had just suddenly escalated and there was just something too … theatrical … about it all. I started to have doubts. But then, from somewhere else, I *felt* an interior thought:

"You are in great, great, great danger. Get out of here."

But at that point Father May intervened and said.

"OK. You need to go back to your hotel now, and I will call you in the morning."

When were on our way back I asked Kristy, "Well, what do you think?"

"Just follow your heart," she said.

As he'd promised, Father May rang me in the morning and said, "I've prayed over this. You definitely qualify for an exorcism. Please come back to my house in a couple of hours."

We were back in his lounge room. Anne was sitting on a chair, independently praying.

"I'm going to say a few prayers," said Father May.

I don't recall the specific prayers, but he did give me a purple sash, and a cross, which I held.

"It's important that you have something from God touching you," he said.

I was sitting on the couch. Kristy was also sitting on the couch, to my left. Anne is in her chair sitting opposite to me. Father May is in a chair, diagonally across from me to my right.

Father May starts praying, and, well …

I stand up, and I have this, powerful, overwhelming urge to dry retch.

I'm going to vomit all over his floor.

And I was doing my best to hold it back.

Holding it back.

Holding it back.

And something takes over me.

I'm still in control …

and I could stop it at any time …

but I choose not to …

so I let it take over me …

and I say:

"I am not afraid of you, Priest!"

It was me. But it wasn't me. I knew I was saying it. But I wasn't saying it.

I sensed Father May's fear. He got so scared, he started rushing his prayers.

I looked behind Anne, and there was a cabinet there. And I had this overwhelming sensation that the cabinet was going to tilt over and drop on the floor.

I looked back at Father May. He started to shake and I could really sense the fear. He rushed through his prayers, stopped abruptly and said, "OK. Good job! You're done."

Well, *I didn't feel any better!*

Nothing really happened. Not for me at least.

"Is that it?"

"Yeah."

"Well, I really wanted to vomit on your floor."

"Thank you for not. That's it. You're done. See you later."

I told Anne about the cabinet.

"Yes," she said. "You were about to manifest, and I knew that. I prayed to stop the manifestation."

Father May then just gave me a few prayers to recite on my way home. And that was it, pretty much. We said our goodbyes. Wham, bam, thank you …

On our way back to the hotel Kris said, "You seem better."

"You think?"

"Yeah. Um … lighter …I don't really know."

And on the plane back home I started reading the prayers that Father May had given me, softly to myself, and underneath – I don't know any other way to describe it – underneath, something was *laughing*.

Laughing through me.

Laughing at the prayers.

Just laughing and laughing.

The next day or so, Kristy had been doing some more research on the internet, and came across some stuff about "Self-Deliverance" – doing exorcism for yourself at home.

"This is for you," she said to me, handing me a Self-Deliverance Prayer Program that takes you through the classic four-stages of Self-Deliverance – stuff like asking for forgiveness, breaking curses, identifying the "afflictions" and the types of spirits and finally, the casting out of demons.

In the Self-Deliverance guidelines there was an instruction to "ask the name of the demon." So, I tried that out.

"Demon, what is your name?"

And some sound tried to come through my voice, in that growling voice that demons like to use. It wasn't so physical as a full-blown voice, more like an undertone of impulses that couldn't quite come through. The thing identified itself as "Rencray" or "Renkre". I'm not sure about the spelling, but that's what it felt like. A French-speaking friend I know said it could be *rencré*, which, weirdly, means "renounced", but I have enough trouble with English, and I had no idea that is what it might have been. For all I know it could have been Ancient Egyptian.

I went to Kristy and told her what happened.

"No, it didn't", she said.

"I'm telling you. *I am telling you*. This happened!"

"Well, I don't know, Paul. I don't know what to do. Keep saying your prayers. I don't know."

So, I went back to the bedroom and continued.

"Demon, leave!"

And I sensed that "it", whatever it was, wasn't going anywhere.

I learned much later that to be effective against demons, you need to develop some level of faith, some level of *spiritual authority*, otherwise they just sense your fear, sense that the foundation of your life is built on sand, and they don't take you seriously. My spirit was so weak, that my attempts at eviction were hopeless. That's why I felt the undercurrent of laughter. And Self-Deliverance rarely works when you're dealing with a serious infestation, you need someone far more grounded in spiritual authority than I was at that time. It would be like attempting open-heart surgery, *on yourself*, when you're always on the verge of having a heart attack.

But I didn't know that at the time.

So, I kept trying. I must have tried casting the thing out about thirty times. I was going through my rosary over and over, but whatever inside me must have sensed that I was so spiritually weak by then, such a spiritual loser, that it wasn't even going to lower itself to even pretending that I was in the slightest way intimidating it.

In frustration, I rang Barry May. I told him about the Demon naming itself to me. I told him I was trying Self-Deliverance, saying the prayers he had given me and there was something *underneath* laughing at me and NOTHING was working.

"Hmmm. Yes. Very interesting."

"Now, I don't want to be rude, but I was wondering how many times you'd done an exorcism because it doesn't appear to me that you've done this very well."

"Oh, I've done this a lot. I know what I'm doing."

By now, I was getting a bit pissed off.

"Well, I tell you what. If you *did* get rid of something, then there's now something else in its place. *It's still there.*"

"OK. OK. I get you. Why don't you send me an email describing exactly what's happening and I'll look into it."

So, I sent him an email. I didn't hear back for several days, so I called him again.

"I've been trying to reply to your email," he said. "But for some reason, it won't let me."

"What?"

"I can't type a reply. It just doesn't work, or I write something, and it gets deleted. Or if I manage to finish something I press 'send' and nothing happens. I just couldn't get in touch with you."

Oh, great.

"Well, thanks for trying, Father." And even though I said that half-sarcastically, I was scared.

And I still got the sense that he was scared too and that he'd bitten off more than he could chew. Whatever he'd done in the past, he didn't know what he was dealing with, *this time*. He was out of his depth. I needed a better doctor, and this doctor was terrified and had, I suspected, only ever performed "minor operations". I had, inadvertently, chosen a dental hygienist to perform brain surgery. Bizarrely, there seemed to be some ego thing there on his part that couldn't let him admit to himself, or anyone else, that he wasn't up to the job. Even more bizarrely, I was dealing with an *anointed Anglican minister*, who, I assume, had a *vocation*, and whose *entire reason for being* was to help people in my position. Call me selfish, but I assumed that he had a duty of care to souls in danger, and that if he wasn't up to it, as part of that duty of care he had an obligation to call on a more experienced person, or a higher authority.

"Look, Father. I'm in trouble here, and I don't know where else to go."

"Isn't there someone in Melbourne who can help you?"

"If there were someone in Melbourne who could help, I wouldn't have crossed the country to see you! I don't know anyone in Melbourne, do *you*?"

"No … OK. I'll help you. But it's coming up to Christmas and my son has just moved in for his usual two to three-week stay, and I won't be able to see you until the New Year."

OH GREAT! You don't obviously want to see me because you've just asked me if there's anyone in Melbourne who can help me and I'm … I'm just … possessed … and I'll just have to wait until the peak of the season is over. Wow! I really hope that demons take holidays!

So, I felt completely and utterly cut off.

Again.

Brilliant!

And that is where we left it.

"OK. Thanks. I'll call you in the New Year."

I never spoke to him again.

Much later I found out that Barry May was the first ever full-time chaplain appointed to the WA police. I never knew that at the time because he had retired from that role in 2007 and he never mentioned that to me. He was also a recipient of the Centenary Medal, the Police Commissioner's Medal of Excellence and in 2008, the Order of Australia Medal. None of which I knew at the time either. He had published a book, a few years before in 2012, about his experiences with Near Death Experiences, Out of Body Experiences and as an exorcist. It's called *Back from the Brink A Glimpse of the Fourth Dimension*, which I didn't know about at the time and that I still haven't read. If nothing else, he had at least *financial* integrity. He never asked me for any money for his services or a donation for his church. Whatever help he had been to other people, which must have been considerable because he was obviously well-loved and respected, I regret to say that he did virtually nothing for me and for what was going on with me. Father Barry May died in March 2015, not long after I saw him.

Sometime later I found out that if you wanted a Catholic exorcism you could go to confession, and the priest could begin a process. However, the Catholic church seems to be in two minds about this. Cases of demonic possession nearly always present as mental health issues, thus paranormal phenomena are dismissed as delusions of a deranged mind. So it's quite possible that you could go to confession and the priest will tell you to see a mental-health professional *immediately and without further thought* and dismiss the whole "possession thing" out of hand without investigating further. Now *you'd think* that an organization with two thousand years of experience in these sorts of matters would have a policy that all priests were uniformly briefed on. But no. You can also bypass the lower echelons altogether and approach your local archdiocese directly, and the church would then arrange to examine your case and determine that what you had was actually a spiritual issue, and that you weren't just some nutcase. Only if they evaluated or even discerned that you really were in some way demonically contaminated, would they then send someone 'round to see what they could do.

But that wasn't to be my path, exactly.

A WORD ABOUT THE CATHOLIC RIGHT OF EXORCISM

The Spiritual Affliction "industry" is unregulated.

There are no universally agreed international standards of what constitutes the circumstances for intervention.

There are no common protocols for treatment.

There is no ecumenical committee somewhere that decides what "professional best practice" is with regard to Exorcists and Deliverers and what such practice might look like.

Perhaps that's a good thing, perhaps not. The reality is that even in the 21st century, Spiritual Affliction is a cottage industry, about as professional in most cases as psychiatry was in the Middle Ages.

What's worse, it has a stigma attached to it that is difficult to shake. People would rather admit that they were the victims of child sexual abuse than that they were the victims of demonic possession. Certainly, mainstream science thinks that Spiritual Affliction is just another form of mental illness, cloaked in a mantle of superstition.

Mainstream churches aren't much better. At worst they talk about Spiritual Affliction in hushed voices; at best they send mixed messages about it. They certainly don't advertise themselves as offering anything like a "Clinic for the Spiritually afflicted" and some don't even believe in it in the first place.

One would think that with a history stretching back 2000 years, the Catholic Church, and its close cousin, the High Anglican Church would be a little more organized about such things, but they're not. Perhaps this will change in time. At the time of writing, the office of the Exorcist no longer officially exists in the Catholic Church.

There are biblical references to Jesus casting out spirits.

"When He arrived at the other side in the country of the Gadarenes, two demon-possessed men coming out of the tombs met Him. They were so extremely fierce and violent that no one could pass by that way. And they screamed out, "What business do we have [in common] with each other, Son of God? Have You come to torment us before the appointed time [of judgment]?" Some distance from them a large herd of pigs was grazing. The demons began begging Him, "If You drive us out, send us into the herd of pigs." And He said to them, "Go!" So they came out [of the men] and went into the pigs, and the whole herd rushed down the steep bank into the sea and died in the water." *Matthew 8:28–34 Amplified Bible (AMP)*

The Catholic Church developed rites of exorcism using Biblical authority over a long period of time in response to needs in their communities.

As a Uniting Church minister, I am not an expert on the Catholic Rite of Exorcism. But from what I can tell, the principal differences between what I do and what Catholic Priests do is the following:

The Catholic Rite of Exorcism is standardized. It is a fixed set of prescribed steps and prayers that follows a particular script. Much of this script was originally inspired by Saint John Chrysostom, who lived between the years 344 and 407 AD. St. John's words are used in the Orthodox Churches.

An example of his work, translated from the Greek in which he wrote, looks like this:

We beseech Thee, O Lord, Almighty God, Most High, untempted, peaceful King. We beseech Thee Who has created the heaven and the earth, for out of Thee has issued the Alpha and the Omega, the beginning and the end, Thou Who has ordained that the four-footed and irrational beasts be under subjection to man, for Thou hast subjected them. Lord, stretch out Thy mighty hand and Thy sublime and holy arm and in Thy watchful care look down upon this Thy creature and send down upon him/her a peaceful angel, a mighty angel, a guardian of soul and body, that will rebuke and drive away every evil and unclean demon from him/her, for Thou alone are Lord, Most High, almighty and blessed unto ages of ages. Amen.

The full Catholic Rite can be found in a book called the *Rituale Romanum* (the Roman Ritual), which includes, among other things, texts for other services like baptism, confirmation, penance, the anointing of the sick, extreme unction (the blessing of the dying), matrimony and the rite for the ordination of priests among other things.

Exorcism, in fact, is one of the *last* things mentioned in the *Rituale Romanum* and only takes up about eleven pages in a book over 400 pages long, so exorcism is by no means the main focus of the book.

In spite of the long history of Roman Catholic rites, the *Rituale Romanum* was only properly codified after the Second Vatican council in 1964 and on 26 January, 1999, the Catholic Church, under the supervision of Cardinal Jorge Arturo Medina Estevez, published *New Rite of Exorcism Guidelines*. It is not without its critics, even within the Catholic Church. It does not, for example take into account the expulsion of demons from physical objects and it leaves the priest two options for the expulsion of demons, one of which, a "deprecatory prayer to God" is judged by some, to be useless.

It is not my intention to take you down a theological rabbit hole and argue over fine points of practice, or to get into an argument with the Catholic Church. I simply wish to emphasize that while the Catholic Rite of Exorcism is highly scripted, the Deliverance process is not.

This is the main difference between Exorcism and Deliverance. Deliverance is, at least in my mind, a much more dynamic, responsive and organic process that what I understand Exorcism to be.

I personally do my best to "get out of the way" and allow The Holy Spirit to flow through me and guide me, in the moment, to what I need to do. Yes, there is a process and yes, there is a plan in the form of – what's the expression? – "boxes that have to be ticked" but the process I take the afflicted through is a dynamic one that is not easily scripted and requires considerable openness to improvisation, guided, as always, by The Holy Spirit.

For those who are interested in taking a further look at the Catholic Rite, you can find it here:

https://www.catholic.org/prayers/prayer.php?p=683

If you have a leaning toward the traditional and you like the idea of reading the rite in Latin, go here:

http://www.catholicdoors.com/prayers/latin/latin040.htm

And for at least one point of view of a deeper analysis and critique, go here:

https://www.fisheaters.com/praeternaturalworldfrx.html

JS

CHAPTER SEVEN

EMBRACING A HIGHER AUTHORITY

"... it doesn't matter what you become. Ultimately, you will end up doing this work, bringing people out from the darkness, bringing them into the light. I think you're going to say 'yes' to this ... in the end."

Joseph

Of course, as a young man I knew very little of the complexities and subtleties of the Deliverance process yet. I had barely a hint of the many traps that an exorcist can fall into. And I knew nothing of what the experience of affliction was like for the afflicted.

But I became acquainted very quickly.

And I know what I have witnessed.

I remember a lady who practically flew across a church and when she landed, she coiled, contorting herself like a snake.

I remember others swimming on the floor as if they were in the sea.

I remember others screaming. Just screaming and screaming. Screaming things like, "Who do you think you are? I cannot leave! I cannot leave! You do not have the *authority* to tell me to leave!" Even screaming in languages that the speakers didn't even know.

Often they simply faint, collapse, as if someone had just switched off every muscle in their body. This can happen at any time during a Deliverance session.

After witnessing many such things, I felt the need to confess something to Pastor Apie.

"You know, when you do that, when you order the demons to leave," I said, "and often when you talk about Deliverance in church, but especially just then, when you do the Deliverance, I feel a strong heat in the palms of both my hands. I don't know what that is."

"Whenever anyone asks for prayer, and you are in my presence, and you feel the heat in your palms, with my blessing and permission, I want you to lay your hands on them," he said.

And yet, for several meetings after my confession, even though I had Pastor Apie's blessing and permission, even though I felt the heat, I didn't lay my hands on anyone.

I was too scared. I was too young and I wasn't always prepared to do what The Holy Spirit demanded of me.

But it wasn't long until Pastor was conducting a church service and people were lining up to be treated in a public Deliverance. I felt an impulse to lay my hands on someone, so I placed my right hand on someone's shoulder, and they collapsed. I felt the impulse again and laid my hand on someone else.

Bang!

Collapsed right down on the floor again.

Then I raised my hand right up because I was shocked by what was happening. Twenty, maybe thirty people on the left-hand pews just collapsed onto the ground. The Holy Spirit had come upon them. They trembled, they shook, and they fell under the power of The Holy Spirit. Those who did not, those who were quick, jumped in to help them down before they injured themselves. And if those who had collapsed were afflicted the demons now began to speak through them. Some, who were not possessed, began to speak of the wounds that they had, wounds that required healing.

Even more shocked now, I wept.

Holy Spirit, I am unworthy to do this. Who am I? I am nothing.

And I wept and I wept and I wept …

Pastor came over to me. "Why are you crying?" he asked.

"I'm not worthy to do this sort of thing," I said.

He paused, in that way that adults pause before they have to tell children something obvious.

"It's not about *you*," he said. "It's about what The Holy Spirit wants. The Holy Spirit *chose you*. This has nothing to do with you. You are just a vessel. The Holy Spirit is the one doing the work."

It's not about me. My opinion about my worthiness is irrelevant.

"You need to understand something, Joseph," Pastor said. "These people, these *broken* people who come to us. They are God's children. They are *Children of the Light*. They need healing. *You are God's vessel.* Never feel unworthy. When The Holy Spirit comes upon you, think about *them*. Think about the people. You are there for *them*."

And even though I had not been ordained by the church, even though I was still in high school and I had not even begun my formal theological training, that day I first laid hands on one of the afflicted, when the Power of The Holy Spirit flowed through me so that the afflicted might begin their journey to ridding themselves of the evil that come upon them, to begin their path to healing. Even though later I would acquire more knowledge and formal training, it was at *that* moment and on *that* day that was the beginning of the Deliverance ministry that The Holy Spirit had ordained for me.

There are often-posed questions:

"Why would an all-powerful God who can do anything, choose *to work through human vessels* to fight evil?"

"Why would God not simply act directly?"

"Why would God work through humans, with all their faults, flaws and imperfections, when a direct approach would be so much better?"

These are fair questions and they have several answers.

Firstly, The Holy Spirit *does* act directly and intervenes in human affairs. Most of the time, the interventions are subtle and go unnoticed by the vast majority of people. Sometimes though, the interventions are more dramatic, and we call these "moments of grace" and in the most spectacular and obvious of cases, we call them miracles.

Putting aside for the moment that our very existence is miraculous.

In many other cases The Holy Spirit works through imperfect, faulty, flawed vessels like Joseph Wisdom Sesay because of a pact that God made with humans long ago.

This book is not an attempt to "preach to the converted." I hesitate to include too many verses from the Bible because I am aware that not everyone in the world follows the Judeo-Christian path of spirituality. There are other valid paths to the Divine, and even the word "Christian" can mean very different things to different people. So, I do not wish to alienate people with what some call "Bible bashing", but in this particular instance I need to make a point that comes from Genesis, Chapter 1, verses 26 to 28.

26 And God said, Let us make man in our image, after our likeness: and let them have dominion over the fish of the sea, and over the fowl of the air, and over the cattle, and over all the earth, and over every creeping thing that creepeth upon the earth.

27 So God created man in his own image, in the image of God created he him; male and female created he them.

28 And God blessed them, and God said unto them, Be fruitful, and multiply, and replenish the earth, and subdue it: and have dominion over the fish of the sea, and over the fowl of the air, and over every living thing that moveth upon the earth.

There is a lot to unpack here, and others have written volumes on the meaning of these verses alone, but I will try to summarize the salient points.

When God created man "in our image, after our likeness" this does not mean that God, in the ultimate sense, has ten fingers, ten toes and a nose that is runny sometimes and sneezes. It means that we are created as independent, conscious beings of free will – autonomous extensions of divinity who can make choices and who are creative *in their own right*.

When God blessed humanity and gave us "dominion over the fish of the sea, over the fowl of the air, and over every other thing that moveth upon the earth" the key word here is "dominion".

"Dominion" does not necessarily mean "domination". It can have meanings like "ownership" or "power", but at its root the word comes from the Latin – *domus* – meaning "house" or "home". You could interpret the verse as meaning, "Make the Earth your home."

We are also told to "replenish the Earth" not to rape and pillage it. After all, would you rape and pillage your own home?

Of course, "human dominion" does not mean "absolute power" as anyone who has ever seen the ruins of Pompeii or the devastation wrought by the Indian Ocean tsunami of 2004, or the COVID 19 crisis of 2020–21. But even the most atheistic materialist would admit that there is something extraordinary about human beings and the power we wield upon the Earth. We have not always used that power wisely, but the power exists, nonetheless.

In giving us *dominion* over the Earth, God gave us *power*, but also *responsibility*.

Above all else God gave us a *custodianship*, which carries with it a *duty of care*.

It is a care that we have not always honored terribly well.

And in giving us free will, God also gave us autonomy.

But this power and autonomy exists not only in the physical Earth, but in the whole *Earthly Realm*. This realm includes us and our choices. Even though God is all-knowing, all-present and all-powerful, much of what happens to us in the Earthly Realm, especially in our culture, societies and history, is of our own choosing.

Even when we make spectacularly bad choices – the Spanish Inquisition, the Holocaust, colonialism in Africa and the slave trade to name just a few – God will not, for the most part, impinge on our free will. So powerful is our free will that even God will, for the most part, allow us free reign on Earth, even if we create Hell, even when we waste the opportunity to create Heaven.

God has set up a reality in which we have the opportunity to make good choices and achieve paradise, but we can also give ourselves enough rope to hang ourselves. God allows evil to happen because evil *must* be an option among beings of free will. Without "evil", the choice for "good" becomes meaningless.

So powerful is our free will that God, for the most part, will only intervene when and if we ask for help, and even then, there's no guarantee. God has access to information that we don't have access to, information that might explain decisions that God makes that might seem incomprehensible from a human point of view.

We are also God's children and children need to mature, to know how to be in the universe, how to learn to make good decisions.

Wise parents know what is best for their children until the children know enough to make better decisions.

But so powerful is our dominion over the Earth that God will not crash into our dominion, our home, except when God has to – no more than a wise parent will crash into school and interrupt a class unless they have to. A parent who crashes into school *all the time* to interrupt class and do all the work for the children or do all their assignments or take all their tests makes the whole idea of being a child, having lessons in classes and taking tests in the school *meaningless*.

So, because of the way that the reality is set up, when it comes to the Earthly realm, through which humans have dominion, The Holy Spirit works both directly but also indirectly through human vessels, even if those vessels think that they are unworthy.

And, if you think about it, what an arrogant position it is to believe that you are unworthy to be a vessel for The Holy Spirit. In questioning your worthiness, you are, in effect, questioning the judgment of infinite intelligence. What might seem to be humility, is actually a manifestation of pride.

To think that you know better than God! The very idea is ridiculous!

If God chooses us, *we must assume that God knows what God is doing*.

The Sin of Lucifer was to assume that "He" knew better than God, and we all know what that led to.

And of course, delusion is also possible. If we have fooled ourselves into believing that The Holy Spirit has chosen us *when we have not been chosen*, when we have deluded ourselves into taking on *missions that do not have our name on it*, well, life has a way of knocking some sense into us too. Eventually. Think of the number of times when you have taken on a problem that wasn't any of your business and that you did not know enough about but felt you had to interfere with anyhow. How do those things usually turn out? Fools rush in where angels fear to tread …

I rearranged my work, my school schedule and freed up my Fridays to become a regular attendant not only in normal services, but in Deliverance services as well. Every Friday Pastor and I would pray and fast in preparation for conducting Deliverance.

"You need to be always spiritually ready," he said, "spiritually strong."

My ability to see into the future had not left me. I would get knowledge.

"Tonight, a woman will come. She is not coming for Deliverance, but to tempt us," I declared.

"You mean, she is afflicted and the demon within her wants to compromise us to undermine us and the ministry?" Pastor asked.

"Yes. That's it."

And that day a woman came to us and just hung around the church, chanting under her breath, seeking to curse us in some way. It didn't work. She stayed for the service, and when The Holy Spirit manifested, she did not collapse onto the ground. Instead, she began running around screaming, "Fire! Fire! I'm burning!" Then she broke down and began to confess to us what she was doing. "I came to undo the prayers. I came to infest a body to become an agent of Satan!" Fortunately, we were able to deliver her. Perhaps she was a little crazy, perhaps she was possessed. Whatever she was the Deliverance process stopped her bad behavior and she never troubled us again.

On another occasion, I was sitting in church with a friend of mine when a sudden impulse seized me, another case of spontaneous spiritual communication, or "reading".

I turned to look at him, I said, "David! You will be traveling to a far distant country!"

"Joseph," he said. "I'm not even thinking of leaving Guinea. What are you talking about?"

"I don't know where you'll be going," I said. "But after I while, I will be joining you."

Not long after, another friend approached David and said, "I'm supposed to be helping out on our refugee program. My brother is supposed to be coming with me, but he can't go. I want you to come and take his place. Would you like to come?"

"Where?" David asked.

"Australia," the friend said.

And so, David went to Australia.

And during this time, I was also regularly visiting another experienced pastor, Pastor Timothy, who was able to teach me a lot about the reality of pastoral work. We often stayed up late at night talking. In his household the pastor had an adopted daughter called Fatmata and we became friends. Then the family emigrated to Australia, but we stayed in touch, off and on.

Sometimes Pastor Apie would invite other ministers from other ministries to perform Deliverance and in watching them, something would "speak" to me – an inkling in my mind, an intuition.

"They are doing it wrong," this something would say with unspoken words.

This capacity to discern the effectiveness of interventions came mostly from the ability granted to me by The Holy Spirit. But in other cases, it would have been obvious even to those who did not have the gift of discernment, that despite Deliverances that were stormy and dramatic, with much raising of voices and flailing about of bodies, the entity just would not go.

At those times other impulses would seize me – just do *this* and the demon will go. "This" could be anything, saying a prayer, making an invocation, or discerning a contract and breaking it. But the ministers, out of ignorance, would not be doing what was necessary. But I had the advantage of a direct line to The Holy Spirit in these matters. Even if I was not performing the Deliverance myself, I knew, *I knew in my bones*, what to do. It was very frustrating for me to watch a bunch of amateurs, however well meaning, botch their operations, convince themselves that they had done the right thing and tell themselves, and everybody else, "That's fine now. It's OK. It's OK." And I knew that the Deliverance had failed because at the very best the afflicted would come back with the same "symptoms" and the same problems recurring over and over again. At the very worst, their condition would deteriorate even further and the chaos that they would cause would escalate.

But then my false humility would show up, and false humility is as bad as false pride.

"What did I know?" I would tell myself. I was just a novice, wet-behind-the-ears. In the hierarchical ladders that humans so like to build, I was on the lowest rung. I had no standing, so I couldn't stand up for myself. And, of course, I had my doubts as to how effective a vessel I was. It took me a long, long time before I could summon up the courage to tell Pastor that sometimes things were not quite right. That moment was in the future.

I was young. Even though I felt the heat in my palms, even though Pastor had given me *express permission* to act on my impulses, still I held back because of *propriety*, because I didn't want to *rock the boat*. I allowed consideration of the feelings of the well-meaning but not-always-effective, "more experienced" ordained ministers, to get in the way of doing effective work. I let my fears of what the elders in the church and deacons and other members of the church hierarchy might say or do – *They might throw me out!* – to get in the way of doing what was right and healing the afflicted then and there.

There was some justification for my concerns. My dramatic

debut had started tongues wagging. The community was somewhat polarized between those who didn't care that I wasn't an ordained minister because I had a *gift*, and those who felt that because of a lack of training, I might get myself into trouble.

I began to walk a fine line. People would "pull me aside to have a chat" or call me on the phone and ask, if, I could help them and "No, no, no, please don't tell Pastor Apie."

Naturally, I couldn't do this. I *had* to consult Pastor first. I didn't want to undermine anything, but more importantly, I didn't want to get into a situation that I couldn't get out of and damage myself or the afflicted in the first place, no matter how drawn they were to me for a solution.

And yet, I still had doubts about myself. Pastor didn't doubt, but also felt that I was right to be cautious, "You have the Power, but you also need experience," he said.

And yet, on the other hand, this discernment and the power flowing into my hands was deep evidence of my calling. I had to accept that Deliverance, with a capital "D", was my calling. This was why I had been put on Earth, as a vessel of Holy Power, as The Holy Spirit's instrument of healing.

I was never actively derailed, perhaps nothing would have happened to me. Perhaps I was my own worst enemy. Perhaps I should have had a little more faith that The Holy Spirit would protect me and see that I, the vessel, would come to no harm.

It was, after all, my destiny; I could not escape it.

But because I am a flawed human, I tried to anyway.

And I can't honestly say that, given my youth at the time, I could blame myself too much for refusing the call.

There is no money to be made as an apprentice exorcist. I didn't even have what little money I needed to supply my frugal needs because the church does not provide even a small stipend for such things. The work is entirely voluntary. But on the other hand it doesn't matter that there isn't even a stipend, because, one way or another, The Holy Spirit *always* provides – although sometimes things can get a little tight.

One day, it must have been when I had been "apprenticing" for a couple of years, Pastor took me aside for one of our little talks.

"Do you feel that you still have a calling?" he asked.

I swallowed. I had known for some time that this talk would one day happen, and here it was.

"Yes," I said. "But I don't want to be a pastor."

He paused for a heartbeat or two. "OK, then," he asked, "what do you want to be?"

"I want to be a lawyer."

More heartbeats passed, and then, with that tone that adults use when they have to explain to children about the unavoidable, "OK, well … then … um … I cannot force you, of course, but I believe it doesn't matter what you become. Ultimately, you will end up doing this work, bringing people out from the darkness, bringing them into the light. I think you're going to say 'yes' to this … in the end."

And of course I knew, in the depths of my soul, that he was right. I knew that I could not escape my destiny, but I was in denial.

Absolute denial.

After everything that had ever happened in my life, after everything that I had experienced, despite extraordinary help and "chance encounters" meeting with people who helped me, after all of that support and after having survived so much hardship, having worked so hard, *I still didn't want to do it.*

I didn't want a life of continual sacrifice. By now I really knew what it was like to be a pastor with a ministry – especially a *Deliverance* ministry.

You were on call 24/7 every day.

Always under pressure.

Always under attack or the threat of attack from demonic forces because once you're on their "radar", once you're on their "hit list" you're always going to be a target.

Always having to be a shield *and* a sword.

Always looking into the abyss, into the mouth of Hell.

Always being called upon to drag wounded, injured, traumatized people out of Hell.

Deliverance is time-consuming. It is not unusual for pastors involved in Deliverance ministries not to have any time for their families, their friends or even themselves.

I had experienced this myself. After a long day at school and at work Pastor could ring me at 11:00 pm and say, "Can you come? Somebody needs our help."

"Of course," I would always say.

What was I going to do, leave the poor man to deal with it on his own?

It's arguably more difficult even than being a doctor on twenty-four-hour call. At least a doctor can outsource their diagnosis to a machine or to a lab. For us, even the process of discernment requires our full attention. You need to be spiritually fit to do this job. It's more like being a special force's soldier who has to stay in top shape all the time to go on a mission at a moment's notice. We don't even have the luxury of fighting something material, with physical weapons. Our battles are with invisible energies that are experts in hiding and lying, cunning enemies, malicious deceivers.

How many doctors have to fight an *intelligent disease* that *actively* wants to *harm the patient and you*?

If the Power of The Holy Spirit weren't there to draw upon, if the Authority of the Word of God could not protect you, what chance would we have? But even so, from a human point of view, you never know what you're getting into.

It is not unusual for ministers to be confronted with situations where you know that if you do not intervene then the life of the afflicted is on the line. They are in *mortal* danger. In such cases the exorcist might have to go into isolation for a time, simply to have enough silence so that they can hear the voice of The Holy Spirit to give them the necessary insights into the case and in order for the intervention to be effective.

You can find yourself fasting for days in solitude to get into the realm of the spirit, to dismantle the layers and layers of lies to drag the soul back into the light. This can even leave your family vulnerable, which requires further steps to create protection.

All this requires tremendous ongoing commitment because *you can't be "half" an exorcist.* The commitment is total.

And I just didn't want to go there.

And I also wanted to do something, I don't know, something more … professional.

I wanted to dress up in a nice suit and go to work and have a wife and children and flake out on the couch and watch TV and take a holiday once a year.

I wanted a normal life!!!

But I couldn't get away from all this demonic stuff. It would find me wherever I went.

Some out-of-town visitors of my employer were staying in his house. They were Holy men who had come to give spiritual help for a political candidate. I did my duty and saw that they were looked after. At one point the oldest of them, the leader said to me "You have been good to us. Let me do something for you." Then he gave me a cross and some bangles. "There are three things this will do for you. One. You're going to be very powerful. Two. You will marry a woman who will listen to you. Three. You're going to be protected, because the higher you go, the more people will hate you and you're going to need protection."

There was something about the situation that felt … *off.*

"But I don't want it," I said. "I don't need it."

"Take it anyway," the man said.

Not wanting to be rude, I did.

The next day I received a surprise visit from my mother, whom I had not seen for a while. She had traveled the whole night and hundreds of kilometers to see me and caught up with me just as I was getting ready to go to school.

"Mother!"

She held up her hand, palm facing me. "I have not come here as your mother," she said, sternly, her voice filled with authority. "I am sent by God. The Holy Spirit came to me and told me that you were in danger," she said. "I went almost straight away to my pastor and we prayed together," she continued, "but I knew that was not enough, so I came here to warn you."

"OK," I said. My mother was scaring me a little, but I knew I had to listen.

"If there is anything you have, anything at all, that is not of God, give it back!" she said. "Whatever it is, it will do you good only for a little while," she said. "But after that, you will be destroyed."

I was speechless.

"The Holy Spirit would never lie to us," she said. She gave me some money and then said, "I have delivered my message," and with that, she left.

The meeting had not lasted even ten minutes. I knew that I had to listen.

The next morning, the old man came to me and noticed that

I wasn't wearing the cross. "Why aren't you using the cross I gave you," he asked.

"I don't need it," I said.

"Why?"

"Because everything that you've promised me, The Holy Spirit will give to me," I said.

He laughed. "You are the most studious young man I've met. All these people who come here, they pay me thousands to help them out. Here I am, giving you my help for free, and you don't want it."

"I appreciate the gesture," I said. "Really I do, but I don't need it." I attempted to give him the cross and the bangles back.

"Don't hand it to me," he said. "Just leave it on the kitchen table."

Which is what I did.

Shortly after, the men were due to leave.

"I've left the bangles on the table in my room," the elder said. "Can you get them for me please?"

They were in a hurry, and as I rushed into the room to get the bangles for him, I heard the car pull out. I felt The Holy Spirit "telling me" not to touch the bangles. I went outside again but the car had already gone. When my boss got home, I told him what had happened, and he said. "It's good that you didn't touch that thing." I never saw the bangles again and my boss and I never brought up the subject again either.

I later learned that the candidate that these men had been helping out did, in fact, get elected. Whatever they had been doing worked, I guess.

Later, I telephoned my mother, and told her what had happened. And I felt an even greater desire to escape from all this spooky spiritual stuff.

I didn't initially quite know what to do about becoming a lawyer.

I did, however, receive an offer to have my seminary studies paid for in Guinea. A member of the congregation, Brother Christian, was rich. He had helped me with a certain amount of money every week, just to help me out. He saw that I had a calling and wanted to assist me. But I didn't want to spend the next five years in Guinea studying in the seminary. I wanted to go home. Even after all this time, in October 2003, after my having been away for about fourteen years, Liberia was still home. The Second Liberian Civil war had mostly been concentrated in the south, around the capital of Monrovia, and had ended on 18 August.

My plans, such as they were, were to start university, maybe start a degree in social work, then transfer to law. A cousin of my mother had promised that he would help me. "Come to Monrovia," he said. "We'll work things out." So I went to Monrovia, the capital of Liberia, to meet up with the cousin. Not long after I took the university entrance exam that would be recognized in Guinea and I passed.

Then my mother's cousin had an opportunity open up for him in Togo – about three countries away, some 1400 kilometers or 860 miles east.

"Joseph," he said. "I am so sorry, but I will not be able to sponsor you in school."

I felt let down. But I prayed to The Holy Spirit.

Please. If it is Your will, show me the way. Make the path clear for me.

I was attending the Assemblies of God Church in Monrovia. A friend said to me, "There's an entrance exam in the seminary. Why not apply?"

"I really don't want to take the exam for the seminary."

"You can try!" If you don't get in, it's no big deal. If you get in, you can get a degree, then you can pursue your goals later. It's better than just sitting down, twiddling your thumbs."

"But I don't have the money!" I objected.

"Take the entrance exam first and then see what happens."

I had five, count them, five US dollars in my pocket on the day I did the exam.

They tested my knowledge of English. My English was good enough.

Then they tested my knowledge of the Bible and Christianity. Those questions were easy enough to answer.

Then the questions got personal.

"What do you understand about the Call of God?"

"What makes you think *you* are called to this work?"

"What do you plan to do after you have completed your studies?"

"Do you intend to work with someone else in an existing ministry?"

"Do you intend to start your own ministry?"

I was also required to speak to a psychologist, to make sure that I was mentally and emotionally fit and prepared to do this sort of work.

"Ministry work is stressful," the psychologist said.

"I know."

"You'll be dealing with many different types of people who are often under a lot of stress," he said.

"Yes, I know."

"80% of the work you'll be doing will be with people. We have to be sure that there is nothing that will get in the way of your working with people. We need to know if you've ever had a drug addiction, or if you've ever been to jail."

"No and no."

"What evidence do you have to support your calling?"

"I've been told by The Holy Spirit that I'm going to be a vessel,"

I said. "I have had numerous encounters with The Holy Spirit and a lot of people have confirmed my calling. They've had independent visions and messages and dreams, and I've been approached by many people confirming that this is the work that I am supposed to do. I have felt The Holy Spirit move in me and work through me. People responded very positively because of my Gift of Deliverance even when I didn't know anything about theology because people recognized that I carried that … *grace* … in my life."

"How do you intend to manage conflict with people who don't believe in you?" the psychologist asked.

"Well, if people don't believe in me that's their choice. But in my experience, most people who might have originally doubted me come not to doubt me."

"And how do you maintain your calling?"

"I maintain my relationship with The Holy Spirit through reading and prayer and through my relationship with mentors from whom I seek advice in everything I do."

"What would stop you from pursuing your calling?"

"The day God chooses to stop using me, that's the day that I will stop."

Two days later the head of faculty called me.

"You really did very, very well, Wisdom."

"Oh! Thank you."

"We're very, very proud of you. We think that you're going to be a great example."

Payment for my first trimester was due in two weeks – about US$900, including books. So, I did what I usually do.

I prayed.

God. You have told me time and time again over the years, that you want me to do this work. If you're calling me to be a minister. If you're really calling me, this five dollars that I have in my hand, is my contribution towards whatever you've got in store for me.

And I put that five dollars down on the table I had in front of me.

A few days later, my mother's cousin got a call from another cousin in Canada.

"I heard that Wisdom is in Monrovia," this cousin said. "I want to talk to him."

He passed the phone over to me.

"Wisdom! It's Mariatu! How are you doing?"

"I'm fine," I said. "It's been a long time."

"Years," she said. "I've been trying to call you for ages. What are you doing there in Monrovia?"

"I've just passed the exam to get into seminary here."

"Congratulations!" she said. "That's great!"

"Not really," I said. "I don't have the money to go. I need about $900 to get started."

"Oh well then," she said. "I'll send you some money."

Oh.

Then, a few days later, my friend David, who, you might recall, had gone to Australia to help with our church's refugee program, called me.

"I've heard you're in Monrovia."

"Word gets around," I said. "Tongues have been wagging."

"What are you doing?"

"I've been accepted into seminary, but I don't have enough money."

"I will send you some money then."

Between my cousin and my friend, I received about $1300. Enough to cover my first trimester fees, for my books and for my living expenses.

Three trimesters a year. Four years. So, payment for one down – eleven to go.

Something will happen.

Another friend was working at a computer school. I approached him and said, "I really want to learn how to operate a computer."

"I don't see why you can't," he said.

"I don't have any money," I said.

"Let me talk to the director of the school," he said. "I'll set up a meeting."

I saw the director. "I don't have any money," I said. "But I can clean. I can be the janitor, and you can take that as your fee."

And he said, "Yes. That can work."

So now I was in seminary and in my spare time I worked and studied in the computer school too.

As they say in Australia, "Too easy."

I knew that The Holy Spirit had made it all possible.

Even though I had the opportunity to go to seminary in Guinea and even though I had refused, the opportunity had come again in Liberia.

Either way, it was going to happen.

And Joseph Wisdom Sesay, lawyer, was never going to happen.

CHAPTER EIGHT

THE LONG ROAD TO LEGITIMACY

"You know, there are political realities to this job."

Joseph

Seminary opened my mind to what I was *really* going to be doing.

A seminary is not a Bible college. If I had gone to a Bible college then the primary focus would have been the Bible and the teachings and doctrines of Christianity – particularly the interpretation of Christianity as espoused by the Assemblies of God Church. The focus of Bible college is on Biblical text and the theology that emerges from that text. I could have gone to Bible college, but I decided on seminary instead because seminaries are more open to a broader outlook. Even by then, my experiences had shown me that Satan and demons do not discriminate on the basis of religion, culture, age, gender or anything else. Being a Christian, even being a good Christian, was no defense against the forces of darkness.

There is no "hero shield" against Spiritual Infestation just because you adhere to a religion, whatever that religion might be.

If there is any entry point, a vulnerability that a demon can exploit, then the demon *will* exploit it. I knew that if I were going to be the best vessel that I could be for The Holy Spirit then I would have to learn to engage with everybody, even atheists, because atheists too are not immune to Demonic Affliction. Just because you don't believe in viruses doesn't mean you can't get sick.

The residing pastor in the church I was attending in Monrovia himself would have preferred that I go to Bible college, but I had to be firm. "I don't want *doctrine*," I said. "I don't want to be *indoctrinated.* I just want to know the truth. I want my mind to be as liberal and as open as possible."

"OK," he said. "But if you go to seminary then after you've finished you will still need to do a few other courses before you can be licensed as an Assemblies of God minister."

"That's not a problem," I said. "But I want to do seminary first."

There are three aspects to belief – dogma, doctrine and opinion.

Dogma is all the fundamental stuff that separates different religions from each other.

For example, Christian dogma affirms the fundamental divinity of Christ. So, *by definition*, if you do not believe in the divinity of Christ, you can't be a Christian.

Doctrine, that which separates different denominations, is more about the *interpretation* of particular details, inspired by scripture. For example, the Assemblies of God have sixteen fundamental doctrines that, collectively define the Assemblies of God as an institution that is separate from say Catholicism or the Anglican Church.

Opinion is what you believe on a personal level, based on personal experience. Sometimes there might be some conflict between opinion, doctrine and dogma. From this struggle, I believe, true faith emerges.

It's not that I had a problem with the doctrines of the Assemblies of God church, I just didn't want to be *limited* by them.

The focus of seminary is to broaden your knowledge of religion and spirituality. It is all about the big picture of *all* the world's systems of belief. Only after your understanding has been broadened, do you examine what the Bible and Christianity teaches about the things you've learned. Seminary is essentially a specialist university for matters of religion and spirituality from a Christian viewpoint.

It was intimidating at first, because here I was, a young man, sharing classes with men who were older than me and for the most part already ordained ministers. Their life experience was much greater than mine. But at the same time, I was more open to everything that I was being taught. The problem with coming at knowledge from a place of already having a vested interest in a particular way of thinking, is that you have a fear that you might learn something that will make you lose your faith, or the source of your authority, or your spiritual credentials.

There is a saying, "It is hard to get someone to abandon their beliefs when their paycheck depends on keeping them."

But where they might have been hesitant, I was just open. I had everything to gain and nothing to lose.

And in particular, I resonated with anything to do with the subject of Demonology. When the lecturer talked about the origin, character and nature of demons, I could relate, because I had experienced so much of the work of demons. I'd been through it, while others in the class, who had been ministers for years, had never had any experience with demons, and didn't have a clue. Demonology was not a *theoretical* subject for me; it was something I had *lived*. The lecturer in Demonology, Professor Felix, who was also an expert in Deliverance, confirmed for me many things that I had worked out or guessed on my own. From him I acquired a framework of understanding to make sense of my practical knowledge. We established a rapport, and he took me under his wing.

We exchanged war stories like the spiritual warriors we were. I remember in particular the story he told me that led him to doing this sort of work.

Professor Felix had a vision where he found himself in Hell. It was the classical lava-pit-fire-and-brimstone Hell where he saw the classical red-skinned, black-horned demons writhing in agony as they were physically chained to melting rocks. He said that in that vision he realized that when we expel demons and bind them they *literally* go back to Hell for that bondage. I assume that Satan is punishing them for having failed in their mission, but this is just an opinion. He also said he was given the opportunity to talk to some of the demons. Some told him that they remembered the very day that they were bound. In some cases their bondage had lasted thousands of years. The vision was so powerful that Professor Felix decided that casting out and binding demons was indeed God's work and a worthy way to spend your life.

"I should add," he said, "that when you expel demons it's a good idea to *specify exactly where you want them to go*, like into the very Pit of Hell itself."

Other subjects that we studied included Biblical Interpretation, Christology, Ethics and Morality, Hebrew and Greek Language, Practical Theology, Religious Education, World Religions, Culture and Society and Worship and Prayer.

Aside from Demonology, the other subject I had a profound feeling for was Pneumatology – the dynamics of the workings of and the study of The Holy Spirit. The word "pneuma" in classical Greek means "breath". It's where we get words like "pneumatic" and "pneumonia" from. But in this case the associations are more like "the breath of The Holy Spirit" and ideas like "inspiration", from the Latin word for "breathing in". It is a poetic way of understanding how The Holy Spirit works in the Earthly Realm.

"And the LORD God formed man *of* the dust of the ground and breathed into his nostrils the breath of life; and man became a living soul." – Genesis 2:7.

Pneumatology spoke deeply to me, because I had intimate communion with The Holy Spirit first, before I came to know the entire Godhead.

A lot of people have a problem with the Trinity. They mistakenly interpret the Trinity as "Three Gods in One." So some people go so far as to think that Christians really do worship three Gods, but this is a profound misunderstanding.

One of the best ways I've ever heard the Trinity explained is like this: just as water exists in three states in the human experience – as ice, water and steam – so does God exist in three aspects with whom people relate. There is "God the Father" – God as parent to the universe. There is "God the Son" – God as the human aspect of divinity, or "the children of God", embodied foremost in the body and life of Jesus Christ. There is "God The Holy Spirit" – the aspect of the ineffable energy and infinite power that emanates from Divine Source and that links and sustains all of creation.

I concede that people have a problem with terms like "Father" and "Son", which they perceive as sexist. If it makes you feel more comfortable think, "Creator" and "Child". Fortunately, "Holy Spirit" is both gender and species neutral.

I should perhaps make the point that given the cultural and psychological state of the human race two thousand years ago, if God had embodied as a woman, then people might have listened even less to the Christian message than they did then, or now. When people exercise their free will, they can choose not to listen to God if God shows up in a form that they cannot relate to. Even today, people filter God through their perceptions, which is why people argue constantly over the nature of the Infinite. Of course, God knows this, and will take whatever form God needs to take to get the message through and God will come through, if *you* allow God.

Contrary to whatever fears my classmates were experiencing about their educations, my constant exposure to new ideas and contrasts and comparisons of the way that The Holy Spirit had shown up to human beings throughout history, and in my own life in particular, only strengthened my faith. I remained more and more in awe about the vastness of the universe and the mysteries of our divine origins and essence.

Contrary to whatever reluctance I had previously had about my calling, I felt that I was now in the place where I belonged. At the age of twenty-three I was the baby of the class, but I was surrounded by people who had dedicated their lives to helping others, and whom I regarded as mentors. If I had lacked human role models, guidance and father figures in my earlier years, in my later years with Pastor Apie, and now in seminary, I now had a surfeit of fathers. Even if we did not always agree, just being around such people was inspirational, in every sense of the word. I was amazed that they could handle their studies, and their ministries, and their family lives all at the same time. It wasn't always an easy balancing act, but that they could do it at all was amazing. These were men in their fifties, and sixties for the most part who were also committed to a process of lifelong education, which was something that was equally admirable.

And The Holy Spirit continued to provide. One of my uncles had contacts at a bank and he became the guarantor for a loan for me to open a computer school. Four thousand dollars later I had acquired a space in a good location, some computers, some office furniture and equipment and a couple of teachers who worked on commission. I started trading. Unlike the "developed" world where even children have computers, if you wanted to learn computers there, you had to go to school. We were a nation of entrepreneurs, all starting and running our own businesses, and if you wanted to design your own business cards, or pamphlets, or even just check your emails you needed access to computers, all of which was part of the service, so we did OK – at least enough that I was able to continue to live frugally and pay my seminary tuition.

Everything was working beautifully, until it didn't.

About eight months in, we were vandalized and robbed, and by the time I paid off the loan with the money I had saved, I had lost everything.

A German company were in Liberia to help in the recovery and reconstruction of the country after almost fourteen years of on-again-off-again civil war as we lurched our way into some semblance of democracy.

Through contacts with my brother I found a new job.

For the first time in my life, I was paid really well for my work.

And because I did my usual best, I got recommended for other work, and continued to work in that same job for the next few years in many different areas, including transport, logistics and even finance.

Fortunately, my work was very flexible – as long as my work was done by the end of the day, they didn't care when I finished. The seminary was very flexible too. I had a very good relationship with my teachers. I was able to choose my units and work around my other work hours, and pay a little extra for Saturday classes, which I could now afford. So, I was back to working sixteen-hour days, but my sense of purpose and the feeling that everything was working out just as it was supposed to, carried me through. Every part of my life was supporting every other part of my life.

I was *blessed*.

I was blessed that I had a firm foundation for what I was doing, because as I continued to become more involved in the life of my community, I was confronted by things that meant that I needed every bit of emotional and spiritual strength I had to spare.

As a relatively young man still, I was a natural choice to work with the church's youth support programs. Now, working with young people and teenagers is challenging even if they have had relatively happy lives of material comfort in socially, economically and politically stable countries.

But it takes on a completely new dimension when you are working with people who have been *literally* through the wars.

I initiated a program called Builders of the Bridge in response to the scores of really broken young people who would come to the church for help.

The war had displaced my family, but we had at managed to stay together for the most part. These young people had not merely been displaced. In many cases they had seen their homes destroyed, their families separated. Some of them, never saw their parents or families again. Robbed of their childhoods and left with nothing, they had become street orphans, surviving any way that they could.

We provided them with their basic needs and some stability, often the only stability that they had had in years, sometimes the only stability that they had *ever* had. We created an environment where they could be safe. Through *our* being able to fund small business initiatives *they* could finally give themselves food in their bellies, a place to sleep and an opportunity to resume educations interrupted by guns and bombs. Some of them were already too old to go to "normal" schools, so we liaised with local schools to create special schools just for them. "Dollar Day" schemes, where those who could afford it, provided the said dollar to fund these programs. My contacts with non-government organizations also helped.

We provided pathways to vocational education. Hands that had once held guns and knives were now holding saws, bricks, pots and pans.

When they had some stability, we would do what we could to restore the humanity that they might also have lost. I believe that The Holy Spirit sent me these young people so that I could practice the art of inner healing on others. It was one thing to expel demons, it was another thing to repair the damage that they had done.

Imagine being twelve years old and losing *everything.*

Imagine your parents being killed in front of you.

Imagine militia kidnapping you and forcing you to learn to fire a gun and then to use that gun to kill people.

Imagine being blindfolded and being told to shoot, and after you have shot having the blindfold removed so that they reveal to you that you have just killed your mother, your father.

Imagine the loneliness you would feel, seeking solace in whatever friendships you can find only to have your friends blown to pieces because they were the ones that stepped on a landmine while you were making your way through the jungle at night.

Imagine being covered in their blood, and in pieces of flesh from those blasts and the sticky warmth that soon attracts the flies.

Imagine killing so often that killing becomes nothing.

Imagine being brutalized, raped and violated so often, in every way that someone can be brutalized, raped and violated that you become nothing, just to survive another day.

I have not even begun to describe to you what some of these young people had been through. Every time I heard yet another horror story I could not help thinking: *I could have been one of them. There, but for the Grace of God, I could have been one of them.*

And in the face of such trauma, there would almost always be Demonic Affliction.

What demon could resist entering the gaping wounds of these

violated children? What demon, once in, could resist inviting even more demons in?

What demons could resist creating even more damage, more trauma, manifesting as drug addictions, and constant thoughts of suicide. What demon could resist using a vessel who would kill again for a few dollars, or for a packet of cigarettes, stick a knife into someone because for so long, killing was all they could ever remember doing.

Many would even have the *desire* to kill again. Wouldn't you, if only to avenge yourself on those who had hurt you so badly, if only to get revenge on a society that had rejected you, abandoned you, left you on the street like so much garbage until one day, someone was there to pick you out of the gutter – *literally out of the gutter*?

We succeeded in helping hundreds of these damaged children. We succeeded in helping so many, I think, because we were able to restore hope. Here finally, were people who did not just look at you as if you were garbage, who did not judge you on appearances, who understood, even if you yourself didn't understand yourself, what you had been through. Here, finally, in us, these broken children found people who wanted nothing from them, nothing but the best for them. We couldn't give them back what they had lost, but we could at least show them that there were people in the world who were not going to hurt them, or exploit them physically, or violate them sexually. And make no mistake, many of them were still children, walking around in bodies that were twenty-five or thirty years old because their lives had been frozen in one long nightmare for a decade and a half and never given an opportunity to heal.

My efforts with youth did not go unnoticed. I was promoted from local leader to zonal leader to district leader in the years I worked there in that program. The whole time I was blessed with a very strong team of support workers who would perform minor miracles every day.

I correct myself.

There is no such thing as a *minor* miracle. Nothing about the work they did was *minor*.

I was a very busy person. We all were. You would think that we would be in a constant state of exhaustion, but strangely enough, we weren't and I think it was because we were not drawing on our own power, but we were merely the vessels through which The Holy Spirit did the work, drawing from a font of *infinite* energy and *infinite* patience. And I, personally, at a human level, always derived enormous satisfaction from seeing someone healed.

The testimonies of the healed – that was the source of *my* strength.

Seventy per cent of Deliverance work is healing work and helping to heal children who had been brutalized in the war through the power of The Holy Spirit was excellent training. If you can repair that sort of damage, you can pretty much repair anything. Healing often meant simply giving a safe space in which to live, and meaningful work that gave people a sense of accomplishment, so that they could feel again, something besides fear. If there is one thing I have learned is that demons revel in fear. Live fearlessly, starve the demons. Starve the demons, and you can feel joy again – and love.

The work that we did also increased church attendance. I didn't ask any of the young people we helped to come to church. It wasn't about, "We'll only help you if you become faithful." Such an attitude would have cheapened our relationship with them to the level of a marketplace transaction. But they came anyway.

Sometimes this would cause problems. Healing is not a straightforward path. Sometimes "items" would be "misplaced". Sometimes mobile phones would be "lost". Sometimes wallets would "go missing".

"Wisdom," my pastor and the elders would say, "we know that you love these people and you want to help them, but we might need to stop them from coming. We can't keep having things go 'missing'. It doesn't look good when fine, upstanding citizens don't feel safe coming to church. It's not a good look for the church."

To which I countered, "I understand the position, but you need to open your Bible and look at what Jesus said. What did Jesus ask us to do? He said, 'I didn't come for those who are healed. I came for those who are sick. I came to bring freedom, transformation and restoration.' Jesus went out into dungeons and into brothels. We need to work together to heal these people to become human again. I know that you want a church to be full of good people and *only* good people, but you can't run a church like that. The whole purpose of a church is to take people in a bad place and give them a good place. We can't be a hospital and refuse to deal with sick people. Our church is just two streets away from one of the principle places where these dispossessed people congregate. Two streets away is their ghetto where you can't even walk after 7:00 o'clock at night. They are our neighbors. What do you think this huge church, with our congregation of three thousand is here for? If a phone gets lost, tell me, and I will pay for it. I've had some of your influential pastors come over and see what we're doing, and I've asked for their help. Some of them have said to me, 'Well, I can help, but how much money will you pay me for my help' and I've had to say, 'I don't have any money to pay you because in doing this you would be doing *your job*'. Make of that what you will."

Repairing broken people, dragging them out of the darkness in all its forms and bringing them into the light is some of the hardest work you can do. Sometimes the people whose benefit you work for don't appreciate what you're doing. Often, they don't even *know* what you're doing.

It often seems hopeless.

"I know what I'm doing!" They argue. "You want me to give up drugs. That's easy for *you* to say. But it's in these drugs that I find some peace."

Yes, and they find freedom from their pain and some peace for a while. But I know they're not *at* peace. I know that their entire family is not at peace, if they're lucky enough to even have a family. And if they are lucky enough to have a family then they won't have a family for very long if they destroy its members through the abuse that *they* inflict on them. It's never about *just* you, it's about everyone that you're connected with, everything that you're connected to. If you're corrupted, you corrupt everything you touch.

And whether we realize it or not, we are not only in a physical battle against chemistry, or violence. It is a spiritual battle too.

But there *is* a way out.

Many years later, I would return to visit my old church in Monrovia to attend a conference on youth work.

Thousands of the young people we had helped, who were now adults leading productive, happy lives showed up and I remember thinking, *this is what redemption looks like.*

But back then, as my second year became my third year and then my fourth year, I just continued to do the work and I continued to pay my dues and I continued to grow in influence.

Through all my time in Monrovia I had talked every now and then to Fatmata in Australia. The seed had been planted several years earlier in Conakry and looking back I think that I had fallen in love with her even then, and gradually, even though we were separated by half a world, our respect and love for each other had grown. Fatmata later admitted to me that she had made up her mind to marry me even before she had left for Australia.

"I cannot come to Australia to marry you," I said. "Not just now.

I will, but not yet. I have to finish my studies first."

"Your degree might not even be recognized in Australia," she said.

"That doesn't matter. I have to complete my studies here."

"You can at least start the process of coming. It will probably take a long time anyway."

"You have a point," I conceded.

If it was to take time, it would take the time it took. Fatmata is a patient woman, and I am a patient man.

Near the end of my studies I achieved the status of Attaché Pastor. That worked for me because I could continue to work with people. Pastors tended to be burdened by administrative duties and I wasn't ready for an office job just yet.

At the end of four years of study, I had qualified with a bachelor's degree in theology. In spite of the concerns of my parents, I had made it.

It took a long time for my stepfather to understand my convictions. I think he felt that the choices I was committing to weren't going to be good for me. He had never understood what it meant to have a calling. No one else he knew had ever had a calling. He had never had a calling himself. It was so far outside of his experience that he simply couldn't process it. I don't think he even understood the *idea* of having a calling.

But not long after I finished my studies, my stepdad called me.

"I was wrong," he said. "Forgive me."

"If you hadn't done what you did, I would not be where I am," I said. "I forgave you before you even asked. My only concern now is that you don't forgive yourself. That's something I can't help you with. You have to find a place in your heart to forgive yourself."

Some people insist on putting me on a pedestal.

But the credit is entirely to The Holy Spirit.

Without The Holy Spirit, I would have died long ago.

I hear this all the time, in many ways from people "I" have helped. "Oh, Wisdom," they say, "I'd be dead if it weren't for you!"

I know that these people are just being nice. They mean well, but the credit really isn't mine.

It really isn't.

This isn't about humility. I am not saying, "Awwwww, shucks."

I really mean it. I cannot do what I seem to be able to do. It is entirely The Holy Spirit working through me.

The piano cannot play itself. The piano cannot take credit for the music.

I truly have no idea what I am doing when I am doing it. People come to me from everywhere without warning. I might get a text message:

Pastor Sesay.

Please help my sister.

She is in serious trouble.

We don't know what to do.

That's often all I get. A call for help. So I answer the call. I answer the text messages and every case is different. I seldom know the full story. The Holy Spirit guides me through the whole process on a case-by-case basis. Every case is different, but I will get intuitions, or the right people come to help at the right time to provide the right assistance. If I am called to conduct Deliverance, I am often in an altered state of consciousness during the Deliverance process itself. It can pass like a dream. I play my part and then it ends, one way or the other.

It is not about me.

Even my graduation ceremony was not about me. Because of administrative and accreditation issues, it took a further year after I had finished my studies for the graduation ceremony to take place. During that year I continued to work for money and to work for The Holy Spirit, answering the needs of others when called to do so, being the vessel for the Divine Light not only through Deliverance and healing, but through good works, like teaching a few classes in computer literacy at the college.

When the day of my graduation for my Diploma in Ministry came, in 2008, none of my parents could make it.

My mother felt guilty about that.

"It's not about the degree," I told my mother later. "It's about the journey I've been through. You don't have to feel bad about not being there. I know you were there in spirit."

And I had my family of friends who were there with me. Wherever I've been, I've always created a family around me. The Holy Spirit has always sent me fathers and mothers and brothers and sisters.

I contacted Attem, my biological father, who was still in Sierra Leone.

"What is going to happen now?" he asked. "Are you going to be a pastor?"

"I don't know," I said. "I only know that The Holy Spirit is going to continue to use me to help people."

"Well, I'm very proud of you," he said. "What you've achieved … I never achieved it. Nobody in my family ever achieved it. So, you're the first."

"Thank-you," I said.

"Wisdom."

"Yes."

"I'm so proud of the fact that you've been able to accomplish so much without my being in your life."

"It's all water under the bridge," I said.

When I look at my children today, I make a daily vow that I will not abandon them, because I know what that feels like. But the past is just the way things were. The past does not have to define us.

To make things even stranger I would not get my degree until October 2010, so I was twenty-seven before I received my actual "piece of paper". But I didn't care. I was used to things never being straightforward with me. I am well aware that winding and indirect are the paths of God.

I was doing well on my winding and indirect path. I continued to do healing and Deliverance work as needed in a number of parishes around Monrovia. I was on a mission to create as much value as I could in people's lives. I got better at listening. I listened and listened to people as they revealed themselves to me so that I could do what I could to help them. And as they told me about their lives, and as they revealed things that were often horrible, I developed and honed the skill of perceiving what was positive in their lives and then giving that perception back to them. They could come to me broken, but before they left, they could at least begin to see the parts of themselves that were still unbroken, I could give them a glimpse of how God saw them.

My Deliverance and Exorcism work continued to expand. My ecumenical approach meant that I liberally worked with pastors from a number of different Christian denominations. My youth work continued. I began ministering to diverse congregations in independent churches and educating them about the process and the experience of Deliverance.

The Assemblies of God hierarchy has a long and diligent procedure for recognizing their ministers already, but because of aftermath of the war and all its other complications, they were also still trying to sort out some administrative issues. As a result, the regional pastor's association granted me a license to practice in August 2010, even though I was not yet ordained. I was prepared to wait because I was in no hurry to go to Bible college to do the necessary subjects to ensure that I would be following the correct doctrines. Ordination was not a top priority. Being an Associate Pastor allowed me the opportunity to do everything that I needed to or wanted to do at the time. Three other churches offered me ordination. I declined them all. My personal ministry, my calling, was to help whomever I could without being limited to a particular church. This has always been my intent. To help anyone who needs it, regardless of where they come from, no matter their affiliations. None of that matters. What matters is to bring people out of the darkness and into the light.

People would come to me with disturbances. I would put them on a program of prayer. If they were afflicted, whatever "symptoms" they had presented with – anything from things going "bump" in the night to feeling overwhelmed with feelings of dread, to drug addictions, violence or worse – these things would sometimes get even worse as the disrupted contaminating demons reacted to the increased spiritual activity caused by the prayer work.

The Gift of Discernment also helps me in the diagnostic procedure. I pray for the afflicted and I get "readings" – direct inner messages from The Holy Spirit about the specific person involved and their challenges. I do this description of readings an injustice by implying that they are just thoughts. There is an unmistakable, palpable quality of *power* behind the readings sent by The Holy Spirit, there is a *presence*. Every now and then I still feel the heat in my hands, but by now I can really feel The Holy Spirit – everywhere.

I never charge for the gifts of The Holy Spirit, because these gifts are priceless. I believe that you should be wary of churches that overtly charge for their pastoral work. There are many ways that The Holy Spirit supports its Workers of Light. The Holy Spirit will always determine what your reward is going to be.

I know that there is always a provision. I know that there is always going to be enough. I know that it will always be like that.

Australia, and Fatmata, continued to loom in the background. At the end of 2010 I prayed about it.

Holy Spirit. I am doing well here. I don't want to go to Australia just because I want to go to Australia.

I want to know that it is Your Will.

And as I prayed, I received another vision, another of those waking dreams that come to me in quiet moments, without warning, unbidden.

I am standing on a big bridge. I know I am in Australia. In my hand I have a scroll. I am praying. Countless people of all types are rushing towards me. There is a dust storm. The people are covered in dust. The scroll, in my hand is turning of its own accord. I know that as the scroll unfurls the names of the people rushing to me are revealed, and as their names are revealed, as the people approach me, the dust falls off them.

When the vision ended, I knew it would be my fate to come to Australia. And the memory of my earlier vision before the Throne of The Holy Spirit came to me.

Fatmata, meanwhile, was putting wheels in motion with the Australian Department of Immigration. I felt a sense that Australia was inevitable.

When I would speak to the immigration lawyer on the phone he'd say, "Wisdom, there are no guarantees. You're too confident about this."

"I know I'm going to come. Don't worry. Just do your job."

A few months after my vision, my mother called me.

"You know, you are not just going to Australia to marry this girl," she said. "You are going there to work."

"Yes, I know."

"The Lord showed me a vision. I saw you standing before thousands of people, healing, healing, healing. There are a lot of broken souls. You are going there to set souls free."

And then on 14 April 2011 my spousal visa finally came through. I could now come to Australia to marry Fatmata. Everything was in place. I just had to tie up a few loose ends, including an important conference I had to attend in July.

"Really? You're delaying because of a *conference*," Fatmata said. "I'm not happy!"

"Don't worry," I assured her, "I'm coming. Relax. It will all be OK."

The head pastor of the Assemblies of God in Monrovia was the Senior Pastor. When I told him I was emigrating he said, "Don't tell anyone else you're going."

"Why?"

"The young people you work with are very attached to you. I don't know what their reaction will be."

So, in the end, practically no one knew I was going.

Then, two weeks before I was due to go, I discovered that Liberia had changed over to using bar-code scanned passports. The passport I had was old and no longer strictly valid and I would have to wait a month for my new passport. I explained the situation to Fatmata.

"That's OK," she said. "Just take the time you need."

"Don't worry. I'm not delaying. I'll arrive in Australia with the passport that I have."

"Oh really? How is that going to work?"

"I don't know. I just know."

It was September 2011 before I finally took my flight. They stopped me in Dubai.

"You can't enter Australia with this passport," the authorities said as people were boarding the flight.

"Is there any place around here, a quiet place to wait?."

"Go over there," said the officer, pointing to an alcove. I sat down and prayed.

OK. Holy Spirit. I'm here, but I can't seem to get past this point.

Then I felt the Presence, that feeling of power, that feeling of an infinite intelligence gently touching my life, closing doors, opening others, the voice that speaks without words.

I WILL TAKE YOU TO AUSTRALIA.

The authorities meanwhile called Australia. The officer had just hung up when I had finished praying.

"OK," he said "Immigration says you're OK to go. Now we have to run."

He rushed me through security I was the last to get on the plane.

"Safe journey," the man said, waving me goodbye.

I arrived on the morning of 13 September 2011 at Melbourne's Tullamarine airport.

It was the first time I had ever been out of Africa. It was my first experience of the West.

It was an exciting thing, and yet, I wasn't as excited as I thought I would be.

Why was that?

I think it was because my focus was already on the future.

There were too many things that were *about to happen.*

Too many unknowns.

How was this all going to work?

"Now it's you who's not happy," Fatmata said, picking up on this.

"No, I'm happy," I said. "I'm thinking about how I'm going to overcome my limitations. There are all these technical problems."

"Technical problems?"

"I don't know how things are done here," I said. "There are systems here and I don't know how they work. This is a country of hundreds of nationalities. How are they going to react to me? How am I going to navigate the process? Am I going to be able to do the *right* thing? How is this whole thing going to work?"

"You'll work it out," she said.

My visa allowed me to work, legitimately, full time. I had a connection in Perth and there was a church over there ready to welcome me with open arms. I figured that Fatmata and I would get married and then we'd go there. But I didn't know how long that was going to take and I still needed a job.

On my second day here a friend who worked in a factory took me into his work where they made ducts for heating and cooling buildings. They gave me job then and there.

Within a couple of weeks, I approached the Assemblies of God Church in Clayton, a south-eastern suburb of Melbourne with my qualifications, and they recognized me as a minister.

A week before I was due to go to Perth to check out the situation there, I entered into a series of deep prayers – just to make sure I was on the right track.

Then, my mother-in-law came to me.

"You know, I cannot stop you going to Perth," my mother-in-law said. "You know that you can do whatever you want to do and I'm not saying this because we want you to be here close to us. But …"

"But?"

"The Lord wants you to be here in Victoria, in Melbourne."

"What makes you say that?"

"The Lord has shown me a vision."

Okay.

"I had a vision of you on the Westgate Bridge, the bridge on the way to Geelong. I think you're meant to be here, in Melbourne, working in Melbourne," she said. "If the Lord wants you to go anywhere later, that's fine. But right now, you're needed here."

The Lord had spoken – to me, to my mother and to my mother-in-law. The Holy Spirit had once again chosen to speak through many minds, through many intuitions, through many visions from many people, just so that I would get the message loud and clear.

So, I didn't go to Perth. I talked to my friend.

"Look, this isn't final, but I need to seek God in everything I do, and I don't know where God is going to lead me. But right now, I'm not being led to Perth."

"I understand," he said.

Of course, he understood. He understood the mysterious ways in which God works.

Then I reached out to the national assembly of the church. They confirmed my status and after a test and an interview that was very much like the test and the interview that I had to do to get into the seminary they put me on probational license for two years, so I had yet another piece of paper to legitimize me.

Fatmata and I were married in November at home. We only wanted something small and private.

The legitimization process continued apace. Within a matter of a couple of months I had emigrated, gotten a new job, been recognized as a Minister in the Assemblies of God Church and I had gotten married.

I became very involved in the Church in Clayton.

It was all very intense. I had hit the ground running and Fatmata and I barely had a honeymoon, but my wife always knew what she was getting involved in. From the very first she had always known that she would have to share me with God. *That was part of the deal.*

I'm given to God's work. This was and is my calling – to bring freedom, transformation and restoration.

God sits right at the top of everything. Anything that God wants, God gets.

It cannot be any other way.

I must always be in a constant battle in the realm of the spirit.

I am someone who must go into an enemy camp and pull people out of bondage, out of darkness.

I became involved in nearly all aspects of the activities in the Clayton church. It was not a large congregation at that time – no more than a couple of hundred – but it was enough to get me started and I had a hand in almost everything.

Some of my reputation in my spiritual specialty had preceded me, but that was not all. As I became more and more involved in the church in Clayton people started noticing the strange "something" that surrounded me like a cloud all the time.

People began contacting me privately for healing and Deliverance, or even sometimes just for a few words of kindness. Tongues started wagging. I met dozens, then scores, then hundreds of people. Without even trying I was building a network and a spiritual family all over again. Gradually, simply through outreach, and later through a cross-cultural program, I learned how things worked here, thanks to the work that the Church in Clayton allowed me to do. Compared to where I came from, everything is well-systemized and programmed. On the other hand, some things are slower and harder to do, precisely because things are so well systemized and programmed. It's not perfect, but Australians must be doing a whole bunch of things right, because we have peace, the streets are clean, the lights are on, few people starve, are kidnapped or are shot in the street. No government in Australia has ever fallen because of armed insurrection or revolution. There is a fundamental stability here that is the envy of the world.

But.

This systematic approach doesn't always work quite so well with matters of the spirit, because you cannot put spirit in a box. Also, back in Africa, the existence of God, the Devil, demons and Demonic Affliction is unquestioned. *They are facts of life.* In the secular West, you are always fighting a little bit to convince people, especially people in authority, that these realities even exist. Secular materialism and the scientific approach have brought enormous benefits to the world, but these positions have a tunnel vision that ignores the non-material, less measurable parts of the totality of existence.

How do you measure evil?

How do you measure love?

You can detect abnormalities in brain function and brain chemistry with expensive machines, but there is no machine yet invented that can detect Spiritual Affliction with the same consistent level of accuracy that an X-ray can detect a broken bone.

No machine has ever imaged the soul.

My reality exists in a worldview, a paradigm that many here simply do not share.

But we who work in this field do what we can.

I'm not here to prove anything to you. The Holy Spirit simply offers a process through me that can help you. If you need help, I'm here to help.

And as it would turn out, one person in particular needed an unprecedented amount of help.

CHAPTER NINE

SUBMITTING TO A LOWER AUTHORITY

"Satan and the demons, or entities, or whatever you want to call them, were gaslighting me."

Paul

Looking back, I believe that demons had planted the vision of abuse with the *express* purpose of giving me feelings of betrayal, grief, vulnerability violation and self-loathing so intolerable that I would kill myself just to be rid of them.

I wanted relief.

I just wanted relief.

But that was still some way in the future. And, as I would later find out, I would not get relief until I accepted what was really going on. I had to recognize that this ongoing mess that my life had become was because I was dealing with a spiritual issue, that what I was dealing with was not "all in my mind", that it was *real*. I had to accept that to have any hope of having any relief, *ever*, I would have to undergo some process that would result in some form of eventual Spiritual Liberation.

But at this point, I wasn't there, yet, because I was still in denial.

This might not be the best analogy, but I'll use it anyway.

Recognizing that what I was going through an ongoing spiritual crisis was a like admitting that you're a drug addict. Although I was, at various stages of this ongoing Hell, drug dependent, I was never drug addicted.

But for those who have it, drug addiction is itself a form of affliction. You have it, you have some responsibility for having it. You have only limited control over it. It's screwing up your life. It makes you make really bad choices that escalate into worse choices. It's isolating. It's definitely not socially acceptable. People will shame you for it, or run away, unless of course they're either used to it or being around it or are equally screwed up with their own addictions. It makes you hate yourself, even if you don't admit that to yourself because you're in so much denial. There's so much shame attached to it why wouldn't you go into denial, but the very fact that you're in denial makes it impossible to fix it.

You can be a high-functioning addict in other areas of your life – as long as you're bringing home the bacon, especially if you're bringing home *a lot* of bacon. And because you're pushing people away constantly, you end up with a perfect storm of other people not wanting to rock the boat too much. No one wants to kill the goose that's laying the golden eggs even if the goose is a total drug fuck. And, as my professional life showed, I was a very high functioning, deeply spiritually disturbed person.

It's only when you accept that you are a drug addict, and embrace that reality, however unflattering that reality is, that you can find some possibility of relief from the all the darkness and the torment and self-loathing and into the light of self-understanding, self-compassion and self-love, so that you can have even a fighting chance of getting some fulfillment of your potential as person, as a friend, as a colleague, as a partner, as a parent.

But this is where there's yet another obstacle to overcome.

Being profoundly spiritually afflicted is in many ways worse than being a drug addict. At least the culture I was living in recognized that drug addiction was real, it was *a thing*. But spiritual affliction isn't *a thing* where I came from. Practically everyone around me just thought I was crazy.

It's hard to get out of denial when everyone else around you is in denial too.

Effectively, there comes a point where if you're in that position you have to find the strength to say, to yourself and everybody else, "You know what? I am under constant attack by demons that are eating me alive and I have to do something about this."

In the last fifty years our society has made great strides in understanding addiction. Sure, lots of churches still regard it as a "sin" and some sort of aberration, and lots of people still have an aversion to it and think it's disgusting and dangerous – with some justification. It elicits little sympathy. It's hard to feel compassion for drug addicts when they've trashed your house and robbed you so that they can get their next fix.

But at least now there are clinics where you can get sympathetic treatment for drug addiction.

But when it comes to demonic possession, or whatever-the-hell this is, we might as well still be in the dark ages. For years, in fact for *decades*, I received virtually no help and no support. I barely even received acknowledgment that what I was experiencing was even remotely real. The closet door was effectively locked. Could you imagine what would have happened to me, my business and my livelihood if it were known that I thought I was possessed? Could you imagine how my employees would have reacted? Would my clients have had any faith in any decision that I had made, or trust in my word?

Would you have taken legal advice from this man?

Would you have asked a possessed person to represent you?

I don't think so.

So I was effectively in the "possessed closet" and would continue to be there. Despite having made at least one small step out of denial that was enough to make me make at least one sincere attempt to get professional spiritual help, I was still largely, generally in denial about what was going on. I was still thinking that my problem was mostly some sort of mental illness, so I was still in the closet even to *myself.* My partner, who was living with me and who had the best outsider's perspective about what was going on, was largely in denial too, and couldn't deal with something that was still largely outside of *her* experience. My mother was in denial, and my brother and sister were no help, mostly because I wasn't sharing what was going on, because on the rare occasions when I had, they'd brushed me off. I had "friends" in the past, but for the most part they were drug friends, who were only there to get high with me, so they weren't really friends either.

Of course, all this isolation is exactly what demonic entities want to do to you.

They *want* to cut you off from all of your support and make it look like you're mad so you feel alone and helpless and that cuts you off even further so you look even more crazy and … their plan was working.

They are very good at their job.

Have you ever heard of the term "gaslighting"?

It comes from an old play, *Gas Light*, written in 1938, which was then made into a movie, once in 1940 and much more famously in *Gaslight* in 1944. In *Gaslight*, a psychopath marries a rich heiress with the express purpose of sending her insane by a subtle and ever-escalating process of changing her reality, and then when she notices it, he denies it. He moves objects in the house and when she says, "Where's the painting that's on that wall?" he says, "You mean that painting on this wall here? Why, that painting's *always* been there!" Then he moves the painting back to the original wall and when she notices he says, "Why! That painting's *always* been there!"

Imagine somebody constantly and persistently changing the goalposts on what you think is real, so that you question everything, until nothing makes sense. Watch the movie and you'll really know what I mean. The gaslighting technique is a monstrously effective form of mental and emotional abuse.

Satan and the demons, or entities, or whatever you want to call them, were gaslighting me.

Why wouldn't they? It's a tried and true method of sending someone mad and if demons like anything, they like to send people mad.

But society was gaslighting me too. Practically no one was acknowledging that what I was going through was real, and even when they did, they'd abandon me, through fear, ignorance or incompetence, or all three.

I even abandoned myself. I had been given a gift, an ability to be sensitive to the realm of the spirit, a gift that's given to everyone. Yes, everyone has the capacity to access other realms of reality besides the mundane and material one that we live in day-to-day. Many people don't because they're in their own form of denial. But this sensitivity, for whatever reason, was for me a lot closer to the surface than for most. From my earliest memories I recall being fascinated by spooky stuff like spirits and mediumship, psychic abilities and other paranormal phenomena. I clearly remember wanting to be a ghost hunter. But this gift was a double-edged sword. It made me more susceptible to spiritual infection. I couldn't come to terms with the reality that access to this realm was an essential core part of me, and because of that, I had inadvertently left myself open to being spiritually exploited and abused. I was, at this point, a long way from owning my spirituality enough to fight off this infection, this disease.

In some sense, I was being called to do battle with the forces of light and darkness, and I was refusing the call. Can you blame me? As I said right at the beginning when I started telling you all this, there's nothing easy about it. It's fucking complicated, you know. There's this whole other world there that people generally can't perceive. It's like having a radio in your head and you can tune into stations and people who haven't even heard of radio keep saying, "I don't hear anything. Are you sure that you're all right?" And you're not all right because while some stations play heavenly choirs some play death metal 24/7 at full volume and you don't know how to tune the radio, so you're stuck with it. I was on the point of being driven mad by my own sensitivity and clumsiness. And "they", whoever they are, want you to go mad and to commit suicide. Because they know that death is no release from the torment. They know that if you die, you take yourself, and all your torture, and your Hell, with you. But you don't know that at the time. At the time when they've taken up residence, all you know is that you're getting weaker and weaker and that you're in more and more pain and self-ending seems like a bloody good option.

The demons were winning.

I was trapped. And my first child was on the way now.

The stakes were going to be getting higher.

The New Year of 2015 began with my continuing efforts at Self-Deliverance/Self-Exorcism. My internet searches for "find your friendly neighborhood exorcist" were going nowhere.

Then a thought came to mind. A former employee of mine, whom I was still referring clients to, and with whom I was still on very good terms, was a religious man. He was an honest, hard-working man of good character with strong Christian values, and I trusted him. It wasn't too foreign an idea to reach out to a fellow person who "spoke Catholic", even though I wasn't a practicing Catholic, or a practicing anything for that matter.

I thought, "I don't have anything to lose here", so we arranged a meeting.

As I prepared myself for our conversation thoughts went through my head like, "Is this for real? Am *I* for real? Can I actually talk to somebody else about this?" Part of me didn't want to go through with it. But I didn't have a choice and at least I felt that I could feel safe with him.

So, we got together, and I told him about my problem.

"I believe you," he said. "What you're experiencing in real and true. I've had my own experiences with demons. I've fought my own battles.

Hearing him say this and seeing the expression on his face while he said this to me and the tone in his voice as he was saying it, made me think that perhaps it would be a good idea if *he* saw a psychiatrist. But that was really a passing thought. What was more important is that I got a taste of what it might be like for someone else to hear this sort of stuff, and, looking at it from the outside, I wasn't surprised that people thought I was crazy. Who was *I* to judge *him*, when I had a similar story? I just think it's interesting that in spite of everything that had happened to me, even *I* had a little trouble believing him.

But more importantly, he validated me and that was incredibly comforting.

He put me in touch with a pastor working in Melbourne. And even though this was an Assemblies of God church, my friend attended because it was a ministry that offered Deliverance services.

"They do Deliverance every week," he said. "It's a regular service."

Really? This is so common that it happens once a week?

"They also have a session which they just call 'prayer'," he said. "And that's like a collective prayer experience where you go up on stage, you share what's going on with you. The Pastor invokes The Holy Spirit, and the congregation as a whole pray for you and for the resolution of your problems. So, through the power of prayer, the intentions of the congregation, and the power of The Holy Spirit, the collective prayer transforms the experience itself into a Deliverance. Makes sense?"

"Yeah."

I left that meeting with a lot of hope and so grateful that I had followed up on my intuition to talk to my friend. Now, maybe, we could get somewhere!

I attended at the first opportunity.

This is a small church. Well, that's not what I was expecting.

And it's a converted factory. That really wasn't what I was expecting.

But it was a good conversion job, nonetheless. Good lighting. Good audio. An excellent set up all round.

In a sea of Sri Lankan, Indian, African and Islander faces, with the odd Caucasian, here and there, I felt like a minority. Not that that was a bad thing, but it wasn't a scenario I was used to.

The Pastor had a passionate, evangelical zeal thing going on – a forceful personality who gives you the impression that he's involved in a holy war. To me he came across like a stern but loving parent, which is just the sort of thing that some people need.

I didn't immediately avail myself of the prayer intercession. My desperation at that point wasn't acute enough for me to overcome my shyness. I did see the Pastor after the service and told him my story and "symptoms".

"I agree," he said. You need Deliverance," he said. "Come back to me next week and we'll do a Deliverance."

"OK," I said.

I agreed to a Deliverance, but I wasn't looking forward to it. I'm an intensely private person and the possession was intensely private. I was a little turned off by the idea of having to get in front of a bunch of strangers and bare my soul, literally. To me it felt like undergoing an operation in front of an audience while still conscious – not my thing at all. It was too much like an American-style, charismatic … how do I put this nicely?

Circus?

I felt that there was an element here of "we need to do this publicly to convince the people."

I didn't feel comfortable with that, but, again, I didn't really have a choice. Anyhow, he said a few prayers for me and sent me on my way. The next week, there I was again, in church.

Well over a year prior, and before I had even met Kristy, the memory of snorting cocaine off prostitutes' breasts and having what was for me, at that stage, a merry-old-time, was still fresh enough that there was a major disconnect between those sorts of experiences and now being in a Bible-bashing church, on my knees, on stage, while a pastor was laying hands on me and invoking The Holy Spirit while a big room full of people prayed for Divine Intervention for me.

Fuck! I just don't feel right. I just don't feel comfortable with all this – at all.

He began speaking in tongues. For those who don't know about this, when a person starts speaking in tongues, they spontaneously start saying sounds that sound like real words in a real language. For all I know, sometimes they are real words and might be from a real language from the present, or even from the past, but from what

I can tell, they just sound like words that aren't exactly gibberish, but that don't correspond to anything anyone else other than God, or the spirits, would understand. Whatever these sounds are, the speaker is usually making sounds close to the sounds they make in their native tongue, and will then revert randomly to English, or whatever language they normally use in a service.

I wasn't feeling anything but confusion, cynicism and sore knees at the moment. I had put on weight and I wasn't exactly in peak athletic condition.

This is soooo fake. This guy's full of shit. This whole thing is a con. I'm an idiot for coming here. How much longer am I going to have to listen to this crap before I can go home?

"Ask Jesus for forgiveness!!!"

"Forgive me, Jesus!"

And, just like happened the first time, I started to dry retch. I was dry retching uncontrollably. My cynicism and impatience had quickly turned to terror. I was so scared in that moment that any minute now the dry retching with turn into *wet* retching and the stage will be covered in my technicolor yawns.

I collapsed onto the stage. I started rolling around like someone having some sort of mild seizure.

I was moaning and drooling, coughing, dry retching, still rolling on the ground, back and forth, back and forth. A part of me was thinking – *I could stop this. I could just stop this.*

But the greater part of me just submitted to the impulses that had taken over my body. Like scratching an itch and having a need to continue to scratch it until its gone, it was easier to just go with it than to stop.

I surrendered to the process.

I experienced some pain, some physical discomfort, but it was nothing compared to the nausea.

The nausea was unbelievable.

"Lord! Let the white light of heaven come down upon your servant!"

And in my mind's eye there was light. With my eyes closed I really did see this white light.

The Pastor is totally animated, I hear sounds coming out of his mouth and occasional gasps from the congregation. But I'm barely aware of this – after all I am in some sort of trance and in that moment. Everything is about me.

"I cast you out in the name of Jesus!"

And then, as suddenly as it had started … It stopped.

No more white light. No more dry retching. No more rolling around like an idiot.

Oh! … That's it! … I'm cured! … Oh!

He helped me up and I sat down on a chair on the stage. He wrapped up the service and afterwards he said to me, "I need you to come back next week."

"Are we done?" I asked.

"I *think* we're done."

So, I did come back. And I we did the same thing again. And the same things happened in the same order, and then at some point in the process, I don't know when because I'm definitely not in a normal state of consciousness, everything stopped, and I was back to what passes for normal.

And, again, the Pastor asked me to come back. And since I was feeling a bit better, I agreed. At least now, I thought, we were getting somewhere.

So, I came back and went through the same experience.

Again.

And again.

And by about week five I'd already been thinking, *well something's happening, obviously, but whatever it is, this isn't working.*

And to make matters worse, at each session, I was getting this escalating feeling of fear. An interior thought, as these thoughts would come to me, was telling me:

Leave! Leave now! You're in great danger!

These thoughts were telling me to run. That this wasn't real. They were trying to get me away from what I was doing. One time, after a Deliverance I felt this overwhelming need to go out drinking and gambling and I did. The demons were saying, "Yeah! We've still got you! You think that THAT worked? Ha, ha!"

I persisted. I'd started off simply as one member of a group of people who were all going through the same process, but over the weeks, as other people got cured, or at least seemed to, I still wasn't getting any better and the process concentrated more and more on me. No one seemed to be in as much trouble as me. No one was dry retching like me. I was really spiritually sick in comparison to the other people who were going there.

One night was different. I stopped dry retching. I felt as if I had had some sort of breakthrough. At this one point, I had definitely felt that some energy had dissipated or gone away and that some interior fog had lifted. And I got it into my head that my measure of success, my "sign" that I had beaten this, was that I would stop dry retching and since I had, I thought, *finally!*

I got excited about my feelings of relief. Imagine this. I had been carrying around something that had been weighing me down for years and it was finally gone and I was *elated.*

I was so elated that I went on a booze and cocaine binge, effectively undoing any good that I had done. Bit silly, I guess, in hindsight! Bit of an idiot!

Looking back, I don't know if I was genuinely delivered at that moment and I had stupidly undone the whole thing with drugs and alcohol, or if the spirits had played a trick on me, lulling me into a false sense of security.

So, I went back.

Again.

And again.

And at some point, the Pastor felt that it was over.

But what he didn't know is that I was still spending the weekends in an alcoholic stupor and come every Monday I'd be back in a state of fear and paranoia.

So, I went back.

Again, and again and again and …

In all I went back fifteen times over fifteen consecutive weeks.

And still it went on.

Clearly, this wasn't working.

So I asked my friend if maybe there was another church or person I could try.

And my friend said, "Well, there is someone …"

And that "someone" was Joseph Wisdom Sesay.

CHAPTER TEN

WORLDS COLLIDE

"Please, please, please, does someone, anyone, know what they're doing?"

Joseph

During these first years in Melbourne I continued to work to support my family.

Our son was born in 2014.

I spent three years at the duct factory, then, briefly, I did nightshifts in a factory that used injection molding to make seats for public transport – buses and trains. Then I moved on to a company doing air-quality testing in industrial settings and operation theaters. I was not in a position to become financially independent until I began the processes to establish a new ministry in the middle of 2016.

The subject of money is always a tricky one when it comes to churches. You should never charge for pastoral services but at the same time pastoral services require money to function. A pastor, no matter how frugal, still needs to put food on the table and a roof over their head. Volunteers freely give their time, but they need some support, some resources to do their work. People need to congregate in buildings and rent, or mortgages, need to be paid. And when people can't congregate, internet services must be built and maintained and paid for.

Like it or not, churches are businesses. We are in the business of saving lives and souls, but businesses have operating costs, no matter how small. I grew up in Africa, where we can run churches on the smell of an oily rag, but the rag still requires *some* oil. The "oil" usually comes in the form of donations and fund-raising activities.

Although I was able to keep things together for a while, there came that inevitable point when The Holy Spirit began to nudge me in the direction of establishing this new ministry.

It was a subtle, but incessant pressure. A persistent feeling that would not leave me, that wouldn't let me go. That's one way that The Holy Spirit "speaks" to me, like an interior wind, blowing me in a particular direction.

Paul

My first experiences of Joseph came from those moments when he would co-participate with another Pastor in the process of the Deliverance sessions.

And yet, even though at first, he was just another face, I very quickly knew, in the way that I know things, that there was something special about him. I felt drawn to him because some part of me recognized his, *power.* Whenever he was helping out, the treatment, if that's what Deliverance was, just felt that little bit more powerful, more effective.

In spite of this, I still wasn't making any progress, at least as far as I could tell.

Joseph must have sensed something too, because at one point he approached me.

"Ah … look … ah … Paul. I don't want to talk out of turn … but

I don't think that this is working," he said.

"Oh! *You reckon*???" I said with a sarcasm not directed at him per se but more in frustration about the whole process and how the whole process wasn't getting me anything but an ever-growing despair, impatience and gastric reflux.

"Listen", Joseph said. "I need to tell you that I'm in the process of leaving the congregation and starting a new ministry, principally focused on Deliverance because that's my calling."

"I see," I said.

"I can help you," Joseph said.

I was in two minds about this. On the one hand I was grateful that everyone before had been making these heroic efforts to cure me of my spiritual disease. On the other hand, I had the sneaking suspicion that the way things were going at the moment I was inadvertently making things worse, in much the same way that Father May had perhaps made things worse. All these pious men and women were doing their best, but this patient wasn't getting any better.

In medicine there's this idea called "iatrogenic illness", which is just a technical way of saying that sometimes doctors, even with the best intentions, are, through their treatments and interventions, just making a particular patient worse." They might be great doctors. They might have great batting averages, but sometimes some patients don't respond to the particular treatments offered by particular doctors, but the doctors still try on the same stuff that works for everybody else, and inadvertently make that non-responsive patient worse.

No one, after all, is infallible.

And some of these ways of doing Deliverance weren't working for me. Every time I'd ask, "How long is this going to take? When is this going to stop?" a pastor would just look at me and say: "I don't know, but you'd just better walk a tight line with God."

Well, that's not very useful, is it?

So now I'd been to two specialists and I was getting the feeling that this whole thing had been very, very poorly handled. Yes, I had been through the Deliverance process, by now many times. Yes, I'd been dry retching and rolling around on the floor and that is what they show you in the movies and so, yes, by now, or rather, for the time being during my constant vacillation between what was real and what wasn't, *at least for now*, I was not in denial that, yes, I was demonically possessed.

I wasn't in denial – at least to some degree.

So, was I in more danger than I can imagine right now? Was something going to happen to me?

A demonic voice, had, after all, spoken through me not so long ago. So naturally, my patience was wearing a bit thin.

Hello! Hello! Hello! I've got spiritual cancer and you're telling me to 'walk a tight line with, God'?

Are you fucking kidding me?

Puhhhlease!

Now this other, new specialist spiritual doctor had come along, and with the same level of sincere desire to help, he was offering me even more help.

I needed help.

I wanted help.

I had to have help.

But at that stage I was feeling a constant, low-level despair. I felt that perhaps my case was incurable, and that this would go on forever.

Yet, for whatever reason, I wasn't ready to give up, and, at least for me, Joseph Wisdom Sesay seemed to be the closest available viable life ring to keep me from drowning.

"OK, Joseph. Can you please help me?"

"I can and I will."

And, fortunately for me, within a couple of weeks he established his new ministry. I followed the doctor to his new practice.

Joseph

People were kind and gave me money that I could channel into the work, but it was not enough to sign a lease on a building, or modify it for church purposes, which is something that would have to be done if I went out on my own.

I prayed to The Holy Spirit about it.

If you want me to leave, you're going to have to provide me with the means of supporting that.

Of course, The Holy Spirit *knows* that, but prayer is often more for the sake of clarifying things for the one doing the praying, than to "tell" The Holy Spirit what to do.

I spoke to my wife about it.

"I need to stop working in these jobs for money. I need to channel my energy into my mission and my pastoral work. I cannot continue to be split down the middle and be effective."

"I understand," she said.

"I need to go out on a limb. I must make an act of faith knowing that The Holy Spirit will provide."

"As we have always done."

"As we have always done," I agreed.

I went back before The Holy Spirit.

Is this what you want me to do, start a new chapter of this congregation?

Then came the strong, interior message, the voice that speaks with no words, but that I have to put into words anyway.

NO. I DID NOT CALL YOU TO DO THAT. I HAVE GIVEN YOU A MANDATE AND ONLY YOU *CAN SECURE THAT MANDATE.*

The message was loud and clear.

Still, I was hesitant.

Then people from prayer groups, who knew nothing about what was going on with me, started calling me at random. After all, they had their *own* lines of communication to Infinite Intelligence, through their own spiritual gifts, through their own intuitions as a result of their own spiritual connections with The Holy Spirit, through their own conversations without words.

A typical exchange, one of many, would go like this:

"The Lord says you have to go from where you are," someone would say.

"How do you know?" I said.

"Because we were praying, and the message came through loud and clear."

And *still*, I hesitated.

Then my mother called me from Africa.

"I am not calling you as your mother, but as a messenger of the Lord."

Oh, here we go again.

"The Lord is giving you one last chance. If you don't leave and start your mission, you are on your own."

Well then, this is the time.

So, I went to the Pastor I was working with at the time and said, "I've had a great time. It's been a wonderful time. But I have to leave."

"Why are you going?"

"The Lord is asking me to leave. The Holy Spirit has given me instruction. He wants me to leave."

"Do you think you're going to make it on your own?" he asked.

"Well," I said, "if I don't make it, it won't be because of lack of trying on my part. The Holy Spirit has said I should leave. The only thing I need from you is ten minutes on the stage to thank everyone and acknowledge all their fine work."

"OK," he said. "You can have your ten minutes."

So, the very next Sunday, I said "good-bye" to the congregation.

As one door closed, another opened.

That was the beginning of the Cross Purpose Church.

My wife was doing part-time work, but it wouldn't be enough to make ends meet. We didn't know what we were going to do, but I had to focus my attention on my mission. We were only twenty-seven people who wanted to establish the church.

Of course, The Holy Spirit came through. Even before you take the step, The Holy Spirit already has things in place.

Tongues wagged again.

As soon as I quit my job, to work full time on the church, there were offers of help. Donations suddenly increased to a new level.

I went back to the church hierarchy and told them of my intention to start a new ministry. Another set of interviews later, they approved of the plan and gave me a provisional license to operate a church under the auspices and with the approval of the Assemblies of God, subject to revision and review in two years.

Over two months the seven of us met in a community hall in Dandenong to discuss the vision of Cross Purpose.

Someone who understood about such things approached me and said, "As soon as you secure a property for the location of the church, you're going to have to modify it for church purposes. Let me know when you find something, and I'll give you everything you need."

Then I had another conversation with Fatmata.

"Listen," I said. Everything that we have saved, we need to put into what God has called us to do because we need to lease a location."

"OK," she said. She really is a very understanding woman. Amazing really.

The Holy Spirit continued to bring people on board who could see the vision and contribute both their time and money to making it happen.

Then, in early November 2016, one of the team came to me and said, "I've seen the building where you'll be able to start."

It was a dilapidated ex-factory in the outer Melbourne suburb of Hallam near where my family was now living. Seen with mortal eyes you would not have been impressed. But the moment I saw it The Holy Spirit "spoke" to me.

THIS IS THE PLACE.

THIS IS THE PLACE WHERE I WILL BRING FREEDOM, RESTORATION AND TRANSFORMATION TO MANY SOULS.

There would always be enough for everything we had to do as a ministry. The Holy Spirit continued to provide, and I continued to refine my Deliverance process, that could be modified as circumstances dictated, always under the guidance of The Holy Spirit.

Paul

So now we get to Paul's Deliverance Stage III.

Poor old Paul is scared shitless. He doesn't know what's going on. The other pastors had given him gobbledygook and a Bible to read.

It would have taken me ten years to read and understand the Bible and by then I could have been dead and in hell for all I knew. I didn't want indoctrination all I wanted was to be delivered of this sickness, this *curse*, and get back to a normal life.

I'm well over my neck here.

Please, please, please does someone, ***anyone****, know what they're doing?*

At least I could take some comfort in knowing that there had been no more weird paranormal experiences. But it was a pretty chilly comfort. My life, in almost every other way, was totally dysfunctional. I had stopped using drugs, mostly, by about Deliverance 15, but there was still …

Drinking. Walking dead. Drinking. Gambling. Walking dead.

I should clarify that I never felt that the gambling was anything more than a hobby. It never really got out of control, although it might have destroyed me if this whole thing had persisted for much longer.

The alcohol was a major problem though. Fortunately, if "fortunately" is the right term under these circumstances, it was mainly beer, and there's only so much beer you can drink, no matter how enthusiastic you are. I could do seven to ten cans in a sitting and that would do the job.

And "the job" was to relax me enough so that I would stop obsessively worrying, get my mind off the otherwise constant state of fear and dread, the persistence of the abuse scenario from my childhood, and all those other feelings of terror that I was doomed to an eternity in hell. Beer binges let me numb my way into a comforting, false sense of security and when you're desperate, a false sense of security is better than a true sense of insecurity.

Somehow, and I still don't know how, somehow, I managed to stumble through, fumble through, work.

Somehow, my business made millions of dollars through all this.

Go figure.

Makes you question how much intelligence or competence you need to make money as long as you've got the right set up, doesn't it?

Which is lucky for me, because my highly functional "money channel" was underwriting and funding every other dysfunction in my life.

Here's an observation. The fact that I was still making money during all this insanity might be part of God's plan. Without the money I would not have survived long enough to get through every stage of this journey through Hell. It's like I'd been given a scholarship at the University of Spiritual Hard Knocks, except that I don't remember making an application for admission to a Degree of Bachelor of Fuckupedness – despite my one-time willingness expressed in a prayer to the Devil to spend another year in Hell in exchange for money.

Kristy, at least, was performing her role as rescuer to a wounded puppy very well. She fully supported what I was doing, and she knew I had to get things sorted. But she was also realistic.

"This is your journey," she said. "I can't help you."

My first session with Joseph at his new ministry went like this:

"I need to do a discernment on you," he said.

Spiritual diagnostics.

We were alone in a small room in his new church. We sat in chairs, opposite each other. He looked at me with that intense but gentle gaze that he has – eyes slightly narrowed in concentration as he listens to me speak.

"I need to know if you are still spiritually contaminated," he said.

"OK."

He placed his right hand, palm down, on my forehead. He placed his left hand, palm down on my chin.

He began to pray.

I started to produce another one of my semi-involuntary guttural growls. In my own voice and with my own consciousness I said to him, "I'm not doing that. That isn't me."

"I know." Then, not to me, not to anyone, more like a general declaration, he said, "In the name of Jesus Christ I forbid anything to manifest."

Then, speaking once again to me, he said, "OK. I need you to come back, within a week."

"OK."

"We have a group of people who are going through a similar process."

The next week we met in the main auditorium of the church. Joseph was sitting on the stage with three other people whom I understood were there to help.

In the front row of the seating section I sat with three other people, whom I also understood were, like me, spiritually "contaminated".

Joseph said, "Please stand up," which we all did. "We are going to start praying."

And as soon as they started praying, a sort of panic set in. I started coughing and coughing and coughing and dry retching. As before, some instinct told me to just submit to the process. I didn't know whether the coughing and retching was a good thing or a bad thing. I didn't know if this meant that I was under attack or if this was part of a healing process.

I collapsed onto the floor, still retching and now thrashing around. As before, I was in a state of consciousness where I was both vaguely aware of what was happening and at the same time not aware of what was happening. I could see myself, but I couldn't see myself.

It was the same as I have described before. I could have ended it at any time, but there was also an overwhelming urge simply to submit to the process. It was *easier* to go with it, as if going with the process was the path of lesser resistance. Like dealing with and itch. You start scratching and even though you could stop at any time, it's easier to just follow the itch and keep scratching.

All the while Joseph and the others continue to pray. I was

barely aware of this or of what might be happening to my fellow "contaminated."

Then at one point, Joseph commanded, "Manifest!"

And immediately I start to wriggle and writhe on the floor on my belly, like a snake.

The rest of this Deliverance session is a blur to me, but somehow it all came to an end.

Joseph

The Devil is the master of deception. Satan and the demons will use whatever they can to deceive you into entering into a deal with you. They will promise you the world, but they never deliver anything of true value.

It's always a bad deal. I cannot emphasize this enough. It is *always* a bad deal.

If you've allowed yourself to be deceived, the deception can continue until the very end. I've been with people on their death beds and *only then* do some realize how badly they've been cheated. They've never embraced living in the light. They've never tapped into their true essence, their birthright to Divine Energy, to True Inspiration. They have had *false* light, though. They have had plenty of *that*. But it's as if they've lived their entire lives living under fluorescent light and have never felt the touch of the sun on their face.

Our souls are meant to feed on the pure energy that comes from The Holy Spirit, delivered to us through our spirit, our unique connection to the Divine and to the Light of the Divine. When we ignore building our conscious connection to our spirit, to nourishing our spirit, then we begin to starve. This spiritual starvation is the source of all our insecurities. Our souls then seek other nourishment in the material world and since the vehicle through which our souls experience material reality is our bodies, then our bodies begin to *crave,* and our material minds begin to *covet.*

The body begins to crave all the classic cravings – superficial sex, shallow sensual satisfaction, affirmation through possessions, gluttony, drug and "recreational" chemistry.

The mind begins to covet all the classic desires – money, status, fame, adulation and validation from others, domination, power over others, alliances with the ideologies of power, self-indulgence and indolence of both the mind and body, the vanity that comes from smug self-satisfaction and the prideful arrogance that comes from believing in your own lies.

And for a time, this seems to work, but the material body and the material mind were never meant to provide for the soul. The sweetness these things bring is like the sweetness of saccharine – sweet but empty of nourishment, empty sensuality, meaningless, false power through false idols. This falseness is true idolatry.

Since these things do not nourish the soul, the individual in a state of sin, in a state of error, seeks ever greater doses of these false idols.

But whatever hit you might get later that hit is never as good as the first time, so the sinning soul seeks even more and before we know it we have full-blown addictions on our hands.

Your soul needs to have love for itself, joy, peace, patience, kindness – especially self-kindness, goodness, gentleness, faithfulness – especially faithfulness to self, and self-control.

False idols can never provide these things and when the self-in-a-state-of-sin begins to be frustrated that it cannot be satisfied it falls into other sins, other errors – envy (maybe *they* have what I'm looking for!) anger and wrath (why isn't this working???!!!) and then finally and most tragically, when none of this is working, when the source of light can't even come from other souls struggling with their own wounds and those souls forsake you too, then comes the ultimate feeling of abandonment – despair.

To heal is to become whole. There is nothing intrinsically wrong with the material. The problem is not so simplistic as that of "bad material" versus "good spiritual". It is just that is no nourishment in *empty* materialism. And here is no nourishment from the spiritually wounded.

There are genuine, wholesome things to be gained from the material world, but the material world is not the whole story. With our hearts in the right place we can find the Divine through the material, but true wholeness requires nurturing our spiritual connection with the Divine.

I repeat. Your soul needs to have love for itself, joy, peace, patience, kindness – especially self-kindness, goodness, gentleness, faithfulness – especially faithfulness to self, and self-control.

These are not material things, nor can they be acquired through possession of material things alone.

Yet the Devil will deny you all these things with lies and empty promises.

The Devil represents the triumph of the shallow material over the profoundly spiritual.

The Devil looks for where your vulnerabilities are.

It might seem confusing. It seems that we are given a choice between a pile of sewerage or haute cuisine. It would seem to be an easy choice. But the Devil does not present "His" dubious gifts in their true form. The Lord of Illusion, Deception and Lies presents a pile of sewerage covered in gold – even if it is fool's gold. Lucifer, the carrier of light, lures you with the bright and shiny, but all that glitters is far from being gold.

In the "developing world", where the vulnerability is poverty and disempowerment, The Devil manifests principally through a desire for *domination* in the material world. It is a practical approach. People who have no material security a search for safety in the material, in *things*. People who live with constant exploitation seek security by finding the means to control people. This is understandable in a place where poverty is a dominant force, and where political and social instability and corruption creates a climate of violence and the constant insecurity that violence brings.

In the "developing world", it is commonplace to seek the death of enemies through witchcraft and through spirits attached to charms, amulets and other tokens of power. The Devil works through witches and sorcerers who promise power through chanting, rituals, sacrifices and bribing demons to work for you. It is the sort of thing that attracted my father.

Even the West is not immune to seeking power in this way. There are any number of cults that prey on the vulnerable. And there is a whole underbelly, a whole subculture of people who use mediumship and channeling not as a path to wisdom and personal empowerment, or as a way of strengthening their connection to Divine Light, but as a means of gaining power over others, of achieving domination in the material world. The subject of the Devil's many tricks would be a whole book in itself.

Any way you look at it, power over others, domination and materialism replace the direct experience of love, peace, joy, goodness, kindness, faithfulness and self-discipline that comes from The Holy Spirit. People fall into the sin, the error, of believing that they can *buy* spiritual fulfillment, *bribe* their way there. They forget that true fulfillment comes through *personal spiritual growth*.

However, personal spiritual growth and the connection with the Divine that comes from it requires some effort, some overcoming of resistance, discomfort, sometimes pain and most of all *time*.

But the Evil one instead says, you can escape poverty *now*, through my gifts! You can make violence work for you instead of against you through my gifts! And you can have it *now*! All you have to do is let me in. Let me help you. And all I want in exchange is that when the time comes, you will do my bidding.

The West also has its poverty and violence, and its own brands of power-hungry corruption, but they are nothing like what people experience in Africa. You hardly ever hear about what is *really* going on in Africa, or in much of Asia or South America for that matter, because for the most part the First World just doesn't care. The First World is concerned with its own First World problems.

In the more materially rich West, in the more *ordered* West, in those countries where the populations mostly have the material things and the stability that the people in the developing world are *literally killing for*, the Devil doesn't use the promise of material gain and power as blatantly. You can't tempt people with something that they already have.

Instead, in the West, the Devil uses the material world to seduce and to blind people to turning away from the true source of nourishment. The predominant vulnerability of the West is in *meaning* and living a meaningful life.

And, of course, the Devil exploits impatience in the West too.

So, in the West, the Devil shows up as an agent of chaos and meaninglessness – in the failure of the material world to satisfy – in substance abuse and the *illusion* that the drugs are somehow "enlightening" and "make you see thing clearly" and help you to "think straight" or that they give you "peace" and "comfort" and "joy" and "love" that comes from sharing chemical experiences. And the "gratification" is *instant*.

The Devil also shows up as sexual abuse or sexual exploitation, in neglect and in taking things for granted, in the failure to respect the things that deserve your respect, in narcissism and entitlement and self-righteousness, in the false power of victimhood and in all the other abuses that can undermine relationships, and, ultimately in the despair that results from the overwhelming sense of meaninglessness when all these things, all these false idols, fail.

People do not give up their false idols easily, even if everything those idols offer is an illusion, because at least the illusions are *something* and the illusions at least continue to be an instant "cure for what ails", even if these cures become less and less potent and less and less satisfying as time goes on.

For healing to work, we have to offer people something other than false idols – something better. But even though The Holy Spirit is infinitely better, we can't offer that while an individual is contaminated with demonic afflictions that block spiritual awareness.

It would seem that we are in a double bind. It seems we can't expel the demons until the spiritual connection is strong, but we can't strengthen the spiritual connection while the demons are blocking it. It seems that we are in a downward spiral – the stronger the demons, the worse it gets and the worse it gets the stronger the demons. In some cases the conscious connection with Divinity is so weak that this is how "perfect" possession occurs.

It might surprise you to know that demons are the *last* thing that this little Exorcist thinks about.

The first thing I think about is: "Where are the wounds? Where are the openings? Where is the *rot*?" Because if you can find the rot, and get rid of it, the flies leave. The rot always happens in the absence of spiritual awareness, so the first step is always to strengthen the spirit, to create a climate of spiritual connection and that only works because, in spite of the illusion of the double-bind, *the spiritual connection is always there* – the afflicted individual just doesn't see it.

Which is why we always begin with self-examination and prayer. This strengthens the spirit and begins to loosen the power of the demons.

The strengthened spirit creates a climate that is incompatible with demonic possession. One-by-one the demons reveal themselves. One-by-one they can be rooted out and the spiritual climate improves, weakening the grip of the demons further. The double-bind is seen to be an illusion, the upward spiral of healing commences. Ultimately, the demons are expelled, the house is rid of its vermin. The house of the soul is no longer afflicted. The soul, no longer in a state of sin, of error, can look in on itself clearly.

What's one more rat in a house hoarded with garbage? But in a clean house even a small speck of dirt is obvious. But now the soul is strong enough and has room to move. It can do its own cleaning. The work of restoration can begin. It can fill in the cracks that were once hidden under tons of spiritual garbage. Then, once the cracks are sealed, the greater part of the restoration can go ahead, and the soul can rebuild its life under the guidance of The Holy Spirit.

The source of corruption is not always obvious. Corruption can appear even in the face of material plenty. Corruption can show up as great fortune. People in some situations of great wealth and power, especially familial wealth, inherited power, will often not question the source of that power. This is not to say that all wealth is evil, but in many cases although you might want to fool yourself into believing that your family wealth has been gained honestly, this is not always the case. Sometimes your family has made a deal. Sometimes an ancestor forms a contract with the Devil and sells off future generations in exchange. Think of what's happened to so many "poor little rich kids" throughout history. If you doubt this, ask yourself how the wealth happens, *honestly*. Look into the origin of your wealth. There are *always* clues that something is not quite right. Even things that appear to be blessings might be curses.

There is no doubt that the survivors of spiritual affliction are *permanently* changed by their experiences. Former alcoholics can't even have a beer without feeling awful. Former pornography addicts find images of loveless sex distasteful. Formerly violent abusers can't even contemplate touching another person in anger.

But the journey from darkness to light is seldom straightforward. *It is certainly never instant.*

Paul

Afterwards, I asked Joseph, "Why all the coughing, retching and writhing?"

"You are spiritually sick," he said, "so spiritually sick that the coughing and dry retching is your attempt to flush out the negative energies that have attached themselves to your body. It is like vomiting after you've been poisoned. It is uncomfortable, but it is a good thing."

"I get it," I said.

"Imagine that you have a glass of full of dirty water," he continued. "Then you put this glass under a tap running with clean water. There is an overflow now of dirty water mixed with clean water, spilling over the rim of the glass and down the sink. The water in the glass does not become instantly cleaned, but gradually the dirty water leaves the glass and eventually the glass is full of clean water. You are full of dirty energy. The light of The Holy Spirit enters you and cleans you out. Gradually, it will all wash itself out, but it is a process."

I thought about this for a moment. "Can't we just empty all the dirty water out in one go and fill it with clean water?"

"Unfortunately, that does not seem to be an option in my experience," he said. "That would possibly be quite dangerous.

Perhaps one day we will be able to do this. There is much that we don't know."

"OK." I was a little disappointed. I was hoping for an instant cure.

"Some people sneeze," Joseph said. "Some people yawn. Some cry. Some even laugh."

"I just happen to be a dry retching collapsing wriggler."

Joseph closed his eyes, tilted his head, held out his hands with open palms shrugged, and gently nodded. "Yes," he said.

Great. I get all the ***fun*** *side effects.*

"I wish I had a camera," Joseph said, attempting to inject a little humor into the situation. "I have never before seen such a pure manifestation as when you started wriggling like a snake."

I just nodded. There wasn't much I could say.

"We're not done," he said.

So much for Deliverance session twenty-one.

But who was counting?

CHAPTER ELEVEN

THE DEVIL HAS YOUR MIND

"Kill yourself. Just fucking kill yourself. You can string yourself up in the garage. It'd be easy. Here's how, just take some rope, loop it over the garage door mechanism …"

Joseph

The telephone rings.

"Oh, Joseph! I heard about you. I heard how you were able to help a friend of my friend. I don't know what to do. I'm overwhelmed by this sense of dread. I feel completely worthless. I'm constantly afraid. I'm confused …"

"What have you been thinking about?"

"I don't know what I'm even doing here. I've been thinking of killing myself."

"Is it possible for me to see you in person?"

"Yes. Please!"

"I'm free on Friday. Can you come Friday morning?"

"Yes."

"In the meantime," I say, "I want to assure you that what you are experiencing might be bad, but it is not abnormal. You are under some form of spiritual attack. Do you understand?"

"Yes. I think so."

"I deal with this sort of situation all the time. I want to assure you that help is available, OK?"

"OK. Oh, thank you. Thank you.".

People usually approach me in a state of desperation. They seldom wait any longer than they have to.

But like so many things people will often wait until they are at their wit's end. They wait until they cannot ignore the weirdness. The dogs barking at nothing, the unease they feel whenever they are in that room, the history of failure at work, or relationships that are always going wrong, the sickness that never leaves them, or the constant intrusive thoughts of wanting to damage people, or the persistent, intangible feeling of dread that makes them want to destroy themselves.

Demonic Affliction doesn't have to be like it is in the movies. People don't start abusing themselves with crucifixes, although they can. People don't have to become serial killers who stage their victims' bodies up in bizarre, ritualistic set ups, although they can. In fact, it seldom is. Furniture doesn't have to move, although it can. Apparitions don't have to scream in the night, although they can. People don't have to start levitating and climbing the walls, although they can.

In the vast majority of cases, the Devil and the demons don't have to resort to paranormal theatrics. In the vast majority of cases, human weaknesses born of fear are more than enough to drive the afflicted into spiritual madness and despair.

"Don't let the fear get to you. You understand?"

"Yes."

"That's more important than anything. Don't let the fear win.

"I understand. But easier said than done."

"I know but do your best. Right now, I want you to understand that the Lord is going to assign angels to look after you until you can see me."

"All right."

"I would like to pray a little with you now, OK?"

"OK."

Asking people not to be afraid is a little like asking you not to think of flying pink elephants. The first thing you'll think of is flying pink elephants. But by beginning to pray with someone, you take their minds off their fear and you take the first step to get them to focus on their spiritual connection. Even if the afflicted is not religious, the simple act of prayer helps because it shifts the focus away from the fear.

Prayer, simply communicating directly with The Holy Spirit, or God, or however you want to think of it, and asking for protect and help, is the very least that you can do to protect yourself.

When I see people in person, the first thing I get them to do is to repeat for me what is going on with them right now. This helps me discern if the problem is spiritual, rather than "simply" being material.

Dreams and nightmares are keys to understanding. It is also important to investigate if there are paranormal manifestations – strange movements or presences in the house. I also need to know if they, in their moments of despair, made a prayer or contract with a demonic entity or even the Devil itself.

In the absence of any discernment that the problem is spiritual, I will refer the person to a number of people in my network who are specialists in dealing with particular problems. These are people with experience, qualifications and the necessary background to understand mental, emotional and physical illness or disorders that are harming people and their lives. The development of this specialist network is ongoing because, naturally, I need people who are sympathetic to, or at least open to, the possibility of spiritual affliction because discernment, like everything else in the field, is not always straightforward. These allied professionals are themselves strongly spiritual, spiritually knowledgeable and have a strong connection to The Holy Spirit in their own way. They know that, or are at least willing to consider that, spiritual affliction might be hidden under more "mundane" "material" affliction and that spiritual affliction might not show up until more mundane forms of treatment have dealt with mundane disorders. In that case, I might end up seeing the afflicted again. After all, the other professionals need to be able to use their own discernment and they need someone like me to refer their clients back to.

The process of discernment is not perfect, but if a pregnant woman has a vivid dream in which "something" is having sex with her and then she miscarries, *and this happens multiple times*, then I'm inclined to accept that we are dealing with Spiritual Affliction – oppression at the very least.

Is the affliction uninvited? If it is, we are dealing with what we call a "stronghold".

Is the affliction invited through some oath or contract? If so, we are dealing with a "legal right".

Strongholds, where there is no "legal right" are relatively easy to deal with because the spiritual connection of the afflicted is minimally compromised, the damage is *relatively* minimal. Strongholds comprise about eighty percent of cases of affliction.

It is important to realize that even demons operate under particular rules. Their power is much diminished if they are purely invasive, if they have not been invited, if they have not been "let in". But "much diminished" does not mean that they are powerless. They still do a great deal of damage, but from the point of view of treatment, they are much more easily expelled than in cases where you have invited them, and where you have formed a contract.

Strongholds are dealt with through an inner healing process.

Legal rights, where there is a contract or pact involved, can get very complicated and might require some investigation. Sometimes what appears to be a stronghold is actually a legal right, but this only comes to light after considerable investigation, "Oh, I remember thinking when I was three years old that I would give anything if …" Sometimes a legal right is the result of a generational problem, as in the case of a patriarch or matriarch that formed a pact in exchange for wealth and power, and who sold out their descendants to have that power.

Regardless of stronghold or legal right, an Assisted Deliverance Prayer program is the initial intervention.

You can find this program of prayer by contacting us directly at Divine Intercession and asking for these prayers: https://divineintercession.org.au/contact/

Because the prayers are bound to stir the demonic entities up, I always ask the afflicted to let me know at any time during the seven days if anything weird, unusual or powerful shows up and to keep a diary or a journal to record events.

All sorts of things might happen when they're doing their prayers. They might feel things, see things, hear voices, smell unpleasant odors and in rare cases experience foul tastes. There might be weird manifestations in the house. It is particularly useful to know during which particular prayers certain phenomena occurred. My phone is always on. It is not unusual for me to get phone calls in the middle of the night during some of the nastier manifestations. People need to know that there is a safety net for them, that there is someone who cares. It is extremely distressing to feel that you are dealing with this sort of thing alone.

The prayer process is also one of self-discovery and disclosure. I encourage the afflicted to go deep into their memories and uncover any trauma that might have allowed the demons a way in.

Of course, as I keep emphasizing, the very nature of this work means that it might be very difficult to separate Spiritual Affliction from mental illness, and if the afflicted has not been properly diagnosed then this complicates matters tremendously.

Sometimes people make mistakes.

Sometimes *I* make mistakes.

And that's when things can go to Hell.

Paul

The next week I was back. This time it was just Joseph and a couple of helpers. I never did another Deliverance session in front of a group of other people ever again. I didn't want to go through another surgery while the peanut gallery was watching. Joseph wasn't going to put me through something that I frankly found humiliating.

Joseph's helpers however were there, and I did find them to be very helpful.

Session twenty-two proceeded much like the previous one, at least at first.

I could really feel the power emanating from one of the intercessors, one of the helpers, even while I was going through my floor writhing.

"I call on the Spirit of Peace," she called out. "Spirit of Peace come through! Come through now!"

And as soon as she said that, the most heavenly, heavenly, heavenly sense of peace came over me. The most heavenly peace that you can imagine.

But it wasn't over.

Joseph pressed on.

And then, all of a sudden, words came into my mind in a foreign language that I had never heard before and I spoke them out loud.

The deliverers began to clap and rejoice.

I later learned that one of the Gifts of The Holy Spirit is the sign that the "patient" begins to speak in tongues. This signifies that The Holy Spirit is in charge and is now in control. The Devil or the demon has now been cast out, and you are now speaking in a private language to God that only God and your deeper self can understand – an encrypted dialog to God, concerning your soul, your spirit and your life – that the demons cannot decode or decipher.

But even as this was happening, even as the deliverers were rejoicing, smiling, clapping their hands and saying, "Hallelujah" all over the place, I was not happy.

My gut feeling was, "*This, isn't good.*"

But since I didn't know any better, I didn't know what to make of this.

One of them helped me up. I was semi-aware that someone was talking to me.

"You've been delivered!" someone said.

Have I?

"Have, I?"

"Yes! We just heard you speak to The Holy Spirit," Joseph said.

"I don't think that was addressed to The Holy Spirit."

"It was The Holy Spirit."

"I'm not sure about that."

"Yes. You have been set free," Joseph said. "Go home. I will talk to you tomorrow. I will tell you what will happen from here."

"OK. I'll go home now."

I was willing to believe him. They had told me I was free! I'm free!

I had never spoken in that strange language before. This is in line with what the Bible says!

I slept well that night. I was OK the following day. Until …

In the mid-afternoon, about four o'clock, Joseph called me. There was an edge to his voice, an urgency verging on panic.

"Paul, Paul, Paul, I'm so sorry. You were right. Last night, after you left, I was praying to God, to get confirmation on your Deliverance, but the Devil came through and said, 'I have his mind'."

Joseph started talking louder and faster. I could hear panic escalate in his voice, "Paul, the Devil's got your mind, you're in big, big trouble."

"I don't believe him. He's just bluffing," I countered. I felt fine. "Don't worry about it. Leave it alone."

"Paul, I don't think you understand, Paul …"

"Don't worry. I don't believe him. I'm fine."

To this day I don't know why Joseph didn't push the matter further. Maybe he did, maybe he did all he could but I was so *enthralled* that I just wasn't listening.

I don't recall how the call ended, but that was it, as far as I was concerned, and I got on with the rest of my day.

At about eight o'clock that night I was lying in bed with Kristy next to me.

I started to obsess, not about anything in particular, there was just the feeling of obsession. I felt a vague, obsessive confusion.

"Kris."

"What?"

"I don't feel right."

Confusion turned into fear.

"What do you mean?"

"I can't describe it."

Confusion turned into terror.

"I just don't feel right … I'm … I'm in trouble and I think I'm going to need some help … I'm really scared, and I … I need help."

I was in the throes of a panic attack.

"OK," she said in a voice that you use when you're trying to calm a frightened child. "We're going to get you the help you need in the morning ."

Blind-sided, I felt like I was on the brink of total and absolute despair. I felt as if I was going to Hell, obsessing over going to Hell. But somehow, I got it together enough to get into some sort of fitful sleep.

The following day, it got worse – more agitation, more paranoia, more obsessing. Thoughts intruded.

Thoughts that were not my own.

Joseph is full of shit. Joseph has fooled you. Nothing he did was real.

After a few days of this, I started calling Joseph every now and then, usually during a panic attack. He explained things to me that I can't remember now because it didn't make any sense to me at the time. He kept trying to reassure me, but the small relief I'd feel after talking to him never lasted. He made no attempt to persuade me to come back. Perhaps something told him that would not have worked.

In a rare moment of lucidity during this time I remember telling him, "I don't think the Devil wants me to see you again."

He prayed for me then.

Joseph is full of shit. Joseph has fooled you. Nothing he did was real. None of this is real.

And after a few more days I didn't want to have anything to do with Joseph. I didn't want to go near him. I had an overwhelming feeling that going to him again would be a disaster. I was terrified and filled with a complete fear of ever going to see him again.

None of this is real. Nothing that you think happened to you ever happened to you.

After two weeks of progressively getting worse, of barely being able to function at all, I decided to see a psychiatrist.

My mind had become so overtaken with irrational thoughts, fears, obsessions and succumbing to panic attacks that by the time I got to see a psychiatrist she said, "I think you're going to have to go to hospital."

I didn't go to hospital, but I came pretty damn close.

The psychiatrist put me onto anti-psychotic medication, but almost immediately after taking it I received other thoughts that were not mine, but that were of a whole different feeling – a calm strength. This was God "talking" to me …

THOSE PILLS ARE NOT FOR YOU.

THOSE PILLS ARE NOT FOR YOU.

THOSE PILLS ARE NOT FOR YOU.

Over and over again.

These thoughts that were somehow not of me, but that nevertheless had a weight of authority behind them were messages as clear as day.

But even in the presence of God's clear "voice", I took the pills anyway because I was desperate, and I just wanted to get better. The pendulum had swung back to my believing that I was going mad. Again, I could not fathom at the time that this was a spiritual issue, not a psychological or a psychiatric one.

I was caught in a place that was both real and not real and it was very, very scary. I couldn't make sense of anything. They put me onto tranquilizers, but just like the anti-psychotics, they weren't working either.

Kill yourself. Just fucking kill yourself. You can string yourself up in the garage. It'd be easy. Here's how, just take some rope, loop it over the garage door mechanism ...

When I wasn't suicidal, I was borderline catatonic. I had to stop working. My mother and my office administrator took over the running of the practice.

I was seeing the psychiatrist three times a week.

"How are you getting to sleep?" she asked. "Are you getting any sleep at all?"

"Well, I've had 20 milligrams of Valium, 10 milligrams of Xanax and 150 milligrams of Lurasidone. I've also had those little red-dotted, top-up tranquilizers, the Quetiapine."

"All that would knock out a horse!"

"I'm barely able to get to sleep."

My mother was counseling me, daily, hourly, minute-by-minute sometimes. And being the observant woman that she is, she noticed that when I was taking the Lurasidone, I'd get worse.

Why don't you just kill yourself?
Why don't you just kill yourself? Why don't you just kill yourself?
Why don't you just kill yourself?
Why don't you just kill yourself? Why don't you just kill yourself?
Why don't you just kill yourself?

Maybe you can have a thought like that, going through your head, from an entity, that you don't even know is real. They were also other thoughts filled with authority, but of a totally different quality, a malevolence, a character different from any thoughts that might come from and All-Loving God.

Maybe you can hear a malicious thought like that thought a thousand times. Maybe ten thousand times.

But after the ten-thousand-and-first time, *killing yourself becomes a real fucking option.*

You know what I mean?

One morning I called my mother.

I was off the wall.

"Did you just take the anti-psychotic?" she asked.

"Yes."

"Stop taking it. You need to talk to the psychiatrist immediately."

"Mum, I know this sounds crazy, but I think I'm under satanic attack."

"You are NOT under satanic attack!"

"I just can't tell you how bad … I'm under satanic attack."

"YOU ARE NOT UNDER SATANIC ATTACK!"

"I know," I said, half lying, "but that's what my brain is telling me. My brain is telling me this and I'm absolutely convinced of it." There was no way that I could shake this feeling.

"Stop taking the medication. You need to talk to the psychiatrist immediately."

Within a couple of hours, I was back in her office. She agreed I had to stop taking the Lurasidone.

"I think I'm under satanic attack."

"You're in psychosis. But you're having a severe side-effect to the Lurasidone. So, I'm going to put you on to Risperidone. And you have to stop drinking alcohol."

"OK."

We were swallowing the spider to catch the fly. I was jumping from the frying pan into the fire.

I wasn't in psychosis, but at the time, that's what everyone was telling me. I was in no position to judge what was going on for myself. I had no way of understanding this for myself, so I just believed her and kept taking the medication. I still had no intention of going back to see Joseph.

Don't go near him. Don't go anywhere near him.

I did slightly better, especially at night-time, and I'd look forward to going to bed like a kid does on the night before Christmas, and I was still taking enough drugs at night to knock out a horse.

I had convinced myself that I had entered into a contract with the Devil.

That I was going to hell.

That I had, in fact, at one point in the past, prayed for money, which is why my business was going so well, even though I was a drugged-up-to-the-eyeballs zombie.

That The Devil had "given me" my first-born child.

And during a particularly bad day, in the midst of this full-blown mental breakdown and in the depths of despair, God spoke to me as a very definite, authoritative tone of thought.

*"WHO DO YOU THINK GAVE YOU YOUR BUSINESS? THE DEVIL? **I** GAVE YOU YOUR BUSINESS.*

*WHO DO YOU THINK GAVE YOU YOUR CHILD? THE DEVIL? **I** GAVE YOU YOUR CHILD."*

THE PILLS ARE NOT FOR YOU. THE PILLS ARE NOT FOR YOU."

So even though God was talking to me, I couldn't believe that. I couldn't process that. There's was no way I could digest that. So, I just started crying.

And my mind was still so hijacked that there was another tone of thought, with less authority, but with relentless persistence.

You're going to hell. You're going to hell. You're going to hell.

I remember one day sending a text message, typing my name and the message auto corrected and wrote the words "Hell" instead.

"Paul" and "Hell" are nowhere near related and so this could not have been me making a mistake. *I assure you.*

In an attempt to not die from alcohol poisoning I had stopped drinking for a while.

Sobriety didn't help. I noticed that whenever I stopped doing anything that would ultimately kill me, this *thing*, or these *things*, inside me would just bide their time until they could pounce for maximum effect.

And pounce they did.

Oh, God, I can't handle this. I can't handle this. You opened my eyes to this, but I can't … I … please just close my eyes again. I saw but I can't handle this. Please shut my eyes.

Under persistent psychic attack, again, I couldn't even pray to God anymore. I was too scared.

I'm scared because when I pray to you it gets worse.

Psychiatry and prescription medication weren't doing much for me. The alcohol and valium I had renounced had at least given me *some* relief, but I needed more, so I started exploring alternative therapies.

I tried going to the hot-tub at my local gym, marinating myself in the warm water chlorinated womb and saying affirmations to myself.

I am safe. I am safe. I am safe.

That helped … a little. It worked … a little.

But even a little was better than nothing.

Then one day, it didn't. My do-it-yourself spiritual aqua therapy failed me and I felt like crap.

So, I sat in the car park, in the car, with my tablet after the failed womb session, feeling spiritually … how do I say this? Hijacked.

Some instinct, some inspiration, directed me to a website called bible-knowledge.com. As I was led through the site by some unknown force I came across some information about "binding and loosing spirits"; https://www.bible-knowledge.com/Deliverance-system-for-casting-out-demons/

"Binding" in this sense, meant effectively putting the demons in spiritual handcuffs. "Loosing" meant breaking the attachment, breaking the connection that they had to you. So, there were two steps – "shackling" the demon, so that you limited their freedom of movement, and then, step two, cutting them away.

I learned that there were different types of demons, each with their own hellish specialty; https://www.bible-knowledge.com/different-kinds-of-demonic-spirits/

There were spirits, it seemed, for every nasty thing you could think of – anxiety, depression, doubt, obsession and compulsion.

The particular exorcist on this site, Michael Bradley, would anticipate the presence of these spirits during a Deliverance session and say things like, "Spirit of Depression, I bind you in the name of Jesus Christ and I loose this spirit from this person in the name of Jesus Christ.".

I figured I had nothing to lose by trying this on myself.

"Spirit of OCD, I bind you in the name of Jesus Christ and I loose myself from you in the name of Jesus Christ."

Instantly, *instantly*, my mind was given some sort of relief and I started dry retching uncontrollably until there occurred a sudden release of energy.

Emboldened, I tried the next thing I could think of:

"Spirit of *fear*, I bind you in the name of Jesus Christ and I loose myself from you in the name of Jesus Christ."

Again, I started dry retching and coughing.

And the fear went away.

I went through a whole series of Spirits of Darkness, and it worked!

Anxiety, depression, doubt, confusion. One-by-one I went through them.

Confusion was a massive one.

Even in the middle of an exorcism, the Spirit of Confusion will come over you, leaving the way open for the Spirit of Fear to attack you.

And Spirit of OCD will send you mad. It will send you *stark, raving, mad.*

Conventional treatments will only deal with conventional "mental illness", but Spiritual Infestation is a Spiritual Affliction. I repeat myself. It can disguise itself as mental illness, but it isn't.

And the situation is even more horrible when you realize that the two states of being aren't mutually exclusive. You can have mental illness *and* spiritual infestation at the same time, complicating an already complicated situation. The stigma of mental illness doesn't help. To this day I'm discredited in the opinion of a lot of people because I was once on anti-psychotic medication.

In some eyes, once a nutter, always a nutter.

But in that moment, in the car park, for the first time in a long while, I felt some relief that did not involve drugs – prescription or otherwise.

I went home.

It almost terrified me that the relief worked, because a spiritual solution had confirmed for me that my problem was a spiritual issue. Now the pendulum had swung back again, and a part of me had to acknowledge, yet again, that *there are such things*.

My do-it-yourself Deliverance didn't last. The feeling of being overwhelmed by everything started up again within a week. Whatever I had done to rid myself of this thing hadn't stuck. Whatever I needed to do or be to make it all go away, I couldn't maintain it.

I compulsively surfed the internet about paranormal phenomena, deliberately setting myself off into yet another obsessive spin, another panic attack, constantly triggering myself.

And all the time there's this *insane* level of fear.

And if it hadn't been for my mother, I would have killed myself. I would tell her my deepest, darkest thoughts, and she'd simply be present there for me and say, "I understand. I understand." And even though she didn't deny me the reality of my *feelings*, she did come up with a rational explanation for all this which would help at least a little and for a short while, before there'd be yet another attack and the cycle of pain, confusion, panic, unreality, fear and terror would begin all over again.

Without my mother, I was gone.

From that first night, when Joseph first told me that the Devil had a hold of my mind, and I had brushed it off, in just three months I went from being a fit young man who surfed on the weekends, to ballooning to a 300-pound, dysfunctional, shattered, shell of a human being. Beer made a major contribution to my weight gain. Beer, in fact, became my savior, beer became the only drug that gave me any real relief at all.

Three months passed until I was anywhere near functional again.

"I can't … I'm sorry … I can't keep going … I just can't go on like this … I'm going to have to kill myself …" I told my mother.

When a mother hears this sort of thing coming out of her child's mouth, you leave her with few options.

"I don't know what to do for you," she said.

"The only thing I know, that I can try, is to have a few beers and a valium," I said.

"OK, then. I'll go to the shops and get some," she said. "If that's what'll help then …"

And I did get my relief. Whatever was trying to fuck me over I guess didn't care as long as it killed me one way or another, but at least I could get some relief. The only way I could get out of this was to get out of my head. And the classic way to get out of your head? Drugs and alcohol.

Right?

I know that you don't want to hear this, because it's not "ideologically sound" or "politically correct", but it was *the alcohol* that got me back on track, at least to a point where I wasn't on the brink of doing myself in all the time. It wasn't a long-term solution, but in the short term it worked *just fine*. That's why PTSD sufferers like it so much. It offers relief. And when you're doing THAT badly any relief is a step in the right direction.

At my next session with the psychiatrist I brought my mother along. We told her what had happened.

My mother said to the psychiatrist, "Before you say anything, I did what I had to do. He was going to kill himself. So, don't you tell me that he should not have had the alcohol." Under the circumstances, the psychiatrist was forced to agree.

I asked her to add an anti-depressant to the drug mix.

"It will work," she said, "not as effectively because you're on alcohol, but it will have an effect to some extent."

So gradually, I got semi-better and semi-functional. What could I do? My brain was fried.

"There is only so much the human mind can take," the psychiatrist said.

I'm in psychosis. This is not real. You are a psychotic.

That's what I was telling myself again. But was that true? Or was that just another demonic voice tricking me with the oldest trick in the Devil's book – *the trick into making you believe that the Devil doesn't exist?*

Later, I learned that while this was going on, Joseph had set up a "Prayer Warrior Team" who would get together and pray for me. They knew that there, in me, was a soul in major trouble. They never gave up on me, even when I gave up on them. Even though there was still a little part of me that wanted to go back to Joseph. But every time I seriously considered it, the spiritual anxiety would flare up and I'd get a panic attack.

My mother, however, blamed *them* for what had happened.

"Don't go back to that pastor," she said in her way of coming up with a rational narrative, "He's what caused it."

It was the same old story. As wonderful as my mother was, there was only so much that *her* mind could take, could understand.

And how do you explain to a psychiatrist?

"Well … I was lying in bed one day … and I said 'Fuck the Devil' … then something spoke through my voice … so, I went to do these exorcisms … and the pastor said that my mind's going to break."

???

Of course, she's going to say, "Well, you've been delusional for a while, you need an anti-psychotic."

There were all these competing realities, and "reality" was up for grabs. The demons had achieved their goal.

But, in the background, unknown to me, there *were* angels looking after me.

One night I was so screwed up I popped three Xanax, went to the casino, drank three beers, felt a bit woozy, thought, "I better get outta here", drove down the coast.

It's important for you to understand that one Xanax and one beer has the same effect as drinking four beers. So, at this point, I had had the equivalent of drinking *twelve beers* in less than an hour.

And the effect is instant, like a single, punch of beer in the face.

Out of the blue, *out of some instinct*, my mother called.

"Where are you?"

"I'm driving,"

"Where are you?"

"I'm fine."

"Don't you tell me that. Stop wherever you are. Stay there. We're going to pick you up. Tell me where you are right now!"

I told her.

"Pull over. We're coming,"

So, I did.

She sent my brother. When he found me, I was in the car, practically comatose. Somehow, he managed to lug a 300-pound dead weight into his own car and got me home. My mother called an ambulance to get them to look me over.

If my mother had not called, it was possible that I might have crashed the car and died, and taken God knows who else with me.

The next day she asked me, "Why did you do that?"

"I can't stand the fear. There's this fear all the time and I just wanted to be away from it. I just need to be out of it."

But I wasn't going to be out of it for a long time yet.

And I still didn't go back to Joseph.

In the midst of all the fear and anxiety I honestly thought it would make it worse if I did.

CHAPTER TWELVE

HITTING BRIMSTONE BOTTOM

"I can't help but feel that something deeper is going on than just a 'mental health issue'."

Joseph

It goes almost without saying that significant trauma creates a very friendly environment for spiritual affliction. You can easily imagine what chronic, repeated mental, emotional, physical or sexual abuse does to a person. There is even such a thing as spiritual abuse. If a person that you trust, someone in authority, creates and environment in which your spiritual connection can falter, if someone belittles your soul, that's spiritual abuse. If someone, or some*thing*, tells you that God *hates* you, that's spiritual abuse.

But even "banal" trauma can cause a big wound. What others might shrug off as inconsequential might be extremely significant if the trauma happened at a time when, for whatever reason, you were feeling particularly vulnerable, or feeling emotionally fragile at a particular time. Maybe you were scared of going to the dentist once, or you had to go into hospital for an operation. Maybe a parent was late picking you up from school one day and you got very, very frightened.

Regardless of the nature of the wound, *all forms of abuse take away your power and integrity*. Powerless people have wounds that compromise their integrity. An unidentified or unhealed wound remains open, remains unhealed. One trauma can lead to all sorts of other trauma, like ripples in a pond, like dominoes falling. Even a small thorn in your shoe can create all sorts of problems if it is never removed. Even a small leak in a roof, barely detected, can let the rain in and can destroy a house unless it is fixed in time.

But no matter how far you've come off the track, *there is always a way back*.

The way back always involves giving The Holy Spirit *consent* to heal you.

We must establish a contract with The Holy Spirit for healing.

Once we establish consent, the process of healing involves me making some things absolutely clear.

The Holy Spirit is here, always present in essence to heal you.

Always.

You need to give yourself over to healing. Whether these afflictions are "your fault" or not is irrelevant. The only thing that matters now is that you surrender to the process that The Holy Spirit, through me as an instrument if necessary, will put you through.

The process often requires that the afflicted go back to their trauma in their imagination.

We might imaginatively reenact the moment of trauma, the moment when, for example, a father came back home drunk and beat the mother and then the child. We retell the story together. We use every memory of senses – how things looked, sounded, felt, smelled, and tasted.

At this point there is usually a tremendous outpouring of emotion, great weeping. The afflicted, the wounded, are right there in the moment.

At that point I invoke The Holy Spirit.

"O, Holy Spirit, come now to this child."

But now the child knows that they are safe, and they can allow The Holy Spirit to enter every part of their being, and every aspect of their life.

In such an environment of affirmation of the power of The Holy Spirit and the consent for the entry of The Holy Spirit, the demonic entities are now in an environment that is completely inimical to them.

And The Holy Spirit might speak through me.

"MY CHILD. I SEE YOU. YOU ARE SAFE NOW."

But often The Holy Spirit speaks to them directly, usually through that intangible voice without words in their minds and hearts, in some internal dialog that only they and God are privy to, but I see them calm down and find peace.

I will ask the afflicted, perhaps now less afflicted, what they "hear".

And they might say, "The Holy Spirit said that He loved me. That I am safe now. That I should not be afraid. He is with me."

Time means nothing to The Holy Spirit. The healing takes place in the past and in the present and in the future – simultaneously.

And I might ask the afflicted, "Can you let that young child you once were go? Can you release that child?"

"Yes," they will say. "I see that child going into the light."

And now I say, "O, Holy Spirit. Heal this child of Yours. Heal them of their fear." And I might say to the afflicted, "Give your fear to The Holy Spirit."

And they do.

And then I might ask the afflicted, "Can you forgive the person who did this evil to you? Can you forgive them now?"

And weeping, they will say, "Yes, I am willing to forgive them. I forgive them."

And in forgiving, the afflicted are set free.

Set free from guilt of believing that your abuse was your fault.

Set free from anger.

Set free from the hold that the event, the trauma, has on you.

Set free from the bondage to the drama.

Set free from the attachment that comes from hating.

Set free from the need for revenge, for violent retribution.

Then, the afflicted is no longer afflicted, at least not by their own trauma, at least not for now.

Then the wound can close.

The entry point of affliction can close.

And then they can *finally* begin to heal.

Or, if the afflicted is contaminated, or possessed, we now know that any hate and anger or violence in them is not theirs, but belongs to the demons inside them, the agents of infection.

You can always tell demonic anger because there is *enjoyment* in the anger. It is an anger that *revels* in the possibility, in the overwhelming desire, of destroying the person that the anger inhabits.

You can always tell demonic despair, because it *revels* in the possibility, in the overwhelming desire of driving the person the despair inhabits into destroying themselves.

The tell-tale sign of the demons is that in the midst of horror, *they are having fun.*

And sometimes they will lead you down many blind alleys, and fool you into thinking that you're free, so that they can continue playing you, like a cat playing with a terrified mouse.

And sometimes they need to almost destroy you before you can muster or rally your forces and ask for help from The Holy Spirit.

Paul

For better or worse, the alcohol kept my anxiety levels down to the point that every now and then I could function. By now I was about six-weeks into this bout of madness, and it felt like six years. The psychiatrist continued to believe that it was the anti-psychotics that were having the effect of making me "better" but the reality was that it was the alcohol, with a little help from the anti-anxiety medication that I had *to ask for*.

I couldn't exercise. I could barely move. I continued to put on weight.

I could work, if only a little. It was enough to distract me during the day but come five o'clock the anxiety would build up and I was straight onto high-alcohol Belgian beer, heavily medicating and self-medicating every night to the point where I could get nine-hours of fitful sleep. Over the months to follow I would eventually be drinking the equivalent of a bottle of vodka's worth of alcohol in beer *every night* – four champagne bottle's worth of beer within about three hours, my 5:00 pm to 8:00 pm daily beer shift. I could no longer pretend that I was drinking just to "take the edge off". By this stage I was getting drunk, passing out on the couch. When I woke up, usually at about two in the morning, there'd be all these empty bottles around me. I couldn't remember drinking the contents. In the two hours leading up to bed I wouldn't remember saying "goodbye" to anyone who might have visited. In my more lucid moments I'd ask myself, "Did I offend anyone? I wonder what Kristy thinks about me?" but for the most part I was oblivious, all I cared about was the relief that my "medicine" was giving me. But the "medicine" was destroying me, *which is exactly what the demons wanted.*

At least I wasn't harming anyone but myself. Kristy was occupied with the baby, leaving *me* to deal with *me*.

The dream or vision of the traumatic abuse that might or might not have happened continued to play in my head. I read on the internet that "you can't get PTSD from a dream" and other mental health professionals were of that opinion too. So, I found myself down that rabbit hole again. If the psychiatrist is telling me that I have PTSD, then the "dream" *must* have been real. Alternatively, if the abuse was "just" a dream, then I don't have PTSD, I have something else, like demonic possession. But if demonic possession isn't real, then it must be PTSD, which means the "dream" was real, but I'm also getting told that the abuse, the trauma, never happened. So 'round and 'round and 'round and 'round we go …

But my nervous system responds to energy, and wherever that energy came from – whether it was a "real" event, or a "paranormal" event or a self-inflicted event of the "psyche" – that energy is real *to me*. That event is *indistinguishable* from reality. It's ludicrous to think that you can't be traumatized by an experience that is indistinguishable from "reality". But I didn't know that at the time. I was still in the hands of "experts" whom I trusted in, whom I believed in.

Because I was in this PTSD state, normal human relationships were impossible. Whenever my mother or sister would visit, they'd encounter someone who met their attempts to engage me with a glassy-eyed stare, staring into the abyss. Or they'd see someone "watching television" but not watching anything at all. I'd "go to work", but it was all a pretense and it was unusual if I spent more than a few hours there at most. The gambling increased to a point where if it didn't stop soon it would stop being a "hobby" and it would turn into a *major* problem. At the worst of times I'd be in a psychic-attack storm, at the best of times, I was just going through the motions of living as the walking dead.

And yet, in spite of all this, there was still enough of a healthy part of me that realized that something needed to be done.

"Kristy, I have a problem."

"Well, I'm glad you've admitted it."

So, I got my psychiatrist to do some research to find a place for me and I requested a booking into a rehabilitation center in Far North Queensland.

The center got back to me one afternoon in late November 2017. I was drunk, in the casino, gambling. Great timing.

"We've got a bed for you. When can you come up?"

I was there within a week. I lied to everyone at work about what I was doing. I cited a "family emergency." I guess it wasn't a *total* lie.

I was just so thankful to be there. It was such a relief. I'd been carrying the burden of running the business for so long – which is ridiculous, since I was barely functional, but in my mind, I was the one who was ultimately responsible. Fortunately, I'd put good people in place, to the point where I think my mind finally said, "It's OK. You can have your full meltdown now," because I was exhausting myself even further keeping up the pretense of being barely effective, while constantly crying inside. Blind Freddie could have seen that Paul was in trouble. But what exactly was his trouble? That was still anyone's guess. I know that my family and friends were doing their best to support me, but *I* didn't feel supported. *I* felt that everything was on my shoulders. They didn't know about my abuse trauma. They didn't really get that I was constantly afraid of going *literally* to hell.

If you've never had the experience of going to rehab, it works like this.

Doctor's appointment to check on your physical health, or lack of it.

Psychiatrist's appointment to check on your mental health, or lack of it.

They take your phone away from you, and only give it back to you at certain times during the week, because they want you to concentrate on getting better.

We had morning walks on the beach, maybe a swim. There were morning meetings so that you could share basic housekeeping stuff with other people, so if you've got a beef with someone you can clear the air and not let things fester.

There are a lot of classes on psychology, to help you understand your condition, learning how to manage your feelings, learning how to communicate with other people better, setting boundaries, that sort of thing. You're assigned your own psychotherapist. This particular place did equine therapy, so you got to commune with horses. There were bushwalks, art classes, a whole program of activities to help you relax and bring some joy back into your life, and massage, spas and acupuncturists to help you heal.

Relaxation and therapy. All this and more is yours for at least a thousand dollars a day!

But it was $40,000 well spent. A better buy at any rate than the thousands I was spending gambling and drinking myself to death.

I started getting back into prayer. I started saying the rosary, praying to stop drinking. I started symbolically flagellating myself as an act of repentance. I would pray to the Virgin Mary, and when I felt her presence coming through, I would start weeping.

I was still making attempts at Self-Deliverance, "St Michael, loose yourself upon these demons", which brought on the dry retching again.

One night, after another bout of Self-Deliverance, I went to the dispensary to get my medication. An overwhelming urge to dry retch came upon me. The facilitator noticed something was wrong as she handed me my pills.

"I'm very spiritual," she said. "I see spirits."

"I'm sorry, I've got to retch again," I said. I headed to a near window just in case I needed to throw up. After I was done, she said, "I saw two spirits leave you. Two things just zapped out of you right now."

Oh, shit.

"Oh well, you don't need a priest now, do you?" she said, and chuckled, and walked off.

Great! I've had a bit of a breakthrough! Fantastic!

Another time I asked another facilitator about the dry retching.

"Your body … knows," she said. "It knows that you've been hurt, somehow, even if your mind has forgotten."

It was amazing that someone, finally, was affirming that regardless of whether or not the abuse had happened to me, it didn't matter, because it was real to me, because my *body* knew.

The suicidal thoughts started up again, but I didn't want to kill myself, it was just the thoughts and they went away after a few days.

After weeks of this treatment I returned home for Christmas and for the first weeks of 2018 – not because I felt truly better, but because Christmas was Christmas.

For some reason I got it into my head to acquire an Electro-Magnetic Field (EMF) detector specially designed and calibrated for ghost hunting, to see if I could detect spiritual entities. Quietly in my study at home, I turned on the machine and the meter and display read, *Spirit Detected.*

Friend.

Reading accuracy 95%.

But then I freaked out and started dry retching. I started panicking again, furious at myself because I felt like I had just undone all the work that had taken weeks at the rehab center. I threw the machine away.

I went back to rehab. The facilitator didn't know what to say to me. I went onto my anti-psychotic medication again. I stayed another week in rehab, which completed my treatment program.

On the night before I was due to fly back home, something extraordinary happened.

By now I was used to being clairsapient, or claircognizant – acquiring psychic wisdom or knowledge through thoughts, through simply "knowing" things, but I was about to experience the next level of that ability.

I was lying in bed and I felt my eardrums throbbing, stretching and a thought came into my head from what felt like another plane of existence in what I now call "a reading".

I know you can hear me. I'm Elaine. Everything's going to be all right.

Okaaaay …

I want you to verify my name with your mother tomorrow, when she picks you up at the airport. I'm Elaine, and I'm your great grandmother – your mother's, mother's mother.

Even though I knew such a woman had to have existed, no one had ever spoken to me about her, much less given me her name.

I was stunned, but what was one more paranormal event in a lifetime peppered with them?

So, when I did go to the airport to meet with my mother …

"You know I've been on this anti-psychotic medication, right?" I said.

"Yes," she said with that tone in her voice that implied that she was preparing to hear more craziness from her youngest son.

"But," I continued, "I can't help but feel that something deeper is going on than just a 'mental health issue'."

"OK."

"And I really want to see a priest."

"Oh, Paul, not again …"

"I know that last time I saw one you think it was a disaster."

"Yes, but …"

"I need you to support me. I need you to believe in me," I pressed on. "Do you back me?"

She paused, in the way that mothers do in these cases, when they realize that they have to do what they can to help their children. "Of course, I'll back you," she said, "I'm your mother."

"OK," I said.

"But at least let's see if you can see a priest in a controlled environment because the last time didn't seem to do much good," she said.

"OK."

"And I want to look much further into this mental health thing because I think we need to change your psychiatrist. I'm not sure that the one that you've got is any good."

"OK." I said. "By the way, Mum …"

"Yes?"

"Who's 'Elaine'?" I asked.

"The only 'Elaine' that comes to mind was my grandmother, your great-grandmother. Why?"

"She spoke to me last night."

My mother looked at me with her "My son's gone crackers" expression. You'd know the look if your mother's ever thought you'd gone crackers.

"No, Mum, you've got to believe me." I continued. "She spoke to me last night and said that 'Everything's going to be all right.'"

"You're hearing voices in your head again. Oh great!"

"It's not like that. It's more like a … knowing. I just … know."

"OK," she said. In that tone of voice that says, 'I give up.'

And then we got on with the business of flying back home.

I went to a confession box at the Catholic parish of St Francis on the corner of Lonsdale and Elizabeth Street in the heart of Melbourne CBD. I asked for help. Through the window grating that separates the priest from the penitent I could see the priest looking at me strangely. He did some basic prayers which did absolutely fuck all and again and let me go.

We did manage to find yet another priest. I gave him a brief sketch.

"I don't know what you're talking about," he said. "I've never really dealt with anything like this before."

Great.

"Well, do you know anyone who does?" I asked.

"No. But tell you what, see me next week."

This guy isn't really filling much confidence. He's probably just going to say some prayers over the top of my head, sprinkle me with Holy Water and send me on my way, with a "You'll be right!".

"Um … OK … I'll think about it and ring you back if I decide to take this further."

What are these people on? Their whole lives are supposed to be about helping people, especially about spiritual stuff and this attitude is just unbelievable. Vow of poverty notwithstanding, how do they justify their paychecks? How do they justify their collars? How do they justify their existence? Do they think their job is to just stand in front of a quarter-filled church (if they're lucky!) on a Sunday, droning on and waving wafers around?

And at that point I decided that there was only one person I trusted enough to know that he knew what he was doing, and that was Joseph.

Bugger it. I'm going to see Joseph again.

I went back to Joseph. I was scared, but by now I'd recovered quite a lot.

At least Joseph was happy to see me.

I didn't feel abandoned and he didn't hesitate to help me.

But even then it was three steps forward, two steps back.

So we started the whole process again. Same reaction as last time. The same ol' drill. Dry retching, spinning out, zoning out. I even started speaking in tongues.

This was an extremely intense session. No walk in the park, not by any means.

Initially, nothing was budging. I could feel something inside me *decidedly not budging*.

In the privacy of my own mind I found myself praying to St Michael and the Virgin Mary for help, for their intercession.

Then Joseph, without knowing what I was thinking, and I assume acting on the same knowledge, called out aloud to The Holy Spirit, and in that moment a malevolent "voice" spoke to me and "said":

NOW YOU'RE GOING TO GET IT.

All Hell broke loose. Literally.

As I felt a break in the energy, for the first time the dry retching turned into a fully-fledged vomit.

Something, whatever was in me, had broken. I felt 'it' come out.

I felt afterwards that now, finally I could get on with my life.

I was fine. I wasn't drinking. I had not touched a drop since rehab. I got my diet under control. I lost a lot of weight.

At the direction of the rehab center as part of the aftercare program I contacted Alcoholics Anonymous, just to be sure that I wouldn't get back into drinking. But the idea of getting up in front of a group of people and telling them that you were defective for the rest of your life and the only one who could save you was God didn't work for me. I categorically *refused* to believe that "Once an alcoholic, always an alcoholic." I didn't want to become an AA groupie, addicted to a false sense of security that this group of dysfunctional people were providing, dependent on meetings that if they didn't happen would turn you into a wreck again.

Again, there was an inner knowing that there *had to be an end* to the process. After all, you're either free or you're not free. I'm the sort of person who needs *closure*. As compulsive as I am, and as obsessive as I can get, even though I tend to go over the same ground over and over and over again, at some point, *I have to stop*. Hypocritically and ironically, I have no patience when other people go over the same ground again and again because it reminds me too much of myself and it's bad enough when *I* do it. When I sat in an AA meeting and realized that I'd heard the *same fucking story* from the *same fucking person* for about the *fortieth time*, I just couldn't do it anymore.

Things finally came to a head when I asked my sponsor, "What is the point of me listening to the same guy tell the same story and crack the same joke, when I'm not allowed to tell *my* story or grow from articulating *my* experience?"

"You need to learn the ways of AA before you can do that. We don't let anyone share their story until they've been with us at least a year," he said. I just looked at him and huffed. He must have sensed something in me and continued, "Look. I don't think this is working. I don't want to be your sponsor anymore."

I felt relieved. "That's OK. I don't want you to be my sponsor anymore either. I'm done with this. I'll leave you with your little addiction to AA," and I left the conversation and never saw the guy again.

On the spiritual side, at the beginning of 2018 I felt that we were finally getting somewhere, I still didn't quite feel that my soul was safe, but the rest of that year passed without incidence. I went to Joseph a couple of times for a 'top up'. Dry heaving was my sign that things were bad, but in subsequent Deliverances there was no excessive dry heaving and no more actual vomiting, so there was no sense of urgency on my part.

Then I had a MAJOR breakthrough.

During one of the Deliverances with Joseph, I got a reading from The Holy Spirit.

Through that reading, God showed me that demons had implanted, in my mind, the childhood abuse scenario that had haunted me for so long. The demons had exploited a weakness with exquisite precision and timing.

My recollection is only hazy. But the demons had exploited a time in my childhood when I was generally feeling unsafe and very, very vulnerable. There are unrelated events that happen often enough in anybody's childhood, events that you usually get over – a parent being angry with you, being unfairly treated by a teacher, even a movie that you shouldn't have been watching that later gave you an nightmare or two. But the demons had manipulated and distorted my memories, conflating and exaggerating unrelated events so that the events had come together, much more traumatically than the sum of their parts. They constructed a vision to manifest with the help of a little … malign intervention.

Somehow, in all this time, I had never revealed this to anyone, even to myself, so neither me nor anyone else had ever put two and two together.

Except the demons *had*.

This reinforced yet again that the Devil and the demons will use any opening, any opportunity, to exploit a vulnerability.

It was all … diabolical.

And it had taken a Deliverance process to uncover this trauma and heal me of it.

Deliverance had worked where hours and hours and thousands of dollars of conventional therapy had completely failed. It's really important to know this if you or someone you love is experiencing something that psychiatry and psychotherapy are failing to treat, that Deliverance might be an answer that will work for you.

Understanding the mechanics of the "trauma abuse implant" had brought me great peace.

I was out of PTSD. I cannot describe how incredibly healed I felt about this aspect of my affliction – the enormous … *relief.*

Of this haunting nightmare, I had been truly delivered.

It was now New Year's Eve, 2018.

So, I had a beer, didn't I?

That beer turned into four beers.

The next day I had another four beers … and the next day … and the next day …

It took me until April to realize, "Hmmm. This is a pattern."

And I had to admit to myself that I had a drinking problem, even though I refused to label myself as an alcoholic. After all, AA was always telling me that alcoholics couldn't stop once they started, whereas my pattern was that yes, I could stop, I could say "no" after four beers, but I still had to drink *every day*. In that sense, I couldn't stop, but I believe, to this day, that I wasn't *addicted* to alcohol, so much as I was *alcohol dependent*, in the same way that I was prescription-medication dependent, because of an underlying problem.

Amazingly, the childhood trauma abuse scenario started playing in my head, yet again. Not nearly as traumatic as before but …

Oh for fuck's sake.

So in mid-2019 I went back into rehab.

But by this time the staff had changed over completely. I expected to have a safe haven, but I was an outsider again. The culture of the center had changed, and I couldn't settle. The OCD started up again.

The anti-psychotic I was on, that I had been on for over a year, was known to have weight gain and low sex drive as a side effect, and the new psychiatrist there changed my medication again. He was amazed that I had been on that type of anti-psychotic for so long, it was only meant to be a *short-term* treatment.

Unfortunately, the new anti-psychotic was completely ineffective. My OCD was going through the roof, the same old repetitive, obsessive thoughts and feelings were driving me crazy and now I had this feeling that I had to constantly defend myself. Every time someone would get physically close to me, I felt I had to distance myself because they were either going to hurt me, or I was going to hurt them.

The staff and I weren't getting along at all. I didn't feel stable and I didn't trust that I could tell the people there what my thoughts or problems were. I lasted all of two weeks.

Strike one.

I tried my hand at AA again. Didn't understand it. Didn't work. Left again.

Strike two.

After five weeks of further sobriety I started drinking again.

Strike three.

I went back on to the old anti-psychotic again, just *because*, and I drank my way through the rest of the year at a steady average of four beers a day, six on a Sunday. Fortunately, it was nothing like last time, and the beers were spaced out over four or five hours.

I guess I was making *some* progress???

And I was functional! You could at least say that! My business thrived.

In October 2019 I did make an attempt at abstinence. It lasted all of two weeks.

Strike four.

It was inevitable that I would fail because alcohol was still the only thing keeping the anxiety away. There was an irony to this. I developed a phobia about letting the alcohol get out of hand, so if I found myself "getting drunk" I'd get a panic attack and stop drinking.

Then my psychiatrist told me that she was retiring from her private practice and that she'd no longer be able to look after me. She didn't refer me to anyone else, but suggested I talk to my GP again. So I did and I started seeing a new psychiatrist.

In our first meeting he conducted a new assessment and ascertained that I was not psychotic, I had never been psychotic, that the medication I had been on was totally unsuitable and that I should *stop taking it immediately*.

The dose I was on was doing nothing anyway, he said that being on 0.5 of a milligram was unusual and *totally ineffective*. He himself would normally prescribe four to six milligrams of risperidone for a psychotic case – eight to twelve times the dose I was taking. Even more importantly, that particular drug was incredibly outdated and was rarely used anymore.

Then he proceeded to give me a background on my former psychiatrist and said, "OK. Let me guess. She's a GP or has a GP background and is in her mid-fifties"

My former psychiatrist had in fact been a GP for many years before switching and becoming a psychiatrist. This was totally accurate and my new psychiatrist had based his analysis on the dose I was on, the type of drug and the age of the drug which apparently many GPs prescribe because they are out of touch with today's treatments.

"I think you have a strong case for suing for malpractice," he said.

Oh, great. Just fucking great.

"Well, thank-you for validating me," was all I could say. But at least I had some sense of relief.

"I do, however, think, in my professional opinion, that you have an OCD disorder and I'm going to prescribe a standard anti-depressant."

So, my relief didn't last, but at least I had finally, *finally* got an accurate diagnosis at least as far as the psychiatric and psychological component of my condition was concerned.

"I'm also really concerned about your weight gain and alcohol consumption, and I have to warn you that if this goes on you'll be dead before you're fifty."

Wow. No one can say that you pull your punches, Doc.

In the face of this sort of wakeup call about not only my mental and emotional health, but also my physical health, I realized that I had to do something soon. I didn't want to die.

In and around January 2020, I went back to Joseph, this time, for good.

If I hadn't known before, I was finally beginning to wake up to the reality that in my current state of mind, state of heart, state of soul, state of being, I was my own worst enemy.

So my primary motivation for returning to Joseph was simply that I'd had enough of the drinking, and I was aware that, for better or worse, the only thing besides alcohol that had been able to alleviate the anxiety had been the prayer sessions and prayer was a far better alternative than destroying myself with beer.

So, ironically, the chain of events that would ultimately lead to my lasting Deliverance came about not because I had sought Deliverance in and of itself, but as a side effect of seeking Joseph out to liberate me from the hold that alcohol had on me, to break that hold.

And though I didn't know it at that time, this is where the real Exorcisms took place

This is where my real Deliverance finally began, where the deeply embedded demons *could* finally be dealt with, *would* finally be dealt with.

But by now, the pendulum had swung back again, and I thought that my primary problem was the alcoholism.

And so it came to pass that in one of the great ironies of this whole sad saga, I went back to Joseph, not for Deliverance, but because I needed to stop being alcohol-dependent through a fault not entirely my own.

Some of us are born into Deliverance, some of us aspire to perform Deliverance.

It would turn out that I would have to have Deliverance thrust upon me.

CHAPTER THIRTEEN

LETTING THE DEMONS IN

"So, we seek out something, anything, that replaces what we've lost."

Joseph

The afflicted come to me almost always not understanding what is happening to them, or how they got to be the way they are. There are many ways of explaining Spiritual Affliction.

Sometimes you have to explain things in several different ways before people finally get it.

Spiritual Affliction occurs either through deliberate or accidental "invitation", or opportunistically through some act of violation or some trauma.

It is useful to think of the parallels between physical illness and spiritual illness.

Your physical integrity and health depend on a sound physical structure and a sound immune system. If you don't wash your hands or practice basic hygiene, or if you are wounded, and the wound is left untreated, you leave yourself open to infection by bacteria, viruses or other poisons.

These agents of infection make you sick because they feed off you in one way or another, using you as nourishment to reproduce, weakening you further and making you less capable of fighting them off. If they don't kill you, they are parasitic. If they have no restraint, they are predatory, and they will ultimately kill you.

If you don't have a strong immune system the infection can take over your body, invading and spreading and wreaking havoc which in extreme cases *will* be fatal.

Similarly, your spiritual integrity and health depend on a sound spiritual structure and, for want of a better term, a strong "spiritual immune system" – a strong connection with The Holy Spirit, the Source from which all existence and all spiritual health, or holiness, derives. If there is a "natural entry point" to your soul, or if you are wounded psychically – and by this I mean you are traumatized mentally or emotionally – then that trauma creates a violation of your psychic integrity and leaves you open to spiritual infection. In the case of Spiritual Affliction, the "infectious agents" are Satan, demons, evil spirits or entities or negative energies – however it is that you want to think of them. Although I must stress that there is a difference between a malevolent energy, which is not sentient, and an entity, which is.

Unlike bacteria and viruses, diabolical entities are conscious beings that are predatory or parasitic and are attracted to the "smell" of psychic injury in the same way that a shark might be attracted to the smell of blood seeping from an open wound in the water. As conscious, sentient entities, with malicious intent and an agenda for destruction they can inflict considerable damage. Like physical infections, they feed off you, particularly your fear, to the point where they might, if left untreated, also ultimately kill you.

But unlike physical infections, where the infection dies with the host, demonic entities are immortal, so they can kill you at no great cost to themselves, unless we intervene.

This makes them even more dangerous, because they have no *restraint*.

Your spiritual immune system is strong when the conscious connection between yourself and The Holy Spirit is strong. Sin, or spiritual error, compromises that conscious connection leaving you diminished in your capacity to fight off a spiritual infection if it occurs. Demons can invade, encouraging you to sin even further, creating more compromises to your integrity and allowing the infection to become worse and creating further damage, and on and on it goes, in a reinforcing downward spiral of ever-greater degradation.

Invitation and Trauma

There are natural entry points in the body that can grant access to disease. Obvious ones are the mouth, the ears, the genitals. Although these entry points have their own defenses, these points are easily compromised if you fail to practice simple hygiene, like washing your hands regularly, or keeping a neat house.

In spiritual terms, our natural entry points are our psychology, our general state of being, and our free will.

If we make bad decisions out of ignorance or worse, anger, pettiness, spitefulness and unforgiveness, we open the door to bigger trouble. If we deny our spiritual source of power, we invite even bigger trouble.

Amazing as it might seem to me, from all I know, some people, in and of their own free will, motivated by greed or laziness or both, actually send out an invitation to demonic forces to "cut a power deal".

In other cases, the entry point is trauma, either self-inflicted or other-inflicted. The trauma creates a psychic wound that leaves the door open for Spiritual Infestation and the resulting manifestations of spiritual sickness. One particularly vulnerable entry point is sexual abuse, because sexuality requires exposure of the self. Sex is fundamentally intimate, no matter what people who treat sexuality casually might tell themselves. As you can imagine, dealing with spiritual afflictions caused by sexual abuse requires considerable sensitivity, perhaps more so than any other type of affliction because the entities that exploit sexual abuse are among the most malicious of all.

Spiritual Affliction as an Opportunistic Infection

Demons are fundamentally *opportunists*. If there is a way in, they *will* find it, and if they find a way in, they *will* cause the maximum havoc that they can. They can't help themselves. They are the agents of chaos.

They are, in a sense, *the adversaries of spiritual integrity.*

You are already familiar with the idea of an opportunistic infection, if you are familiar with HIV and AIDS.

The parallel between Spiritual Affliction and AIDS is actually quite striking.

In the disease process of AIDS there is at first, some form of trauma, some break in the protective skin of the body that allows entry to the Human Immuno-Deficiency Virus (HIV) through body fluids. The HIV then attacks your immune defense system, doing what it can to kill the army that's protecting you from disease.

If the attack, *the infiltration*, of the HIV is successful – and it almost always is – cells that are vital to your immune defense are compromised and you have now Acquired the Immuno-Deficiency Syndrome (AIDS). Your immune system is now *deficient.* With the defensive army gone, the barbarians can invade, and unusual, weird and downright rare diseases that normally wouldn't stand a chance in a healthy person can make real trouble for you – diseases like candidiasis, toxoplasmosis or cancers like Kaposi's sarcoma.

Spiritual "infections" work in the same way. Sloppy spiritual hygiene, a conscious invitation, or some trauma – violence, violation or abuse happens. This then weakens your conscious awareness of your spiritual connection with God. You effectively deny the source of your spiritual well-being.

Because our connection to God IS our life, when we lose it our true self, our soul craves the lost connection in the same way that a tree would crave the loss of rainfall and sunlight.

We begin to wilt.

We begin to suffer.

We wither.

From this perspective, we can define suffering as a disconnection from our divine source.

It is a terrible, terrible feeling. I think it is the worst feeling you can have. All the afflicted whom I have ever dealt with speak of the suffering that they undergo – the suffering of losing their conscious connection with The Holy Spirit. That alienation, that *loss*, is intolerable.

So, we seek out something, *anything,* that replaces what we've lost. In the absence of our awareness of the true nourishment that comes from The Holy Spirit, we will seek "nourishment" from sex or co-dependent relationships or alcohol or other drugs or gambling or money or power – *anything* to take away the pain of our lost connection. But seeking false nourishment from earthly dysfunctional things is futile. It's like substituting the nourishment and healing qualities of a spoonful of honey dissolved in warm milk with a mixture of chalk and water sweetened with saccharine. Yes, it's white, and sweet, but it is empty of any capacity to truly feed you.

All diseases like a particular environment, like the way that mold likes the damp and the dark. It is in just these spiritually deprived environments that demonic forces thrive. They *want* to continue to cut you off from awareness of your source, so that you will seek "nourishment" from them. This too is an illusion. They have no interest in nourishing you.

Their only interest is in nourishing themselves.

Demons are first and foremost parasitic.

They feed off your suffering, without killing you.

At least at first.

It is my professional opinion that demons feed off your spiritual energy so they can feel some pathetic echo, no matter how faint, *of the spiritual connection that they themselves have lost.* Because for all their violence, for all their illusion of power, demons are about as dead as any sentient being can be and still function. Demons crave life. Although their pride would never let them admit this to themselves, they feel the loss of their conscious connection to the Source of The Holy Spirit more than any human could. At their core, they feel dead inside. They want to feel alive and since the only energy they can ever feed off is born of pain then pain is what they feed off.

Any pain will do, including the pain of fear that comes from mental, emotional and physical illness.

They will squeeze every last drop of pain from you. And when they are almost done with you, they become predatory, they will kill you, condemning you to your own Hell – in the way that they themselves have condemned themselves to Hell.

Therefore, for the purposes of our discussion, Hell is more than just a place, it is a state of being, where you believe that you are so separate from your source that in the deepest despair you can no longer even cry out for help.

Hell is a state of being where you are so weakened, so disconnected, that it is almost impossible for you to deliver yourself from it. By the time you reach the point of Hell, you can only be delivered from it through Grace.

Yes, you *can* experience Hell on earth, even without dying.

Spiritual Affliction is as close to Hell as any of us would ever want to get.

While it is indeed possible to have a sex, drug, gambling or power addiction that is entirely psychological, and it is indeed possible to have a mental, emotional or somatic illness that is entirely physical, we should not automatically dismiss a *spiritual* origin or root cause for these diseases. If we do, we run the risk of treating the symptoms – the drug, sex, money gambling or power addiction – not the disease itself.

Of course, we should always eliminate conventional, material explanations first. Spiritual Intervention is not a step that should be undertaken lightly. Spiritual Intervention into a problem that is not spiritual to begin with is potentially dangerous, and psychologists, psychiatrists and mental health professionals are justified in their concern that any sort of spiritual treatment could make a matter which is purely somatic, psychological or psychiatric worse. If badly handled, a clumsy or ignorant spiritual intervention can perpetuate the trauma and the condition the intervention was supposed to deal with in the first place.

But it is equally harmful to dismiss the possibility of spiritual causes too. I think, that at the very least, we should suspect a deeper cause, especially in cases where conventional treatments have consistently failed, when we have tried "everything" and nothing has ultimately worked. In many cases we should look into spiritual intervention in those cases where there is perhaps, little to lose and everything to gain.

Historically, Spiritual Affliction has not always been handled well, or methodically, or intelligently. The phenomena associated with Spiritual Affliction and its manifestations are complex, with many subtleties.

In its usual usage the word "possession" is simplistic, inaccurate and therefore largely misleading.

This is why I prefer to use the term "Spiritual Affliction Syndrome" to describe the full spectrum of causes and manifestations of Spiritual Affliction – SAS.

Conditions that Create the Opportunity for Spiritual Affliction

There are a number of paths to the Hell that is long-term Spiritual Affliction and the development of Spiritual Affliction Syndrome.

The list below is by no means exhaustive, but it should give you an idea of how you can get into trouble.

Psychic Hygiene and Vulnerability

What you experience spiritually is the result of the state of being that you are in. Some people have fallen into the habit of negativity, and negativity begets negativity. Some people are just, by their nature or habit, naturally more susceptible to creating in themselves a state that is conducive to SAS. This is especially true if they already have a strong connection to the realm of the spirit, but they have not or will not acknowledge that connection or learn to use it in a positive way.

It might sound unlikely, but some people can open the door to Spiritual Affliction just by watching horror movies.

Some people can watch horror movies with impunity. They are perhaps cynical or detached or they are simply not psychologically susceptible to being placed in a state of fear or psychic vulnerability through horror movies.

But for others, horror movies lull them into a state of psychic vulnerability. I have delivered people through the power of The Holy Spirit that invited on themselves the spirit of fear just by watching horror movies. Satan can use those movies to masquerade himself. Sometimes after watching the movies, you start to experience strange things happen in your dreams and on the other hand, you can even feel the literal "presence of someone with you".

It is the same with pornography. Some people can watch pornography with impunity. For others it can become the entry point of sexual obsession where you lose all interest in a real, wholesome sexual relationship with a committed partner. What you need to know is that Satan uses these movies, videos or magazines to seduce your mind into creating obsessive sexual images or open the door to demons having sex with you to destroy your capacity to have a normal, fulfilling sex life.

It is the same with other things, like placing bizarre religious images in our homes. Many religious images have a spirit attached to them. Idols can be infested with demons. A key point here is understanding that in order to seduce you, it helps if demonic entities can get your attention, and idols, religious symbols, statues and icons provide focal points for attention, from which demons can begin to focus their dark magic.

Cemeteries are areas where evil spirits live because these are solitary places frequented by people whose personalities might predispose them to focusing on grief – pain again – or morbid thoughts – more pain. In fact any place where there is a lot of pain, like trauma centers, clinics, and hospitals, are candy stores to demons. Culturally, the West is very good at physical hygiene, but almost totally negligent in the realm of psychic hygiene. Delivering "places" of Infestation could be a specialist area in and of itself.

Yet even something as innocent as seashores and rivers have from time to time been identified as places where evil spirits are present. Any place where energy flows, like flowing water, can attract the unwary – a sort of spiritual "honey trap".

Once again, some people have religious idols in their homes and they are nothing more than pieces of wood or stone, nothing more that unusual objects – conversation pieces. Some people can walk through cemeteries and feel and be perfectly fine. Some people are immune to haunted houses, no matter how haunted. These people simply aren't susceptible.

However …

If you have items, idols, images that you are not sure about, or you have noticed something strange in your house or business place or personal life and something just feels off, don't continue to keep that idol around. It doesn't even have to be an idol. It could be some perfectly innocent looking thing. Sometimes the objects are perfectly ordinary. I have been in homes where people got an object from a garage sale and that object was invested with demons who almost destroyed their lives. I began by saying prayers for the occupants. Then I had to cleanse their whole home of the Infestation. It was through the process of discernment that The Holy Spirit revealed to me that all their trouble originated in that one object. Having exorcised it, I destroyed it and since that time their lives got back to normal.

The take-home message is this: It is important to recognize your points of vulnerability. Some people can walk through a field of flowers and think, "Oh, what pretty flowers!" Others walk through that same field and have an allergic reaction so bad that it kills them. Some people can drink alcohol in moderation and think nothing of it. Some people can't even smell alcohol without wanting to binge because they are alcoholics.

It is vitally important to recognize where you might be vulnerable, idiosyncratically vulnerable, to being spiritually compromised or attacked.

Often you don't know if you are vulnerable, until you are attacked. Unfortunately there is no "spiritual allergy sensitivity test" that can tell you beforehand if you are vulnerable. At least not yet. Developing one is potentially an important priority of future research – the "to do" list of things that need to drag Deliverance into the 21st century grows ever-longer.

In the meantime, you can simply practice awareness and ask for guidance. Pay attention to how you feel in certain circumstances, in certain places and around certain things or people.

What is your heart telling you?

What is your gut instinct?

In the privacy of your own mind ask The Holy Spirit for insight, and then listen as The Holy Spirit nudges you through your intuition. Act on Divine Inspiration and Advice, even if it seems irrational. This develops and strengthens your spirit and with it, your own discernment. If in doubt, seek professional help.

Whether you are susceptible or not, there are, however, circumstances that are potentially *dangerous to everyone.*

Some things are poisonous, *no matter who you are.*

Personal Sin

The origin of the word "sin" in English is complicated and interesting. It might ultimately be ancient in origin and might be connected to a legal formula in the ancient Hittite language in which a guilty person confesses to wrongdoing by "it is being" as in "it is being a transgression". This in turn might have originated in the even more ancient language of Proto-Indo-European through a word reconstructed by linguists – *synt-ya – meaning "becoming". Through a long history of mixed association a word that originally meant "being" came to mean "it is true that I have offended" and in Proto-Germanic – one of the root languages of English – "*sundio" meaning "trespass" became the Old English "synn" meaning "moral wrongdoing or injury and "syngian" meaning "to commit a sin".[1]

In other languages the concept is equally ancient but has a different emphasis. "Peccare" in Latin, meaning to sin, originally had the meaning of "missing the mark" as in when you shoot an arrow and miss your target. This is in parallel to the Hebrew word chait, which is usually translated as "sin", but which also means "to miss the mark".

In the Book of Judges (20:16), slingers from the tribe of Benjamin are described as being so good with their weapon that they can "aim at a hair and not chait." This makes sense only if you translate "chait" as "miss the mark".[2]

No matter how you look at it, the idea of "sin" is historically inextricable from the idea of missing the mark. And when we sin, we do indeed "miss the mark". We miss our mark on the path of maintaining our spiritual integrity, which is the only path that can

---

1 Online Etymological Dictionary.
2 Aish.com.

reliably lead us to fulfilling ourselves as spiritual beings – of beings of any description for that matter.

Of course, many will debate what constitutes "sin", and what is considered "sin", in one cultural or religious context might not be considered "sin" in another. As a Christian, I can only say that some things like murder, rape, abuse, deception for gain, theft, exploitation and other violations of the integrity of others are *obviously* sins and *obvious* entry points for Spiritual Infestation.

It is important, however, to acknowledge that there is no sin without the possibility of repentance and redemption. The word "repentance" has its origin in Latin words for "regret" and "to make sorry". The "pen" in "repent" comes from the same root as "penal" – punishment for transgression.[3]

But to me "repentance" isn't just a *feeling*, it is *a feeling that you have to act upon*. True repentance only happens when you make a conscious decision to change the path of your life as a result of what repentance made you feel.

Feeling something without making a change is worthless.

This brings us to "redemption".

"Redemption" ultimately means to "take back" in the sense of "releasing from debt"[4] Thus it is through the recognition of sin and regretting of sin, that one can be released from the debt of sin and it is this acknowledgment of regret that opens the path to restitution.

Soul Ties

A soul tie is an unhealthy, dysfunctional or abusive relationship which has spiritual ramifications. The integrity of the soul is inviolable

3 Online Etymological Dictionary.
4 Ibid.

because the spiritual link between the soul and The Holy Spirit is unbreakable. The soul tie fragments the soul from a healthy state to an unhealthy one.

However …

It is all too easy to sin, to miss the mark and to lose your conscious connection with that link.

Soul ties are "sinful" because they cause you to err, to lead you away from your conscious communion with The Holy Spirit. Soul ties are "unholy" because they distract you the true source of your spiritual power and make you "un-whole". And, as if this wasn't bad enough, soul ties allow a gateway for Spiritual Infestation.

I once helped a young woman who was in a relationship with a man. This girl was a Christian, but she was treated like a doormat, abused and threatened almost every day by a man she "could not leave". Soul ties create an environment which allows one person to control and manipulate another. The controlled person might be unaware of what is going on or knows what is going on, but for reasons that are complex and not always straightforward, allows the control to continue. In either case, a negative soul-tied relationship diminishes *both* parties in a relationship.

Soul ties have their origin in an act of sin that then perpetuates itself in a downward spiral of self-degradation or mutual degradation. There are many ways soul ties can originate.

Unholy sexual relations are one example. A sexual relationship is "holy" when entered into between two people who are committed to each other's spiritual growth. This, for example, is one reason for the institution of marriage.

In contrast, "unholy" sexual relationships are characterized by exploitation, abuse and superficiality. When entered into too often, such relations fragment the soul. People who have many past exploitative relationships find it very difficult to 'bond' or be joined to anybody because the multiple soul ties of abuse remain.

Other soul ties are more exotic in origin. While uncommon in the West, in Asia or Africa the practice of Blood Covenants – contracts "sealed" through the blood sacrifice of an animal are an option for many people. I remember dealing with a girl who made a blood covenant with a boy to "be together forever for life". This turned out to be a complete illusion. The pair later separated, and although this girl was beautiful, hardworking, educated, and very respectful, each time she started a relationship it would just stop for no reason at all. This repeating pattern persisted until the Deliverance process brought this Blood Covenant out into the open. The covenant then had to be broken because the soul tie was still in place.

Soul ties need not be between two people. Addictions are examples of soul ties between a person and a substance or practice that degrades them. What might start as a purely psychological or emotional dependence can easily degrade into a physical dependence, which in turn further degrades into a spiritual matter as the addiction compromises the soul's spiritual connection. The addiction need not be to a chemical. One can become addicted to pornography, to sex, to money, to gambling, to power, to violence – the list goes on and on – and the existence of soul ties is well recognized and documented in the history of Deliverance and Exorcism.

Unholy Contracts

While a soul tie can be considered an unhealthy binding between two people or two "entities" of roughly equal power, an unholy contract or covenant exists between a human being of lesser power and an entity of greater power – or at least something *perceived* to be of a greater power.

Unholy contracts include, but are not limited to, the classic "deal with the Devil". The Devil, demon or evil spirit has some capacity that you perceive that you lack. You enter into a contract whereby the demon does something for you. Demons have no *real* power, but they do undeniably have influence, especially with the susceptible, and they have access to knowledge. They use their knowledge and influence in order "to grease the wheels" and "to clear a path" for things to happen, like "facilitating" a business decision or deal in your professional life, or "making" someone "fall in love with you." Then the demon claims the payment specified in the contract, like Paul's "I'll spend a year in Hell in exchange for money." In fact, Paul spent much more than a year in Hell.

But no matter what the deal, *it is always a bad deal.* You always end up paying through the soul for something that you perhaps should never have asked for in the first place, something that violates the Holy Covenants designed to maintain your spiritual integrity.

Unholy contracts all have a common origin. They come from a place of *perceived disempowerment.*

They come from failing to realize that all legitimate power comes from your connection to The Holy Spirit.

This failure might be the result of disappointment.

You didn't get what you wanted.

You have failed to realize that perhaps the reason that you didn't get what you wanted was because The Holy Spirit knew that *it would have been bad for you and there was something better waiting for you.*

But you, in your arrogant and egotistic pride, think that you know better than The Holy Spirit and you become *obsessed.*

You allow your ego to get in the way, and in your *pride,* you think, "Well, God failed me on this one! Time to look for power from elsewhere!"

So perhaps you try sorcery. You read a "magical" book where you read some instructions and follow directions. Or maybe you decide to "play" with a ouija board "for fun".

Nothing seems to happen at first, but you're already entangled. You will start having bad dreams that can sometimes be very vivid. Some of those dreams come with further clear instructions, for sacrifices, or for magical formulas to say, or places to go to invoke certain forces. You have left yourself wide open for Satan to assign evil spirits to keep giving you those instructions, waiting for you at those places of invocation. For most people, it can start off as fun, but little-by-little, your life comes off the rails and in the end the contract takes over your life. In my experience in the field of Deliverance, I have dealt with some complex issues where people almost lost their lives by just by reading a demonic book or fooling around with a Ouija board "for fun."

The cruel irony of all this is that there is nothing that Satan or the demons can do for you that you cannot have through communion with The Holy Spirit, who is the *true* source of all benefit. And that's just the point. Demons don't care about you. They'll say anything to give you the illusion that they are satisfying your limited ego with its limited perceptions of what the ego thinks would be good for you. Just because a child wants to eat a whole bag of candy doesn't mean that the child should. The Holy Spirit, on the other hand, like a loving parent, knows you better than you know yourself, knows what is truly good for you and would *never* violate you by pandering to your ego.

But this fundamental truth is lost on some souls, and they have to learn the hard way.

And some souls are so deluded that they'll sell out not only themselves, but generations that follow them too, in order to pay for the services of Satan Inc.

Ancestral and Familial Curses

One final point of vulnerability is the case of ancestral and familial curses.

These cases are like, say, genetic diseases that are passed down the generations. This might not seem fair. It might not seem fair that you can be spiritually afflicted, for example, as a child for a problem created by an ancestor that you might not even have known, and yet, in that sense, it is no more fair than when a child is suffering from spina bifida because the mother didn't have enough folic acid in her diet, or be born addicted to heroin because the mother was a heroin addict, or have cystic fibrosis because of a genetic mutation in an ancestor who lived five thousand years ago.

Fair or not – and that is a discussion for a whole other book – ancestral and familial curses are well recognized in the field of Spiritual Afflictions and they are another form of trauma or vulnerability that allow the demons opportunistic entry.

If someone has lost one or both of their parents as a result of alcohol or drug abuse it is easy for Satan to assign familial spirits to that person to deceive them into believing that they will also, *inevitably*, die in the same way. As a result of that deception, that person might find it easy to believe that they too are "cursed" and "destined" to become an alcoholic or a drug addict. This then becomes a self-fulfilling prophecy. The afflicted will start having unexplained panic-anxiety attacks but because the evil spirits have already built a stronghold in the mind of the person then the alcohol or drug becomes the only way of alleviating these panic attacks. It becomes hard for that individual to break from their "only source of relief" even as the "relief" is ruining their health and destroying their life. As the drug abuse escalates, the afflicted is less able to defend against further attack as the demons continue to manipulate them into taking their lives.

Soul ties, unholy contracts and ancestral and familial curses *can all be broken.*

The first step is to acknowledge that they exist, and that at some point they were created through some spiritual error or sin. Even without being able to discern specifically what the problem is, the mere intent to achieve liberation and to consciously strengthen your connection with The Holy Spirit is an excellent first step on the road to Deliverance and healing.

I tell you all this because it's important to know these things, because they are true, and the truth, if used properly, will set you, or someone you love, free.

I tell you all this because you would not have read this far if you did not have some investment in the subject, in every sense of the word.

But, most importantly, I tell you all this because what you are about to read will not make sense without some context.

You are about to read the accounts of Paul's final exorcisms and Deliverances, which took place in the first half of 2020, a year dominated by a plague, during which Paul had his own plagues to contend with.

Remember what you have already learned, while you read what follows.

CHAPTER FOURTEEN

DELIVERANCE

"I came to this body when his father hit him."

Joseph

I have already said that some people are more vulnerable, are more intrinsically susceptible to Spiritual Affliction than others.

If it is possible to inadvertently invite some form of Spiritual Affliction simply by watching an imaginative rendering of demonic activity in a horror movie, then how much more so is it possible to inadvertently invite affliction through actual exposure to a real-life exorcism.

I don't know of any vulnerabilities that you might have, but I have a duty of care for you, and I take that care very seriously.

So I will present this very sensitive material in two ways.

What follows is a summary of how a "typical" Deliverance or exorcism might go, with interjections on my part so that you can further understand what is going on and why I do the things I do.

Although I use Paul's name, this first example is a composite, taken from sessions with Paul, but from others as well. Think of this example as "Exorcism Lite". It should give you a good idea of how things progress from beginning to end in a nutshell.

In the interest of "psychic hygiene", I strongly suggest that you perform an act of prayer for Divine Protection before you read any further to invoke the protection of The Holy Spirit.

THIS IS WHAT DELIVERANCE LOOKS LIKE

We sit down on chairs, opposite each other.

I get him to look into my eyes.

"Repeat after me," I say, "'Holy Spirit. I allow you to enter me. I give you my body, my soul and my spirit. I give you absolute and total control of this time and of my life.'"

He does this.

"Repeat after me. 'I, Paul, am safe. I want my whole existence to know Jesus as Lord and to experience Jesus as Lord. From my birth to my now and to my forever I want to know Jesus as Lord.'"

He does this.

I need him to be spiritually focused. Even if he might not believe in Jesus, even if might not believe in God, the words provide enough consent for The Holy Spirit to enter and to do the work.

"We now divide soul and spirit and we bring your soul into the presence of the Lord."

And from this point I address the demonic forces inside him.

He goes into a trance-like state. He starts coughing, then dry retching, then collapses from the chair that he is sitting on and falls to the floor.

I have asked The Holy Spirit to protect me, so I am also safe.

I too am now in a state that is not like waking consciousness. I allow The Holy Spirit to enter me and work through me. I feel the Power, first subtly, then it grows ever stronger as we progress. the Power is unlike anything else. It is a paradox, it is a gentle rush that draws its strength from Divine Love. It is beautiful, almost painfully, achingly beautiful, and it requires some discipline not to fall into rapture at the expense of the work at hand.

"Holy Spirit, point your Divine Finger of Truth on Your servant. Reveal the truth to us."

With the knowledge that he is safe in the hands of The Holy Spirit, Paul now allows the demon to come through. The demonic personality takes over and speaks through him.

From the mouth of the afflicted a voice might issue.

"Get fucked" it says with an animal growl.

"In the name of Jesus I place you before the Throne of God."

The demon might scream at this point.

"I speak to you Demon! You cannot lie before the Throne. You cannot lie in the presence of God. If you do, we will bring judgment upon you and you will be cast down into fire."

I begin my interrogation.

"Demon! When did you first get into this body?"

"I HAVE BEEN HERE SINCE HE WAS TWO YEARS OLD," the demon says in its deep, growly voice. You can hear the pride and the arrogance in this voice. The tone is constantly saying "You weak, puny human! I have nothing but contempt for you." Even the more sophisticated, well-spoken and articulate demons with voices like honeyed butter manage to convey this prideful contempt.

"Do you have a legal right to be in this body?" I ask.

"YES," says the demon voice through Paul's mouth. "I HAVE A LEGAL RIGHT."

"What is the legal right?"

"I CAME TO THIS BODY WHEN HE WAS INJURED."

The violence opened a door for the demon to enter. There must be a *generational* contract – a *familial* contract, a cycle of violence that will be transmitted down the bloodline unless the contract is broken.

"Do you have any other spirits with you?"

"YES."

"How many?"

"WE ARE SEVENTEEN."

"What are you trying to achieve?"

"WE ARE HERE TO TORMENT HIM UNTIL HE KILLS HIMSELF."

"Have you caused any spiritual damage to this Child of God?"

"YES. WE HAVE CONVINCED HIM TO HATE GOD. NOT TO BELIEVE IN GOD. NOT TO SEEK HELP FROM GOD. TO BELIEVE THAT GOD HAS ABANDONED HIM."

"Have you caused any emotional damage?"

"YES. WE HAVE CREATED RESTLESSNESS WITHOUT CEASE. WE HAVE CREATED *DESPAIR*."

"Have you created mental damage?"

"YES. WE HAVE CREATED CONFUSION. HE NOW HAS TO TAKE MEDICATION."

The demon begins to laugh – a half "human" half "animal" sound.

"Have you caused physical damage?"

"YES. THE ALCOHOL HAS DAMAGED HIM."

"Where do you get your power from?"

"WE GET OUR POWER FROM THE DEVIL."

"Is there any other information that I need to perform this Deliverance?"

"YES. THIS PERSON DOES NOT WANT US TO GO BECAUSE WE BRING HIM MONEY THROUGH HIS BUSINESS."

This hidden information is very common. It could be any "benefit" that the demons provide as a result of the contract. It could be bringing "good luck". It could be that the demons help the person in sexual seduction. It is therefore vitally important to ask this question – that the demons must answer honestly under threat of torment – because unless these hidden forces are dealt with, there can be recurrence, or no effective Deliverance in the first place.

Often the "victim" is a willing participant. This is the classic "contract with the Devil" that has been depicted throughout history. Sometimes the reward is pathetically petty, like luck on the gambling tables. In rare cases the Deliverance stops here.

The afflicted, in such cases might take over, interrupting and saying, "That's enough. It's true. I now know why men / women desire me. I don't want them to go. I don't want to lose that."

In those rare moments I must step back, "I'm here to help you. But if you don't want my help, I can't force you."

They try to bargain with me. "Can't you just get rid of the other demons, and let me keep the ones who help me?"

"It doesn't work that way," I tell them. "You can't have it both ways. You can't have the 'pleasure' without the pain. There's no such thing as being 'semi-possessed'. It's like being 'slightly pregnant' or being 'half a gangster'. We either do this properly, or we don't. We don't do 'demon-lite' here."

When I say 'rare', this might happen in one or two cases in fifty. Still, two to four percent is still significant, when you think about it. Even more rarely, some of them later come back, when they realize how much they have given up for so little. And those who don't come back, or go to anyone else, that's sad, because I know that they're going to be destroyed and they might take their families with them or they will end up in Hell when they die, which is a much harder Hell than Hell-on-Earth. It's tragic when people don't look at life holistically, but I am powerless in the face of free will.

Even the otherwise omnipotent God is voluntarily powerless in the case of free will.

However, there is such a thing as the Gift of Grace.

The understanding of what Grace is, differs from denomination to denomination. But I see Grace as a *continuous* Gift of God – a gift that keeps on giving.

Grace is *always* there. The Holy Spirit always has gifts for you, paths open for you, support that you can rely on. Such Grace is vital in the process of defeating the Forces of Darkness. People, in their arrogance, narcissism and sense of entitlement, think that they can beat the Devil and the demons at their own game. Sometimes the price seems low, "I'll let you play inside me for a while". Sometimes the price is high, "I'll give you my unborn child to possess," or "I'll sacrifice a virgin to you", or "I'll sacrifice my sexual organs to you, after all, I don't want to get married or have a child, but I want power and wealth and lots of it, so feel free to make me impotent."

These contracts are not just theoretical examples. They are real. I have deal with the afflicted who have made such contracts.

Do you think that these stories of "deals with the Devil" are urban legends? Believe me, they happen, and much more often than you think. Western people, in the developed world, are often very sheltered. They live in a bubble. They often have no idea what is even going on in their own neighborhoods. Most certainly have no real idea of how pervasive demonic evil is in the rest of the world.

In their greed and lust for power, and in their arrogance, some try to negotiate a good deal with demonic forces, but this is truly naive. What limited human can compete against entities that are immeasurably old? What mortal can compete with that much experience and intelligence in human psychology, in human nature and human *vulnerability*? What man or woman can prevail against a system of such vast resources dedicated to and fueled by a sheer capacity for wickedness?

No matter what the deal is, *you cannot outwit the demons.* It is *always* a bad deal. You cannot cheat this game and you cannot win this game on your own. The only salvation will come through connecting to some higher power for good, whatever you call that power by – I choose to call that power the Grace of The Holy Spirit.

Fortunately, in most cases, wisdom prevails (no pun intended) and we continue with the process.

Having made a thorough investigation of the circumstances of the Affliction, I now must cancel the contracts and stop the demons' 'right of access.'

"Hear me demons! In the name of Jesus through the power of The Holy Spirit, I cancel all contracts and legal rights. I cancel the contract Paul made to spend time in Hell in exchange for money. Holy Spirit of the Living God, whatever contracts are in place I now nullify them through the Blood of Jesus Christ. Demons! In the Name of Jesus Christ, I bind you and I cast you out to the Pit!"

You can always tell by the reaction when the demons leave. There might be yelling and growling and screaming. There might be thrashing and writhing on the floor. There might be shaking and weeping and running around doing all sorts of crazy stuff. There might be vomiting and self-soiling, but these more extreme manifestations are rare because I ask The Holy Spirit that these external manifestations be kept to a minimum. This is especially important in the case of the afflicted who because of age or a medical condition, should not be writhing around on the floor screaming. And soiling yourself is not optimal no matter what your age.

An extreme manifestation is not necessarily a sign of the power of the demons or of the efficacy of the Deliverance. There are times, of course, when no matter how expert the Deliverer is that you will not be able to stop the demon from thrashing around and screaming. There are methods to minimize these manifestations even when they can't be avoided altogether. However, I should point out that if all the Deliverances performed by an exorcist are always so dramatic it might indicate that the Deliverer is inexperienced or does not know what they are doing and that they are operating under their own power and a low level of spiritual authority rather than allowing The Holy Spirit to act through them freely.

However, when a Deliverance is done properly then the demons know the game is up and staying is no longer in their best interests. The Holy Spirit is the highest authority in existence and trumps everything. The Holy Spirit is a superweapon, but like all superweapons, must be used judiciously.

"I set the body of this Child of God in the Light of Truth, in the Light of The Holy Spirit."

And in the Light of The Holy Spirit the spiritual body of the afflicted is subjected to something like an X-ray that reveals the truth and simultaneously burns the spiritual sickness out of the afflicted. The process is analogous to a combination of a three-in-one shot of accurate medical imaging, radiation therapy and chemotherapy against cancer, only in this case it is a cancer of the spirit.

This process can be short, or long. I usually budget around an hour for this. One hears horror stories of Deliverances or Exorcisms that go on for hours and hours, but I consider this to be spiritual malpractice. The afflicted can only take so much at time. Weakening the mind and body through excessive exertion does no good to anyone. If the deliverer or exorcist does not know what they are doing they can go so far as to drive the afflicted mad from the sheer violence of the demonic manifestations. This is like allowing a patient to die on the operating table because sufficient precautions have not been taken.

This is why I ask the afflicted to make a declaration of safety, of allowing every part of them to experience Jesus and His Love.

Think of this as spiritual anesthesia.

"Holy Spirit, fill this, your Child, with your light and presence."

Finally, the afflicted quietens down and that is the end of that particular Deliverance for now.

The operation has been performed; the rats have been expelled from the building and in their place the gaps left behind are filled with the invited presence of the divine. The gaps have now been filled and the demons can no longer gain entry.

The afflicted is now maybe 'the formerly afflicted', I say 'maybe' because as I have said often enough, it is rare that this process takes place only once. Usually, multiple operations are needed. The average is about a dozen times. This might seem like a lot, but you have to understand that I seldom see people until their spiritual illness has progressed to quite an advanced stage and that there are often other mental, physical and social health issues that have emerged as a result of spiritual affliction, or that existed before, which is why the spiritual affliction happened in the first place.

We might have to do this five, ten, twenty, fifty times if the wounds are deep and the infection has gone rampant. I repeat, Deliverance is like surgery. We can't do this all at once because the experience takes its toll on the mind, the heart and the body. Even though Deliverance is a healing treatment, it can be extraordinarily demanding on the afflicted. Deliverance, especially in very serious cases, requires time and a lot of support. The afflicted must maintain their spiritual connection. The prayer must continue so that the soul can remove their focus from their sickness and continue to focus on their spiritual integrity.

But at least for the moment, after an operation of Deliverance, the afflicted is at peace. They might be tired or even exhausted, but people usually say that after Deliverance they feel *lighter*, they feel relieved.

And now comes the sometimes-long process of restoration.

But that is a whole other subject.

CHAPTER FIFTEEN

DELIVERANCE THRUST UPON HIM

"While it's very hard for me to remember what happened exactly, I recall there were two battles. The first battle was for my soul. But the second battle was for my life." – Paul

Joseph

Compiling the information from which these accounts were written took over a year. Key to an understanding of the Deliverance process were actual recordings of sessions. These were made sporadically over a period of eight months in the year 2020. The recordings were made for the reference of the participants as part of the process of Paul Harrington's ongoing treatment for his severe Spiritual Affliction. These recordings are, for want of a better way of putting it, "clinical documents", they were not intended to be source material for a book. As such, the quality of the recordings was not the best, not all Deliverance sessions were recorded and what recordings we have are incomplete. What did survive however provides a unique insight into the process of dealing with the most severe case of affliction that I have ever dealt with so far. The edited excerpts below are as accurate as they can be and if you note any mistakes in language it is because the participants are in an altered state of consciousness, akin to being in hypnosis or in a waking dream. Accurate grammar and word usage isn't exactly a priority when you're in that state of mind.

Please note that the edited transcripts below represent only a small selection of over five hours of recordings that have survived. These recordings themselves captured only a fraction of what must have been over a hundred Deliverances that took place between 2016 and 2020.

20 January 2020 – Undisclosed Location – Melbourne – Australia

Paul begins this Deliverance convinced that he is going to Hell.

Something speaking through Paul is speaking in tongues, and sighing.

Suddenly, it finds another voice, gentle and almost feminine in tone, if not in pitch.

"The Lord is with you. He will always be with you. He will never leave you. He will never go to hell. You will be a warrior … a warrior … fight back when the Devil attacks."

Abruptly another voice comes through. It speaks in tongues, then laughs.

Abruptly the first voice returns, "Keep coming back for prayer. Never stop praying to me. Keep coming back for prayer."

All the while in the background, in his own reverie, Wisdom speaks in tongues.

The angelic voice returns, answering perhaps a question that Paul asked only in the privacy of his own mind. "You don't have to worry about that …", the voice assures him, and continues, "The Devil is terrified of you now. He is terrified. He is terrified of this prayer. He is terrified of it … You are well protected. You are well protected. You are well protected. You are so very well protected. Pray to me, when you are scared."

Paul begins to weep.

"The prayer you said before," the Voice says, "where I told you the Devil was scared, pray that. Pray that one. He will run like a puppy … You are free."

The Voice is the Voice of The Holy Spirit. The Holy Spirit calls Deliverance "prayer". This is not the prayer where you sit on your knees, hands together, eyes closed and asking God for something, but a conversation affirming the spiritual connection between that person and God. Prayer, as we normally understand it, is when the person talks to God. Deliverance, in this sense, *is when God talks back*.

23 January 2020 Undisclosed Location – Melbourne – Australia

In the background, Wisdom speaks in tongues.

An angelic Voice speaks through Paul: "God is with you now … He is back … He took authority … He crossed out … ahhhh …"

Briefly, cruel laughter breaks through Paul, but it is quickly silenced. The Voice returns:

"The fear in your mind is not real … Cross the dark in the name of Jesus …"

Now Paul's voice comes through, but it is the voice of someone as though talking in their sleep. "I crossed out the fear in my mind in the name of Jesus Christ of Nazareth … in the name of Jesus Christ of Nazareth … I take authority over my mind and my life in the name of Jesus Christ of Nazareth … I command you to stay away from me in the name of Jesus Christ of Nazareth … I call upon the bond and covenant given to me by God to be reinstalled in the name of Jesus Christ of Nazareth … The Father once said, "You come near me, He will release his might and show you who is my Father." I call on God to show him."

Paul asserts control by calling upon the covenant, his contract with God. God's promise that Paul is protected, inviolate. Then, out of nowhere Paul begins violent dry retching, coughing and moaning. Within Paul something that Paul identifies as Satan is losing control. Paul has a sense that God is striking the Devil with an almighty force. This is enough to knock Paul off his feet and onto the ground, where he begins to spasm, and yet something protects him from injury. The Devil has been blindsided. The Devil was not expecting this. This is a breakthrough moment, but the dry retching, coughing and moaning continue as Wisdom begins to cry out:

"Let go in the NAME of JESUS … in the NAME of JESUS … by His HOLY MARK I pray that you let go in the NAME of JESUS … right NOW by the power of The Holy Spirit … let GO … let GO … let every harm, let every thought, let every imagination right NOW let GO in the NAME of JESUS whatever INFLUENCE I pray right now in the NAME of JESUS I pray God in the name of Jesus …"

JOSEPH: "In the NAME of JESUS … Father I pray for the REDEMPTION, the redemption of the mind, REDEEM the mind … REDEEM this mind … REDEEM this mind in the NAME of Jesus … redeem the mind … redeem the mind … I pray for the redemption of this mind … I pray for the redemption of this mind."

Wisdom continues to pray for the redemption of a mind lost for so long under Satan's control.

And in the thrall of this, Paul begins to feel liberated from fear – particularly his fear of annihilation, his fear of losing his mind.

Paul speaks again. Perhaps to Jesus now, "You were the man of truth. Your covenant. You have a covenant of my mind to protect my mind. God … act of covenance … to protect my mind …"

Paul senses that something powerful has happened here, that here, at this point, the battle for his immortal soul was won.

Paul senses the mind of Satan: "*I CONCEDE YOU HAVE WON. THE BATTLE HAS BEEN WON. YOU HAVE FOUGHT VALIANTLY.*"

Is it possible that the Devil is actually being … gracious?

It was like a release from prison, from *unfair, unjust* imprisonment a release from pain so great that Paul often didn't care if he had died.

But now Paul senses the heavens rejoicing. Paul's mind's eye is filled with images of angels rejoicing.

The battle for his soul might have been won. But there remained the battle for his mortal body.

The Voice of The Holy Spirit, if that is what it is, now speaks through Paul, reassuring him:

"He is not here now … you have been suffering … keep praying to me … he is not here … he told you your soul was in heaven with me and that is true but to fight for your life, he wants it."

It is one of the greatest moments of Paul's life that it was not God who told Paul that his soul was in heaven but that it was the Devil who told him this and that God confirmed it.

Paul answers God in his own voice, "God? What is it I must do? What must I do? God? The battles are being won, but when will the war be over?"

The Holy Spirit answers in turn: "The war. The war is already won. We are just going through the process. Do not be afraid. I am here. Give me your fear."

"I give you my fear, God. I give it to you."

"You can always, always rely on the prayer I told you … just now before. The one where I will show him my mind. I crushed him and sent him running. I showed him *who was your Father*."

Touched by the love and compassion of God, Paul begins to weep quietly.

The Holy Spirit continues: "Keep coming back for prayer (Deliverance). He will give up. He will give up. He is already giving up."

The Holy Spirit continues to reassure Paul. "… so you do great things. He knows you will do this. But I will not allow that to be taken from you."

It is strange, this conversation of two minds, two consciousnesses and two voices, alternating out of the one mouth. The parent reassuring the child as the child seeks that reassurance.

"The covenant of my mind, God, is the most precious thing," Paul says.

"I have prevented many attacks," The Holy Spirit says. "Today you were meant to be tormented, but did you? You will not go back to where He was with your mind, for I am in it."

"God, never ever let me doubt. Please. I don't want to be doubt. I don't want to be scared. I want to feel safe. Safety is what I want."

"He is nothing. He is nothing now. He is nowhere near you. He is terrified. He is terrified now. He did not expect that. He did not expect that."

Wisdom intervenes. "Jesus. Thank-you, Jesus. Thank-you, Jesus."

"This will not last long," The Holy Spirit says.

"Thank you, Jesus. Thank you, Jesus," says Wisdom again in a reverent almost-whisper.

"This will not last long. You are nearly there. You are nearly there. It is nearly over. Keep fighting. For you have faith in me."

"I have faith," says Paul.

"You have faith. You have faith."

"God, also, I just need …" Paul says.

"It is nearly over," Joseph reassures.

" … need peace of my mind …" Paul continues.

" … over … over …" Joseph says, as if were a chant.

"I need peace of my mind …" Paul says, as the desperation subsides. "For I am just merely a mortal … just need some peace … heavenly peace of my mind. A rest … I can do this, God. For as long as you have control of my mind … and you diminish the fear,

I can do this. I can do this … keep the control of my mind."

Wisdom too beseeches God, "Ease the fear … diminish the fear, God … diminish the fear … reduce the fear."

"Take away all the doubt," Paul asks. "Take away the doubt …"

"Let it vanish … let it vanish … no doubt, no guilt, no shame, God, I pray that You will seal this man," Joseph asks. "Shield this mind with Your Word. Seal him with Your Word."

And The Holy Spirit speaks through Paul again. "Your soul is in heaven with me and surrounded by angels. Nothing He can do now. He knows that. You won the war there. It's just the battle for your life, and it's nearly won … you will sleep in heavenly peace … keep coming back for prayer. It is almost done. You do not have to do this forever. You do not have to do this forever. It will be won. Just like I won your soul. I won your soul. I won your soul. There is not much more He can do. When the war is won, the door will be shut. No more attacks … Tell Wisdom, the war will be won."

What we cannot hear is the internal Voice of The Holy Spirit as it constantly reassures Paul. Nor can we hear the internal Voice of The Holy Spirit when it speaks directly to Wisdom. When the Voice speaks aloud through Paul, it is to reinforce the message that The Holy Spirit has already communicated in the mind's ear. "Tell him, it is not true you will live like this," The Holy Spirit continues. "It is not true. You will not live like this. Your victory will be assured. I set you free from alcohol. You do not want to drink anymore. I will set you free from this. It's nearly there. Keep coming back for prayer and pray to me when you are scared."

Paul feels assured that God will keep God's covenants. God does not break God's word.

Days will pass. Weeks will pass. Although Paul's soul is no longer in mortal danger, demonic attacks continue as the demons persist in their other agenda, to end Paul's life. Paul remains in mortal danger.

Each time another Deliverance happens Paul's spirit, his connection with the Divine Source, is strengthened. But it will not be enough to call Paul "saved" or "delivered" even if all the demons are expunged. True Deliverance does not end when the afflicted One has been "cleansed". Real life is not the movies. The afflicted One is not all bright and shiny after the last demon goes.

Roll credits.

The afflicted One is still damaged, often profoundly so and needs healing. And while the afflicted One Heals that one will still not be truly safe until that one can protect themselves even without the help of a minister, priest or other Mediator of Deliverance. It is a process.

The prayers, the Deliverances, now take on a greater intimacy.

26 January 2020 – Undisclosed Location – Melbourne – Australia

HOLY SPIRIT: You are in my arm, my hand, but you must keep praying to come closer. I have you by the hand now. I have you by the hand. Pray the rosary. Pray every day. You can come back here for prayer too, but you have come through. Your life won the other day. Your soul with me in heaven. Your fear taken. Your trauma cured. Your alcoholism gone. And I give the gift of my life.

PAUL: My emotions, God? My emotions?

For so long Paul hadn't felt anything but despair and fear he felt that he had lost the capacity to feel anything else.

HOLY SPIRIT: They will come. Keep coming back for prayer then.

PAUL: My emotions? My emotions … my emotions … my emotions … where are they?

HOLY SPIRIT: They will come. Keep praying for them. Today, I give you peace and strength of my hand …

Three months and about twenty deliverances later:

27 April 2020 – Undisclosed Location – Melbourne – Australia

"You were possessed by many demons. Oh, there were many," The Holy Spirit says.

Paul in a small voice, almost a whisper, says, "You touch my feelings. You touch my feelings. My Father said you would get my feelings back. My feelings will come back. Connect me back, God. Connect me back with overwhelming love. Peace, happiness, my childhood happiness …"

At this point Paul begins making sounds resembling corrupt Latin, or perhaps a transitional Latin dialect or early Romance language – "identifiable" words on the recording include: *solamente* – only; *dus, tres, quatros … cente* – two, three, four … one hundred; *elemente* – element.

Paul switches to English, " … practice let me live in peace of mind now, moving forward."

Then the Voice of The Holy Spirit again confirms the expulsion of a demon: "He's gone. He's gone. He's gone. He was the one in your bedroom. He scratched you that night. You know that scratch. That scratch. That was the demon. The one that … He's gone. Your prayers need to be specific. Be specific."

Paul begins to speak in tongues, then, "*e demando de* Jesus Christ" – I ask of Jesus Christ, "*e demand e le sala Maria*" – and I ask of the [Saint?] Mary, "*e questo solo cente*" – and this alone one hundred.

None of this quite makes sense. The word "Sala" could be a corruption of "Santa" or "Saint" and it seems like some dialect of Italian and some dialect of Spanish are being mixed here. We should note however that Paul is not a linguist and has no knowledge of Latin or Romance languages in spite of having been brought up a Catholic. The mutterings might just be subconsciously learnt language, ravings or he could genuinely be channeling a consciousness that, for whatever reason, is speaking in something like a Romance language.

It is not unusual for Paul to have readings that start off in a foreign language that he then has to interpret or translate later through intuition. In one instance the translated message was "My life is in God's hands" and even now, whenever he feels threatened, he says "My life is in God's hands" as a divinely inspired affirmation of peace and protection.

Several weeks and at least ten deliverances later:

22 May 2020 – Undisclosed Location – Melbourne – Australia

There are gaps in the story. Readings from The Holy Spirit between deliverances that continued to support Paul during this time of intensive spiritual treatment. Sometimes the recordings make no immediate rational sense out of context.

For example:

HOLY SPIRIT: It's your left hand … Your left hand will do it.

JOSEPH: A different level of authority has been released.

PAUL: Whoa hoah … Oh, thank you, God, thank you, God, thank you, God …

JOSEPH: A different level of energy has been released.

HOLY SPIRIT: The covenant of security for both of you. For both of you. For both of you. Tell Wisdom it's for both of you. It's your left hand like I showed you in the last … vision. Use your left hand …

Paul explained that, "The Holy Spirit is talking about my left hand. On one occasion I was sitting in my car and I had the uncontrollable urge to speak tongues for half an hour. In that moment I was told that I was given the gift of healing. Now The Holy Spirit is reminding me to use my left hand when I practice my gift of healing. I still have not perfected this. I don't understand what it is exactly however I'm led to believe that later down the track I will do much healing work for people. The Holy Spirit has revealed to me that I will be able to put my left hand on their foreheads and read their problems."

At the very least it seems logical that some of the afflicted might be given Holy Gifts to help not only in their own healing, but in the healing of others. Examples like this show yet again the stark contrast between the way that the media and popular culture portrays Exorcism and how Deliverance *actually happens* in real life.

Paul is nevertheless grounded in the midst of these revelations.

"I can't say that I necessarily interpret all of my readings correctly. I think it's a bit like how a dyslexic person may look at something on a screen and get mixed up. I might misinterpret "writing in the screen of my mind's eye" or "sounds heard in my mind's ear". Many mediums and light workers have the same experience. If things are misinterpreted it's not The Holy Spirit's fault but rather the medium's inexperience in understanding these messages accurately."

Again and again we encounter the word "covenant" – holy contracts between an individual and The Holy Spirit that define and strengthen the relationship between that individual and the Divine.

The ongoing communion between Paul and The Holy Spirit was not confined to the Deliverance sessions alone. For example, in a series of text messages Paul related the following:

2 June 2020 – Text Message from PH

Late last night an urge came over me to pray to Saint Michael and to war with the devil. St Michael and I were warring and in the middle of it a holy sense of relief came over me and I started weeping. This weeping has happened to me before when praying to the Virgin

Mary. The weeping comes because I know that they are there, with me. The weeping is a sign for me of a very strong connection to the Divine. But it is also an indication that beings like St Michael and Mary are weeping for joy when *they* know that *I* know that they are there with me. It's a surreal experience but very satisfying at the same time. I sense Saint Michael encouraging me to come to him in any time of need. I am encouraged to "Loose yourself! Set Michael on to the Devil." This message comes repetitively. I then get a reading to the effect that the Devil is getting his "arse whipped". I'm no longer on the defensive but on the offensive. Hallelujah!

I think it's extremely important that people understand that as they move through Deliverance they move into a new reality in which they become aware that spiritual support has always been there for them. Deliverance isn't just a physical process. It's mental and emotional as well as spiritual.

Two days later, this:

2 June 2020 – Text Message from PH

I thought I would share with you that today for the first time in over twenty-three years I truly feel at peace. I keep speaking a foreign language: "*Num chala masande*," is what I keep saying, a phrase that translates as: "May my spirit be grounded with God." I keep getting readings that it only gets better and what is in store for me is nothing in consideration to what I am feeling now and my spiritual senses will grow. I have no anxiety, no OCD, no fear, just absolute peace of mind and comfort. Thank you, God.

It's important that people understand that what is promised is not given to you instantaneously but that it takes time to develop. I keep getting more instruction: "Play more angelic songs, that is the pathway to your healing."

Six days later, this:

2 June 2020 – Text Message from PH

Last night a psychic attack came over me and I did the usual clearing of energy and various other kinds of things that I usually do when this occurs. However, it gave me a false sense of security and just did not feel right. For approximately one hour afterwards I was getting mentally battered and had OCD-like symptoms concerning faith and what to do next. It even occurred to me that I may have to see Wisdom to help move this along. I asked for spiritual guidance and did some further prayers then went to bed. Before I went to bed I started receiving thoughts saying that was a "test of faith". I climbed into bed and went to sleep and woke up at 3:00 am and was thinking, "It's just a process" and all of a sudden, Kristy, who was asleep and clearly in the middle of a dream said to me, "It's just a process, Paul". Soon, a thought came to mind and said, "God wants you to know that everything is going to be all right" and a chill flowed through my body afterwards. Today I feel more relaxed and less anxious about my mental state. More thoughts came earlier this morning, "This will break soon," but I am constantly and ultimately concerned about having that full-blown mental breakdown occur again and this negative energy likes to test me and use this against me. So far, so good.

Paul as it turned out was right to be concerned. The battle for his life was not quite over.

12 June 2020 – Undisclosed Location – Melbourne – Australia

The transcript below doesn't quite convey the violence in the tone of voice of the demonic entity coming out of Paul's mouth. It's a strangled voice. Oily. Greasy.

UNIDENTIFIED DEMONIC ENTITY: … the Devil's contract …

WISDOM: I command you. You repeat that. Are you in this body by legal right or not?

UNIDENTIFIED DEMONIC ENTITY: Through contract. I came through the contract when He took his miiiiind. He spoke through him. You didn't KNOW you fool! He did not speak The Holy Spirit. He gave his miiiiind! (violent retching)

WISDOM: Right now those words you have spoken you are before God and you don't lie. I ask you again, is it true this testimony? Is it true or false?

UNIDENTIFIED DEMONIC ENTITY: It is truuuuue!!!

WISDOM: It is true. And what damage have you caused to this body?

UNIDENTIFIED DEMONIC ENTITY: Make him go maaaaad!!! Maaaaad!!! I make him go craaaazy … (Demonic laughter)

WISDOM: What other damage have you caused? You make him go mad. You make him go crazy. What other damage have caused in this body? Speak now or I execute a judgment on you right now.

UNIDENTIFIED DEMONIC ENTITY: Aye, nothing. There's nothing. You just …

WISDOM: You make him mad.

UNIDENTIFIED DEMONIC ENTITY: Just the madness.

WISDOM: And make him go crazy.

UNIDENTIFIED DEMONIC ENTITY: He's afraid of it. Afraid … (Demonic laughter)

WISDOM: Have you caused any physical damage in this body?

UNIDENTIFIED DEMONIC ENTITY: Nooo …

WISDOM: Have you caused any emotional damage in this body?

UNIDENTIFIED DEMONIC ENTITY: Yeeeah. Stop his feelings. Stop his feelings.

WISDOM: Have you caused any mental damage in this body?

UNIDENTIFIED DEMONIC ENTITY: Just the OCD … (coughing and dry retching)

WISDOM: Have you caused any physical damage in this body?

UNIDENTIFIED DEMONIC ENTITY: No, no, no, no … no, no …

WISDOM: What other spirits are there with you?

UNIDENTIFIED DEMONIC ENTITY: FUCK OFF!!! Fuck off!!

WISDOM: Right now I command you, I release the fire of The Holy Spirit right now!

UNIDENTIFIED DEMONIC ENTITY: (begins to cough violently and make loud, high-pitched animal-like growling)

WISDOM: Just listen to what I will say I release the FIRE of The Holy Spirit RIGHT NOW.

UNIDENTIFIED DEMONIC ENTITY: (still retching violently, then suddenly in a quiet voice) It's rejection … rejection …it is rejection.

WISDOM: You caused rejection.

UNIDENTIFIED DEMONIC ENTITY: Rejection is in him as well. I am above the rejection.

WISDOM: And what other spirits in him? What have rejection caused to his spiritual life?

UNIDENTIFIED DEMONIC ENTITY: Ahhhh … relationship damage. Her relationships … damage …

WISDOM: What are thus, what does these spirits cause as well with his emotions?

UNIDENTIFIED DEMONIC ENTITY: He can't love. He can't LOVE. He can't love. The rejection. It stops him from loving. (Demonic laughter)

WISDOM: What had rejection caused, mentally?

UNIDENTIFIED DEMONIC ENTITY: Nothing. Just me. The OCD. Rejection stops him from loving.

WISDOM: And what has that caused, physically?

UNIDENTIFIED DEMONIC ENTITY: It's weight gain. He got fat because he … (degenerates into Demonic laughter)

WISDOM: And how many wounds have been caused by the OCD? How many wounds have you caused in this body?

UNIDENTIFIED DEMONIC ENTITY: There are seven.

WISDOM: Can you name them for me?

UNIDENTIFIED DEMONIC ENTITY: SEVEN!

WISDOM: Name them for me right now in the name of Jesus!

UNIDENTIFIED DEMONIC ENTITY: (coughs violently) I can't tell you. I don't know. There are seven.

WISDOM: I don't take "I don't know" for an answer. I speak right now. You are before the Throne of God. You can only say the truth. If not, I execute a judgment or fire of The Holy Spirit consume you. What are the seven wounds you have caused?

UNIDENTIFIED DEMONIC ENTITY: It is on his heart. It is on his mind. It is on his soul. It is on his body. It is in his spirit.

WISDOM: Now. Every other demon that is attached to the OCD, I BIND them right now to it, to that demon, that head demon every other demon that the demon of OCD brought, I bind them right now in the NAME of JESUS.

UNIDENTIFIED DEMONIC ENTITY: … Say that. Don't say that!

WISDOM: In the name of Jesus Christ of Nazareth! …

UNIDENTIFIED DEMONIC ENTITY: (begins to cough and dry retch violently)

WISDOM: … who came in the flesh. I command every demon. Loose!

UNIDENTIFIED DEMONIC ENTITY: (cough and dry retching escalates)

WISDOM: In the name of Jesus! GO! To the PIT! In Jesus' name!

Without repeat and tearing I command you RIGHT NOW to leave …

UNIDENTIFIED DEMONIC ENTITY: (loud, growling and lion-like roaring)

WISDOM: … I BIND you and I CAST you without tearing and without reaping. Right now I command you into the PIT of Hell in the NAME of JESUS Christ of Nazareth …

UNIDENTIFIED DEMONIC ENTITY: (loud dry retching) … WE'RE LEAVING … WE'RE … (can't continue due to the dry retching and coughing)

WISDOM: I set this body on the fire of … ([unintelligible] due to the loud coughing) … right now. I set this body on the FIRE. I set this body on fire …

UNIDENTIFIED DEMONIC ENTITY: (retching and coughing suddenly stops)

WISDOM: Now say, "I break the curse of OCD in the name of Jesus."

And then, another voice, of a completely different, softer nature, issues from Paul's mouth:

UNIDENTIFIED ANGELIC ENTITY: They left. Tell Wisdom they left.

Paul, later commenting on this session said:

I think it's important that people know that the severe OCD attacks that occurred in 2016 was, in this Deliverance, was now confirmed to be a *spiritual attack* and not a mental health issue. This "UNIDENTIFIED DEMONIC ENTITY" was the Spirit of obsessive-compulsive disorder.

I want people to know that if you're ever suffering from these things and you don't know where to go you can simply pray to God,

He and he will lead you to the people that you need in your life at a particular point. "God I am suffering from XXX and I do not know where to turn, please lead me to the people who can help me recover from XXX and I pray that I do not die prematurely with this ailment."

The 12 June 2020 Deliverance turned out to be a particularly grueling one. Later in this same session we identified The Spirit of Rejection, and with it, the revelation of a truly malicious agenda:

WISDOM: … name of Jesus. You're going to be consumed by fire …
SPIRIT OF REJECTION: No, no, no, no, no …
WISDOM: … if you lie in the name of Jesus. How did you get into this body, you, Spirit of Rejection.
SPIRIT OF REJECTION: His girlfriend. It was his girlfriend. He was …
WISDOM: Are you there by legal right or not?
SPIRIT OF REJECTION: It was a spell. It was a spell from Satan, to break up with him and harm him to *kill* him. He has been rejected ever since. God intervened and healed the wound but I'm still here. God sent his wife to help him overcome but I am still heeerreee … ahhhh …
WISDOM: Today is your last day. You're gonna depart today.
SPIRIT OF REJECTION: Nooooo …
WISDOM: You will in the name of Jesus …
SPIRIT OF REJECTION: Nooooo …
WISDOM: Do you want me to execute …
SPIRIT OF REJECTION: Nooooo …
WISDOM: … that the judgment on you right now?
SPIRIT OF REJECTION: Nooooo …
WISDOM: So now you be quiet and listen to what I'm going to say.

SPIRIT OF REJECTION: Ohhhhh … Shut up.

WISDOM: In the name of Jesus …

SPIRIT OF REJECTION: Shut up.

WISDOM: … any word that I don't ask you to say do not say it if not I will release the fire of The Holy Spirit …

SPIRIT OF REJECTION: No …

WISDOM: … upon you. Have you caused any damage you, Spirit of Rejection? Have you caused any spiritual damage?

SPIRIT OF REJECTION: Not spiritual.

WISDOM: Have you caused any emotional damage?

SPIRIT OF REJECTION: Yeeeeesss. Yeeeeessss. Lots. Lots of it. Lots of it.

WISDOM: Have you caused any mental damage?

SPIRIT OF REJECTION: Depression. I make him depreeeessssed. Depreesssed, so he kill himself. So saaaaad. So saaaaad.

WISDOM: Have you caused any physical damage?

SPIRIT OF REJECTION: Hmmm … noooooo …

WISDOM: Where did you get your power from?

SPIRIT OF REJECTION: He came from Satan. He came from Satan. He bound me to him.

WISDOM: How many wounds have you created in this body? In this heart. In this mind? How many wounds have you created?

SPIRIT OF REJECTION: Six … six …

WISDOM: Name them. Name the six wounds .

SPIRIT OF REJECTION: Ha, ha, ha, ha … How do I know?

WISDOM: You will know and right now I expose you to the truth of the Power of The Holy Spirit. I expose you to truth. I expose you to the Word of God right now. You don't lie to me. You said "six". You should know it in the Name of Jesus. How many wounds have you created?

SPIRIT OF REJECTION: His nervous system. His heart and his mind. His health. I put over his health … he used to be fit. Now look at him! A fat piece of shit … (Demonic laughter)

WISDOM: Right now …

SPIRIT OF REJECTION: … there is in the spirit. He's bound in the spirit. The rejection and then all over his body. There is your six (Demonic laughter)

WISDOM: Right now, you, Spirit of Rejection, in the name of Jesus …

SPIRIT OF REJECTION: (erupts into loud wheezing and groaning)

WISDOM: Christ of Nazareth. In the name of JESUS Christ of Nazareth, who came in the flesh, I command every other demon that you brought in this body, right now, I LOOSE in the name of Jesus …

SPIRIT OF REJECTION: (interrupts and talks while WISDOM continues to speak) You don't understand …

WISDOM: … and I ask you right now …

SPIRIT OF REJECTION: It is a spell …

WISDOM: I command you in the name of Jesus …

SPIRIT OF REJECTION: Nooo … you're not listening … there is a spell …

WISDOM: I break that spell in the name of Jesus.

SPIRIT OF REJECTION: (Demonic laughter, more coughing and roaring)

WISDOM: I break that spell in the name of Jesus.

SPIRIT OF REJECTION: … *it was to him* to KILL her … (Demonic laughter, more coughing and roaring)

WISDOM: I BREAK that spell …

SPIRIT OF REJECTION: He was going to KILL her … (Demonic laughter)

WISDOM: And right now I BIND that SPELL – CAST IT OUT – in the name of Jesus … (voice gets louder in an attempt to be heard above the coughing/wheezing and roaring of Spirit of Rejection) I remove that SPELL in the name of Jesus. Let every spell be gone in Jesus' name! And set free and LOOSE from every spell in the name of Jesus.

Then, suddenly again:

THE HOLY SPIRIT: (sudden quiet) Tell Wisdom it is broken. The spell has been broken.

It is interesting to know that demons feel the need to keep the Ministers of Deliverance and the afflicted informed even if they are distracted, the tone of voice when the Spirit of Rejection said, "You're not listening" was sardonically amused.

Later in this session Paul and I dealt with the Spirit of Fear, which revealed yet another layer to the affliction and its treatment.

HOLY SPIRIT: Tell Wisdom there's one more wound …

JOSEPH: Healing … healing … healing … healing …

HOLY SPIRIT: There's one more wound …

JOSEPH: (Speaking in tongues)

HOLY SPIRIT: There was one more wound … (Speaking in tongues)

It is interesting to note that at this point Wisdom seems so enthralled by the process working through him that he seems not to be listening to The Holy Spirit.

JOSEPH: (Speaking in tongues) … the finger of God right now and the light of The Holy Spirit and I search Paul's soul … I search his spirit. If there is anything, God, that is of … that is in him, that needs to be exposed today, pray that you will bring it to light in the name of Jesus. I ask in the name of Jesus …

PAUL: They're saying …

JOSEPH: … what is in you …

PAUL: The crown is wounded. My crown. It's open and wounded.

JOSEPH: (Speaking in tongues)

PAUL: It channels negative energy and is open. And there is the Spirit of Fear. God bound him, but he needs to come out. God bound him but he needs to come out.

JOSEPH: Holy Spirit of the Living God you are worthy to receive glory. You are worthy to receive praise. You are worthy to receive all honor. Whatever you said right now is that, is that flesh or it is spirit?

HOLY SPIRIT: The fear lives in him and his chakra is open.

JOSEPH: (Speaking in tongues)

PAUL: Have God fix the chakra so negative energy does not get in.

JOSEPH: (Speaking in tongues) You, the Spirit of fear …

PAUL: That only God can enter.

JOSEPH: (Speaking in tongues)

PAUL: Fix the chakra.

JOSEPH: (Speaking in tongues)

PAUL: (Speaking in tongues, we can clearly hear the words *mentale contentis* – happy mind?)

JOSEPH: (Speaking in tongues) Fear. That Spirit of Fear that is bound in you …

PAUL: (Begins to cough)

JOSEPH: … Your spirit of fear right now (Speaking in tongues)

Spirit of Fear? (SOF?): … Nooo … nooo … (high pitched Demonic laughter)

JOSEPH: The Lord is in control. If you speak, I'm going to charge the Judgment of God upon you. The Lord is in control.

The Lord is in control. Father, in the name of Jesus, according to Matthew 18, 18, you, Spirit of Fear, that dwells in this body. I bring you before the throne of God. And I ask that you say only the truth …

SPIRIT OF FEAR: But I am so weak.

JOSEPH: I ask that you say only the truth.

SPIRIT OF FEAR: I'm telling you I am weak.

JOSEPH: I ask that you say only the truth.

SPIRIT OF FEAR: God bound me …

JOSEPH: (Speaking in tongues)

SPIRIT OF FEAR: He bound me …

JOSEPH: (Speaking in tongues)

SPIRIT OF FEAR: … through your prayers before, He bound me. I am not allowed to attack.

JOSEPH: I command you right now. I command you right now. You are bound. I command you right now.

SPIRIT OF FEAR: (angrily and impatiently) But I already AM bound …

JOSEPH: … in the name of Jesus TO LEAVE in the name of Jesus. You have no authority. I command you right now …

SPIRIT OF FEAR: God weakened me.

JOSEPH: TO LEAVE.

SPIRIT OF FEAR: He weakened me …

JOSEPH:(Speaking in tongues) Right now, I execute that you will be consumed by fire in the …

SPIRIT OF FEAR: (begins to cough and dry retch very loudly)

JOSEPH: … name of Jesus and I command you right now, to leave, leave in the name of Jesus.

SPIRIT OF FEAR: STOP IT!

JOSEPH: Leave in the name of Jesus or be CONSUMED by the fire of The Holy Spirit …

SPIRIT OF FEAR: (coughing and dry retching escalates)

JOSEPH: Leave in the name of JESUS … I set Paul's soul on fire. I set on fire in the name of Jesus.

PAUL: (calmly) He's still there.

JOSEPH: I set this soul on fire …

SPIRIT OF FEAR: (begins to cough/roar very loudly like and angry elephant) …

JOSEPH: In the Name of the Holy Ghost … in the Fire of the Holy Ghost … Fire of the Holy Ghost … Fire of the Holy Ghost … Fire of the Holy Ghost… consume … consume … consume … consume … consume … in the name of Jesus consume this … [unintelligible] … with the FIRE of The Holy Spirit in the name of Jesus. I consume you in the name of Jesus. I consume you with the Fire of the Holy Ghost in the name of Jesus. I command you OUT!

PAUL: He's out.

JOSEPH: In the name of Jesus and I send you to the pit …

PAUL: He's gone.

Later still there was another revelation when Wisdom and Paul dealt with the Spirit of Disbelief and Confusion.

JOSEPH: Is part of that contract signed?

Spirit of Disbelief and Confusion (SODAC): … in faith of prayer (Demonic laughter)

JOSEPH: Spirit of Disbelief and Confusion, now listen, have you caused any spiritual damage?

SODAC: We nearly took him to hell …(Demonic laughter)

JOSEPH: Have you caused any emotional damage?

SODAC: We nearly make him go mad … (Demonic laughter)

JOSEPH: Have you caused any mental damage?

SODAC: He is not mentally sick … (Demonic laughter) the doctors said he was sick, but he isn't … (Demonic laughter)

JOSEPH: Have you done any physical damage?

SODAC: No …

JOSEPH: Where did you get most of your power from?

SODAC: It came from Satan. He gave it to us … (Demonic laughter)

JOSEPH: So, Spirit of Confusion and Disbelief, do you have any other spirit that you've come with?

SODAC: We are alone. It is just us.

JOSEPH: How many wounds have you caused?

SODAC: Ten … eleven … eleven …

JOSEPH: Eleven wounds . What are they?

SODAC: They are just the same as before.

JOSEPH: What are they?

SODAC: He put it on his heart. His mind. His soul. His body. His peace. His love. His tranquillity. His ability to access energy from Heaven. Why do you think he's fat? He can't access the energy. We have stopped that. It is bound in Heaven and in Hell. There is more, but that is basically it … (Demonic laughter)

JOSEPH: Now, in the name of Jesus Christ of Nazareth, who came in the flesh, I command you, Spirit of Disbelief and Confusion, …

SODAC: It's the contract! You can't take us out.

JOSEPH: … right now …

SODAC: You have the contract.

JOSEPH: I break that contract in the name of Jesus. Whatever contract it is, I use the power of The Holy Spirit to break that contract right now in the name of Jesus …

SODAC: (heavy wheezing, coughing and loud dry retching) …

JOSEPH: Contract is BROKEN in name of Jesus … by …

[unintelligible] … the contract is BROKEN in name of Jesus. And now, Paul I subject you to The Holy Spirit. Say, "I break that contract …"

PAUL: I break that contract …

Paul and I also dealt with the Spirit of Doubt in this session.

JOSEPH: (Speaking in tongues) … are you Spirit of Doubt.?

Spirit of Doubt [?]: … (coughing and dry retching which gradually escalates)

JOSEPH: According to Matthew 18, 18, I bring you right in the presence of God so that you can answer this judgment and I command you that you answer this judgments, this answ …, these questions rightly because you are in the thro … you are … ss … st … standing in front of the throne of God … [unintelligible] … if you lie … I will ask … I ask the Lord to prepare two judgments for you …

SPIRIT OF DOUBT: You could … [unintelligible] … the Devil this way, but not me …

JOSEPH: … and I prepare the judgment that you be consumed by the Fire of The Holy Spirit … you'll be consumed by the Fire of The Holy Spirit. How did you get into this vessel? How did you get into this body?

SPIRIT OF DOUBT: Through his mind.

JOSEPH: Through his mind?

SPIRIT OF DOUBT: Yeeeess. I came through the mind … (sighs) …

JOSEPH: Do you have any legal right?

SPIRIT OF DOUBT: After the contract.

JOSEPH: Do you have any legal right?

SPIRIT OF DOUBT: After the contracts.

JOSEPH: After the contracts.

SPIRIT OF DOUBT: I came through the mind after he entered the contract. When he prayed to Satan in your prayer session here, he gave Satan his mind and then I came in. I came in through *that* way.

JOSEPH: Have you caused any spiritual damage?

SPIRIT OF DOUBT: I have not. I just tormenting him.

JOSEPH: Have you done emotional damage?

SPIRIT OF DOUBT: No, no, no …

JOSEPH: Have you done mental damage?

SPIRIT OF DOUBT: No, he is not mentally sick …

JOSEPH: Speak the truth, in the name of Jesus.

SPIRIT OF DOUBT: No. I tell you. No mental damage.

JOSEPH: Have you done any physical damage?

SPIRIT OF DOUBT: No.

JOSEPH: Where did you get your power from.

SPIRIT OF DOUBT: Power from Satan (Demonic laughter)

JOSEPH: How many wounds have you caused?

SPIRIT OF DOUBT: (sighs)

JOSEPH: How many wounds have you caused?

SPIRIT OF DOUBT: I can only say "one" because that is the truth. I want to say "more" but it is "one".

Fascinating that the demon would love to lay claim to more than one wound, but that before the Throne of God and compelled to tell the truth it can only admit to one wound.

Several more sessions were to follow, but it wasn't until late June that the worst was finally over.

23 June 2020 – Undisclosed Location – Melbourne – Australia

WISDOM: (Speaking in tongues) … in the name of Jesus … (Speaking in tongues)

UNIDENTIFIED DEMONIC ENTITY: You have cast out many … but there are more … ah, he was the strong one, yes, but there are more … oh …

WISDOM: … Who are you?

UNIDENTIFIED DEMONIC ENTITY: … Tantalei …

WISDOM: Tantalei …

TANTALEI: Yes … (Demonic laughter)

WISDOM: What is your mission?

TANTALEI: I come … I come … I come … to harm him …

WISDOM: How? …

TANTALEI: I break his motivation … I break his motivation … I break the motivation …

WISDOM: How do you do that?

TANTALEI: No. It's not contract. It's not a contract …

WISDOM: How did you do it? How do you, how do you break his motivation?

TANTALEI: His energy …

WISDOM: His energy … you stop his energy …

TANTALEI: Yes.

WISDOM: And how do you do that? …

TANTALEI: I stop him focusing … on his mind … I stop him from focusing … and concentrating … I stop him from achieving his goal … (sighs) …

WISDOM: So, do you have a legal right?

TANTALEI: No.

WISDOM: How many of you are there?

TANTALEI: Seventeen.

WISDOM: Seventeen.

TANTALEI: Yeeesss …

WISDOM: In the name of Jesus, I bound all the seventeen to you and let me know when that is done in the NAME of Jesus …

TANTALEI: (coughing and spluttering) … oh, we're bound … no we're not …

WISDOM: I bound them in the NAME of Jesus to you … I bound the seventeen to you, Tantalei, in the NAME of Jesus …

TANTALEI: They are bound … they are bound … they are bound …

WISDOM: Have you caused any damage?

TANTALEI: No.

WISDOM: Physically?

TANTALEI: No.

WISDOM: Mentally?

TANTALEI: No.

WISDOM: Spiritually?

TANTALEI: No …

WISDOM: You just stop his emotions …

TANTALEI: Yes.

WISDOM: Right now, in the name of Jesus, you have no legal contract?

TANTALEI: No, no, no, no …

WISDOM: You have not legal right?

TANTALEI: No, I'll just leave, I'll leave, I'll leave …

WISDOM: I set Paul's body on fire right now in the name of Jesus … I set Paul's body right now in the name of Jesus … in the name of Jesus … in the name of Jesus … (continues in this vein) Let go! In the name of Jesus … I set Paul's body on fire right now … set his body on fire … (continues in this vein) Fire of the Holy Ghost, consume, in the name of Jesus … (continues in this vein) FIRE in the name of Jesus … Paul, say, "I break …"

PAUL: I break …

WISDOM: "every curse …"

PAUL: Every curse …

WISDOM: "from Tantalei …"

PAUL: From Zolo …

WISDOM: "Zolo, in the name of Jesus …"

PAUL: In the name of Jesus …

WISDOM: "Zolo, in the name of Jesus …"

PAUL: Or Tantalei … Tantalei?

WISDOM: (Speaking in tongues)

PAUL: Do that in the name of Jesus …

WISDOM: (Speaking in tongues) right now, wherever your energies have been …[unintelligible] … I open the valve, right now … (Speaking in tongues) I speak energy now in your life … I speak supernatural energy right now … supernatural energy right now … (continues in this vein) I loosen the valve for energy right now …

PAUL: (continues deep sighing while WISDOM continues to invoke)

WISDOM: Let supernatural energy begin to flow in your soul … (continues in this vein) supernatural energy in the name of Jesus … I open the source … the true source of energy … Receive energy in the name of Jesus …

PAUL: I need break … God says I need a break …

WISDOM: (Speaking in tongues)

PAUL: There's more but … he's enough … we're done …

One-by-one, Paul and I work together to expel the demons. It is grueling, painstaking work, but it cannot be avoided. There are no shortcuts. Even leaving one demon undetected, one wound open and unhealed would be enough to compromise the whole process, in the same way that cancer can return if even one cancer cell is left undealt with.

And even though Paul needs a break, I am on a roll.

WISDOM: (Speaking in tongues) (reassuringly) We're nearly there (Speaking in tongues) Right now, I pray, if there is any spirit, that will torment, any spirit that will torment, that has the capacity to torment Paul I command you to speak right now ... speak right now in the name of Jesus ...
UNIDENTIFIED DEMONIC ENTITY: (Demonic laughter)
WISDOM: Speak right now in the name of Jesus ... Speak right now in the name of Jesus! ... What's your name? What's your name?
UNIDENTIFIED DEMONIC ENTITY: Kalmator ... Kalmator ... Kalmator ... Kalmator ...
WISDOM: Kalmator ... What is your mission, Kalmator? ...
KALMATOR: I want to torment his mind ... I'm torment his mind ...
WISDOM: Torment his mind?
KALMATOR: Yes ...
WISDOM: Were you not in the mind when we casted the other ones out?
KALMATOR: I'm sitting outside.
WISDOM: You're sitting outside ...
KALMATOR: Yes.
WISDOM: Do you have any legal right?
KALMATOR: No.
WISDOM: Do you have any access?
KALMATOR: No.
WISDOM: I consume you right now with the Fire of The Holy Spirit and I ask you to LEAVE in the name of Jesus.
KALMATOR: (begins to cough and splutter)
WISDOM: LEAVE in the name of Jesus! ... LEAVE in the name of

Jesus! … Paul's mind is set FREE by the Power of the Holy Ghost …

KALMATOR: I know, I know, I know …

WISDOM: Now LEAVE to the PIT in the name of Jesus! … in the name of Jesus!… Paul's mind is FREE in the name of Jesus! …

KALMATOR: I know, I know, I know …

WISDOM: Now, I command you, right now, I BOUND you now with ropes, and I cast you to the Pit, in the name of Jesus …GO in the name of Jesus … LEAVE in the name of Jesus … LEAVE in the name of Jesus (continues in this vein while Kalmator continues to dry retch loudly) … to the Pit in the name of Jesus.

KALMATOR: (Demonic laughter)

WISDOM: (Speaking in tongues)

KALMATOR: No, I didn't go … ahhh … ahhh … there's light …

WISDOM: (Speaking in tongues) Wherever you are, I release the Fire of The Holy Spirit on you, fire, you'll be consumed …(continues in this vein) … I release THUNDER and LIGHTNING on you … be BURNT in the name of Jesus … are you ready to go? FIRE consume you in the name of Jesus … FIRE of the Holy Ghost … CONSUME in the name of Jesus … and I cast you into PIT in the name of Jesus … (Speaking in tongues) Jesus Christ of Nazareth … come and make this house your home … come and do everything that you can do … (Speaking in tongues) Lord, Holy Spirit, any spirit that has the tendency to disturb, to torment Paul. I command you right now to speak, in the name of Jesus.

UNIDENTIFIED DEMONIC ENTITY: Aha, I'm so weak …

WISDOM: Speak out in the name of Jesus!

UNIDENTIFIED DEMONIC ENTITY: Only the last one …

WISDOM: Speak out in the name of Jesus!

UNIDENTIFIED DEMONIC ENTITY: Yes?

WISDOM: What's your name?

UNIDENTIFIED DEMONIC ENTITY: Tenthei.

WISDOM: Tenthei?

TENTHEI: Yes.

WISDOM: Tenthei's your name, what is your mission?

TENTHEI: I am the last one to torment his mind.

WISDOM: The last one to torment, what is your mission?

TENTHEI: I tried to attack him.

WISDOM: Tried to attack him …

TENTHEI: Yeeesss …

WISDOM: And how many of you are there?

TENTHEI: Thirteen

WISDOM: You are thirteen …

TENTHEI: We are the last ones.

WISDOM: Tenthei …

TENTHEI: To torment him.

WISDOM: To torment him …

TENTHEI: Yes.

WISDOM: How do you do that?

TENTHEI: We attack … we attack from outside the mind …

WISDOM: Do you have legal rights?

TENTHEI: No … no …

WISDOM: Can you reach Paul? Can you reach where he is right now?

TENTHEI: No.

WISDOM: Can you reach him?

TENTHEI: No.

WISDOM: I bound all the thirteen demons to you, Tenthei,

I bound them to your right now. If they are bound you let me know.

TENTHEI: Yes …

WISDOM: Right now, wherever you are, including the thirteen demons, I set you on fire, in the name of Jesus. I set you on fire, in the name of Jesus. I rain fire on you! (continues in this vein, raining fire and burning the demons while they cough and dry retch increasingly loudly) be consumed …

TENTHEI: (Demonic laughter) I am so weak …

WISDOM: (continues the invocation to consume, set on fire and rain fire on Tenthei and the thirteen demons) … I command you to THE PIT and the thirteen demons in the NAME of Jesus … (Speaking in tongues)

TENTHEI: Ooohhh … shut the fuck up! (begins to roar and howl amidst the coughing)

WISDOM: I rain fire in the name of Jesus … (repeatedly and incessantly)

PAUL: OK … he's leaving … he's leaving … God says …

WISDOM: I cast you OUT in the name of Jesus … (Speaking in tongues)

UNIDENTIFIED DEMONIC ENTITY: (Sustained Demonic laughter) Once I leave, you will not be tormented … Once I leave, you are free from torment … Your mind is free, clearly … Now I can't attack you … (Demonic laughter)

WISDOM: (Speaking in tongues) Do you have a legal right?

UNIDENTIFIED DEMONIC ENTITY: Yes … yes …

WISDOM: What's your legal right?

UNIDENTIFIED DEMONIC ENTITY: I came, I came through prayer.

WISDOM: You came through prayer …

UNIDENTIFIED DEMONIC ENTITY: Yes … yes.

WISDOM: Whatever prayers is that?

UNIDENTIFIED DEMONIC ENTITY: He prayed to the Devil.

WISDOM: He prayed to the Devil …

UNIDENTIFIED DEMONIC ENTITY: Yes … yes … yes …

WISDOM: Do you have any contracts?

UNIDENTIFIED DEMONIC ENTITY: Yes.

WISDOM: What are the contracts?

UNIDENTIFIED DEMONIC ENTITY: The contract for his girlfriend … He prayed … He prayed to the Devil … (Demonic laughter)

WISDOM: He prayed to the Devil.

UNIDENTIFIED DEMONIC ENTITY: Yes … yes … yes … many were sent … He did not know many were sent … Demonic laughter)

WISDOM: (Speaking in tongues) What is your name? What is your name?

UNIDENTIFIED DEMONIC ENTITY: Sa … Sabiath.

WISDOM: What is your name? …

UNIDENTIFIED DEMONIC ENTITY: Sabiath … Am I Sabiath?

WISDOM: Are you Sabiat?

SABIATH: Yes.

WISDOM: Sabiat …

SABIATH: Yes.

WISDOM: That's your name.

SABIATH: Yes .

WISDOM: How many demons do you have with you?

SABIATH: Twenty.

WISDOM: Twenty.

SABIATH: Yes .

WISDOM: Right now I bound all those 20 on you and let me know when that is done in the NAME of Jesus … Let me know when that is done in the name of Jesus, Sabiat.

SABIATH: (loud dry retching) It is done.

WISDOM: It's done?

SABIATH: It is done.

WISDOM: Have you caused any mental damage, Sabiat?

SABIATH: Yes.

WISDOM: Physical damage?

SABIATH: No.

WISDOM: Spiritual damage?

SABIATH: No.

WISDOM: No … Right now, in the name of Jesus … In the name of Jesus … I set you … Sabiat …

SABIATH: There's a contract.

WISDOM: There's a contract.

SABIATH: Yes.

WISDOM: Right now, I break that contract, in the NAME of Jesus (amidst much loud, demonic coughing) I BREAK the contract, in the name of Jesus … Tell me when it is broken … I break that contract … I BREAK IT in the name of Jesus … I BREAK IT in the name of Jesus …

SABIATH: It is broken …

WISDOM: I break the contract in the name of Jesus … I set Paul's soul on fire … I rain the fire of the Holy Ghost on you … (continues in this vein while Sabiath continues to struggle, cough and dry retch increasingly loudly) Be consumed … Rain fire! … Fire! … Leave! In the name of Jesus! To the PIT! … Be consumed in the name of Jesus … Destroy every root in the name of Jesus! … I command you to LEAVE and I cast you OUT in the name of Jesus … Fire of the Holy Ghost! … I command you to leave now … Be consumed … I strike you with thunder … I strike you with torment … Strike with THUNDER in the name of

Jesus … I CONSUME you with the consuming fire of the Holy Ghost! …

With that, the last of the demons that had afflicted Paul for so many years was finally cast out.

We can count ourselves fortunate that at least we have a record of Paul's final triumph, when the last of the hold out demons were expelled. From this point, the demons would not, could not, damage Paul anymore.

This is where the fight for Paul's life was won.

And, having been expelled, Paul's consciousness, his awareness, his very soul is infused with Divine Light.

At the end of the recording, we have this moment captured.

PAUL: It's really bright!

WISDOM: (Speaking in tongues) Now allow the power of that light to get in you. Holy Spirit, shine Your Light through … Shine Your Light through, in the name of Jesus … Shine Your Light through, in the name of Jesus …

PAUL: (Makes sighing sounds of awe while WISDOM continues to invoke)

WISDOM: Shine Your Light through, in the name of Jesus … Shine your light through, Holy Spirit … Shine Your Light … Shine Your Light … Shine Your Light … In the name of Jesus Christ of Nazareth, I pray …

PAUL: (Begins to sing to the song of angels)

WISDOM: That you will shine Your Light … Shine Your Light … Shine Your Light … Shine Your Light … Thank-you, Jesus … Thank-you, Lord.

PAUL: I have been set free from torment (continues to sigh and sing)

WISDOM: (Speaking in tongues) Holy Spirit, receive all the glory, honor, and praise. Jesus be glorified. Heaven up your … [unintelligible] … Thank you, Lord … Thank you, Jesus … Thank you, Lord … Every work that has been done here today we seal it with the Blood … of Jesus … We seal it with the Blood of Jesus … Thank you, Lord … Thank you, Lord … Father, I introduce a new pattern … right now … in Jesus' name …

PAUL: I can see light … There's so much light! Oh …

The voice of Paul in these last moments is like that of a little child seeing fireworks for the first time. Words cannot hope to convey the extent of what he must have been feeling in those moments.

In the end, we don't know how many demons entered through Paul's unhealed wounds to come and go, or to come and stay, over the twenty-four years that Paul was afflicted.

We know that at least seventy demons were expelled during the Deliverance sessions with me, including, apparently, Satan Itself. It seems that the "senior" demons were known only by their designation. More "middle management" demons identified themselves through actual names. Both senior and middle demons were more often than not "captains" of cohorts of "junior" demons who would remain unnamed. These junior demons had to be bound to the captains so that they could all be loosed at the same time.

Just for the record.

LIST OF IDENTIFIED SPIRTS AND THEIR ASSOCIATED DEMONS

(Quantity numbered, except designated by a "?" when the number is unclear or unknown)

Spirit of Confusion (?)
Spirit of Death (12)
Spirit of Doubt (2?)
Spirit of Harm (?)
Spirit of Hopelessness (?)
Spirit of Madness (10)
Spirit of Rejection (?)
Spirit of Selfishness (?)
Spirit of Suicide (16)
Spirit of Torment (?)
Spirit of Unforgiveness(?)
Spirit of Vindictiveness (?)

Onomator (7)
Sabiath (?)
Sanmala (12)
Solematu (?)
Sonmalei (10)
Tandalei (13)
Tantalei (17)
Tenthei (13)
Tobartha (?)
Tobias (17)
Zenthei (14)
Zenthia/Zebaiyeth (?)
Zolo (16)

CHAPTER SIXTEEN

SOME FINAL REFLECTIONS FROM PAUL

As I look back on everything that happened to me I realized that even as I was extricating myself from demonic contracts and contracts with the Devil I was entering into new contracts with God.

God makes contracts too and with every step I came closer to God the contracts would be even more affirmed. But for all the assurances that I was now finally safe, I had suffered a great deal of damage.

For many months after my final Deliverance I experienced a hypersensitivity to disturbance which often left me feeling overwhelmed. It was exhausting, but gradually, over time, things have calmed down a lot.

I now pursue a more ordinary life. I have rediscovered what it is to have hobbies and pastimes. I'm finally taking charge of my business again, and I'm engaging with developing my professional life.

Joseph and I have developed a friendship which is a source of great comfort to me, and I do what I can to help him spread his unique message.

I have been free of alcohol for more than a year now without the need for another stay at a rehab facility or any need to participate with Alcoholics Anonymous. In fact, I have no desire to touch alcohol at all.

My relationship with my wife and children has blossomed and I have become a better, more engaged father. I take great joy in raising my son and also my daughter, who was born near the time that I resolved to help Joseph help me again.

My mental health issues settled and diminished considerably. It's nice to be part of a success story that shows the light at the end of the tunnel.

There is a profound peace in knowing where I am going when I die, that my soul is no longer in Hell and that there is no chance that I will go there again.

To this day, I get reassuring readings from my great-grandmother, Elaine, from angelic intuitions, and from The Holy Spirit as well. These readings provide invaluable guidance and give me a sense of security that is incredibly comforting.

If there is one thing I want the afflicted to understand it is this:

It wasn't until God strengthened my spirit and demonstrated that He was there for me each and every time we called on him for help throughout the Deliverance process, that I finally understood that God was in control.

The Devil was never in control.

This truth ultimately set me free. For once I had finally accepted the knowledge and understanding that God was always the stronger power the Devil ultimately lost the battle.

The security that comes from truly knowing the omnipotence of God, that your soul is inviolable and indestructible, that The Holy Spirit is the true source of everything and that your spiritual connection to The Holy Spirit, cannot be severed, EVER.

This realization is what you are ultimately fighting for.

It is in binding yourself to Light and to Divine Love that you are truly set free.

For all their tricks and tactics, Satan and the demons have only one strategy – to separate you from your conscious connection to The Holy Spirit.

For a long time I believed that Satan and the demons were more powerful than anything, but that was the most damaging lie of all.

Nothing is more powerful than our all-loving God, and in that truth, we can always take refuge.

CHAPTER SEVENTEEN

SOME FINAL THOUGHTS FROM WISDOM

As for me, in the beginning I used to find this process very demanding, but that is because out of egotistic enthusiasm, or a desire to help, or mostly because of ignorance and a belief in 'no pain, no gain', I was operating under my own power.

In other words, I was *getting in the way.*

As I have learned to better channel the energy of The Holy Spirit, I find myself less tired, and sometimes even exhilarated, because I draw on a source of *infinite* energy. The more irrelevant I become, the more effective is the process. It's not my job to be yelling and screaming and fighting the demons, giving as good as I get and fighting unholy fire and brimstone with Divine Fire and Light.

I apologize if you ever witness a Deliverance that I conduct, and you find the whole thing underwhelming and not particularly enthralling, but *it is not my job to be dramatic.* My nature is not to be dramatic. My nature is to embrace the Authority of Holy Law and the Power of The Holy Spirit and to let that Power act through me and to let what happens happen, "dramatic" or not.

My job is to get out of the way and let The Holy Spirit do the work.

This does not stop people from projecting on to me qualities that I do not claim and wanting to put me on a pedestal. I have had people come to me and say, "I saw your eyes were red like fire!" Or, "I saw a globe of light around you! It was so radiant!" Or "I saw you like a lion!"

To which I reply, "OK. But I didn't do anything."

I also understand their gratitude and that as the human face of their Deliverance I am the focus of that gratitude, but I always discourage any attempts, however well meant, for them to indulge in hero worship. I can't begin to express how wrong this is, because giving up your power to a hero, or to anything other than The Holy Spirit, is to give up your own Spiritual Authority.

It is vitally important for me and for them to continue to assert Spiritual Authority.

By now, I have taken hundreds of people through Deliverance – Africans, Asians, Middle Easterners, Europeans, Americans, Islanders, Christians, Muslims, Jews, Atheists, Agnostics, Pantheists. I know that people in the depths of their own unique version of Spiritual Affliction Syndrome and in the midst of a session of Deliverance see whatever they see filtered through their culture, their personal history and their idiosyncratic psychology.

They experience, perhaps, what they want to experience.

They experience, perhaps, what they are capable of experiencing.

They experience, perhaps, only what they are prepared experience.

They certainly experience what The Holy Spirit requires them to experience.

By now, you know that Deliverance is not the end of the process.

It is important to continue to practice living a life of integrity, or risk affliction all over again. This is why we must pray, or meditate, or do whatever spiritual practice we can to continue to develop and strengthen our conscious spiritual connection to the Source. We need to feed our soul in the same way that we feed our bodies, or we spiritually starve and become weaker and vulnerable to all sorts of chaos that can do immeasurable harm, over a period of decades, or even for an entire lifetime.

The case of Paul, for example, continued for over two decades and continued to be challenging right up to the very "end". The damage inflicted by such a long period of affliction such as his was extensive. At the very least, the soul becomes somewhat desensitized to normality, in the same sense that a hoarder can't see the filth and chaos that surrounds them.

The Devil is clever, and certainly powerful. The Devil has no ultimate power because nothing beats The Holy Spirit! However, this doesn't stop the Devil from being extremely convincing and seeming to triumph over and over again.

Exorcism or Deliverance is often misunderstood *solely* as a war over the soul. But the war is never only between The Holy Spirit and the Devil over the soul. The war and the numerous battles and engagements are more a struggle between The Holy Spirit and the soul's perception of reality and its conscious spiritual connection with Divinity.

A "win" for Satan would be a case where the Devil succeeded in *completely* ridding the afflicted of any knowledge of or conscious connection to the Divinity of The Holy Spirit. A "win" happens when the afflicted physically dies or exits their mortal body in this state of profound disconnection. This occurs, unfortunately, very often. And it is in this state of abandonment, that persists even after the death of the physical body, that your soul is effectively taken. In this state of abandonment you adopt a point of view so compromised that whatever the ultimate reality, *the soul subjectively feels lost forever*.

Remember that one of the greatest weapons of the Devil is deception.

The enemy will always be ready to create doubt and to cast that doubt into your mind and heart, deceiving you into believing that your condition is hopeless.

Always remember that The Holy Spirit is closer to you than the very book you hold in your hand and in your hands you hold His Words of Liberation.

No matter who you are, no matter where you are in life, do what you can, while there is still mortal life in you.

Act now and be eternally free.

ABOUT THE AUTHOR

Joseph Wisdom Sesay is an ordained minister.

Joseph has a unique connection to draw truth and knowledge from the Holy Spirit – the Spirit of Truth, the Spirit of God – who guides him accordingly through the Deliverance Process and other spiritual matters concerning the Spiritually Afflicted, not only during the Affliction, but in other parts of their lives.

Like many people who have been called into this work, he has a strong spiritual connection to the Holy Spirit. After he discovered that he had a unique gift to help others cleanse themselves of negative energy and entities, Joseph served under experienced Exorcists and Deliverance Ministers, gaining considerable experience working with them, conducting Exorcism and Deliverance Counselling.

He is the Director of Divine Intercession, a specialist Deliverance Ministry in Melbourne, Australia.

This is his first book.

This book was written with the invaluable support of
Divine Intercession.

If you or someone you care about are experiencing spiritual distress, please don't hesitate to reach out to us.
divineintercession.org.au

All enquiries will be dealt with in the strictest confidence.